CATHOLIC SOCIAL TEACHING AS THEOLOGY

CATHOLIC SOCIAL TEACHING AS THEOLOGY

GRÉGOIRE CATTA, SJ

Paulist Press
New York / Mahwah, NJ

Imprimi potest
François Boëdec, SJ
Provincial, Society of Jesus, French Speaking Province of Western Europe (EOF)
December 5, 2018

Cover image by singpentinkhappy/Shutterstock.com
Cover and book design by Lynn Else

Library of Congress Cataloging-in-Publication Data
Names: Catta, Grégoire, 1975- author.
Title: Catholic social teaching as theology / Grégoire Catta, SJ.
Description: New York : Paulist Press, 2019. | Includes bibliographical references and index.
Identifiers: LCCN 2018060661 (print) | LCCN 2019021962 (ebook) | ISBN 9781587687235 (ebook) | ISBN 9780809153565 (pbk. : alk. paper)
Subjects: LCSH: Christian sociology—Catholic Church. | Catholic Church—Doctrines. | Theology.
Classification: LCC BX1753 (ebook) | LCC BX1753 .C3925 2019 (print) | DDC 261.8088/282—dc23
LC record available at https://lccn.loc.gov/2018060661

ISBN 978-0-8091-5356-5 (paperback)
ISBN 978-1-58768-723-5 (e-book)

Published by Paulist Press
997 Macarthur Boulevard
Mahwah, New Jersey 07430
www.paulistpress.com

Printed and bound in the
United States of America

A.M.D.G.

To my parents

CONTENTS

ACKNOWLEDGMENTS

ALTHOUGH WRITING A BOOK of theology is a rather solitary endeavor, it is also the fruit of numerous conversations and explorations in a community of learning, and it would have been impossible to achieve it without the help and support of many people. May they all find here the acknowledgment of my profound gratitude.

Most of the reflections in this book developed a few years ago in my doctoral dissertation. I owe a great debt of gratitude to my professors and colleagues at Boston College, and most of all to Lisa Sowle Cahill for agreeing to guide and advise me on my project. Her generous encouragements and precious comments at each stage of the process were invaluable. I could not have wished for better readers and teachers than David Hollenbach and John R. Sachs. I thank also the students and faculty members of the Boston College ethics seminar who have given valuable input on my work, including James Keenan, Stephen Pope, Andrea Vicini, James Bretzke, Mary Jo Iozzio, Kenneth Himes, Kevin Ahern, Michael Jaycox, René Micallef, Gonzalo Villagran, Hoa Dinh, Joshua Snyder, Christopher Jones, Conor Kelly, Katherine Ward, Marianne Tierney, James O'Sullivan, Bambang Irawan, Katherine Jackson, and Antuan Ilgit. Thank you to the professors of Centre Sèvres—Facultés Jésuites de Paris, and most of all Alain Thomasset and Paul Valadier for introducing me to theological ethics during my bachelor and licentiate degrees. They raised in me an interest that does not dwindle! Centre Sèvres is now a wonderful place to teach and write. Thanks to all my colleagues and to my students there.

I am most grateful to the Society of Jesus and to my provincials, Jean-Yves Grenet and François Boëdec, who entrusted to me the mission of working in the field of social moral theology. I am grateful to the communities of the last few years: the Saint Peter Faber Jesuit Community in Boston, especially Hurtado and Harrington houses, and the Communauté Saint Alberto Hurtado in Saint Denis (France) where I now live. A special thanks to the community of San Roberto Bellarmino in Santiago de Chile that hosted me during a crucial semester of writing on this book. Many Jesuits helped me along the way: my superiors at Boston, Brad Schaeffer and Jim Gartland, and at Saint Denis, Étienne Grieu and Olivier Barreau; James Keenan, Alain Thomasset, Christoph Theobald, Étienne Grieu, Bertrand Hériard Dubreuil, and Jorge Costadoat for their acute feedback and support at various stages of the project. I am extremely grateful to the companions with whom I shared the mission of doctoral studies and with whom I now share the mission of theological work: Román Guridi, Bambang Irawan, René Micallef, Gonzalo Villagran, Mario Insulza, Cathal Doherty, Francis Alvarez, Antoine Paumard, Erwan Chauty, Nicolas Steeves, Pierre Molinié, and Guilhem Causse.

Writing in a foreign language would not have been possible without the generosity and limitless availability of Simon Smith, Paul Harman, and Kenneth Hughes, who reviewed with patience and precision the various drafts up to the final version of the book and drove me through the subtleties of the English language. Thank you as well to Paul McMahon and the editorial team of Paulist Press, for recognizing something of value in my work and for allowing me to share it on a larger scale through the printed page.

As a Jesuit priest, my pastoral work is not separated from my academic work. The people I minister to are my primary teachers and they give meaning to my research. Thank you to the parishioners of Saint Mary of the Angels, Boston, and of Saint Denys de l'Estrée, Saint Denis (France).

Many friends in the United States, Chile, and France contributed to my completing this project with their invaluable friendship and support. May they find here a sign of my gratitude: Andrew and Susan, Marina, James, Kathy (†), Maria, Ana, Valentina and Domingo, Veronica and Martin, Eduardo and Ignacia, Clarisse, Franck and Aurore.

Finally, my heartfelt gratitude goes to my parents, Yolande and Bruno Catta, and my sisters, Yolaine and Sybille. Who I am today, I owe to you. You opened my eyes, my mind, and my heart to the faith I attempt to witness in this work.

ABBREVIATIONS

Ap	*Concluding Document of the Fifth General Conference of the Bishops of Latin America and the Caribbean,* 2007, Aparecida, Brazil
CELAM	Latin American Episcopal Conference
CiV	*Caritas in veritate* (Benedict XVI, 2009)
CST	Catholic Social Teaching
DCE	*Deus caritas est* (Benedict XVI, 2005)
DV	*Dei verbum* (Vatican II, 1965)
EG	*Evangelii gaudium* (Francis, 2013)
ES	*Ecclesiam suam* (Paul VI, 1964)
FCF	*Foundations of Christian Faith* (Karl Rahner, 1978)
GS	*Gaudium et spes* (Vatican II, 1965)
LS	*Laudato si'* (Francis, 2015)
Med	*Concluding Document of the Second Conference of the Bishops of Latin America,* 1968, Medellín, Colombia
MM	*Mater et magistra* (John XXIII, 1961)
OA	*Octogesima adveniens* (Paul VI, 1971)
PiT	*Pacem in terris* (John XXIII, 1963)
PP	*Populorum progressio* (Paul VI, 1967)
Pue	*Concluding Document of the Third Conference of the Bishops of Latin America,* 1979, Puebla, Mexico
RH	*Redemptor hominis* (John Paul II, 1979)
RP	*Reconciliatio et paenitentia* (John Paul II, 1984)
SRS	*Sollicitudo rei socialis* (John Paul II, 1987)
TI	*Theological Investigations* (Karl Rahner)

Citations of church documents are made by indicating the abbreviation followed by the section number. Unless specifically indicated in the notes, the English translation used for papal and conciliar documents is the one available at www.vatican.va. Emphasis in citing these documents is from the original unless otherwise noted.

INTRODUCTION

IN *SOLLICITUDO REI SOCIALIS* (SRS), Pope John Paul II speaks of the church's social doctrine as belonging to the field of *theology* (SRS 41). In what sense is this the case? What does it mean to say that Catholic Social Teaching (CST) is theological? How do we understand the relationship between social ethics and theology?

An obvious answer is the natural movement that goes from theology to social ethics. Theology is a possible and fruitful source for ethical discernment of social issues. Theological ethicists commonly refer to a set of four sources for their reflection: Bible and Christian tradition, philosophical tradition, scientific reasoning, and human experience.[1] Undoubtedly, CST in general, and more specifically, since Leo XIII's *Rerum novarum*, its magisterial component, uses theological concepts and symbols as sources and tools. It is true that, up until the Second Vatican Council, it used principally a form of ethical reasoning based on natural law, which seemed to provide universal principles accessible even outside the context of explicit Christian revelation. However, one should note that, in the Catholic understanding, natural law reasoning is far from being nontheological, because it is envisioned as the expression of God's eternal law imprinted on human hearts and minds. More recently, since Vatican II, the theological sources of CST have become more explicit.

Without denying this first way of articulating ethics and theology, it is possible to consider a second movement going *from* ethics *to* theology. An example of this is a social encyclical that promotes the preferential option for the poor as an inescapable criterion in political and economic matters, and highlights at the same time Jesus Christ's proximity to the poor and that he is met through encountering them. Another example would be how the promotion of integral human development in very concrete options reveals crucial aspects of how the Christian faith envisions the human being. A third example would be the inductive and dialogical approach at work in Pope Francis's reflection on integral ecology in *Laudato si'* that points out how the Triune God reveals Godself within history.

This book aims to investigate this path from social ethics to theology and to show how the relationship between the two can be envisioned through considering how the former contributes to the latter, and not merely how the latter is a source for the former. Catholic Social Teaching is theological in that it offers ethical reflections and practical orientations regarding social, political, and economic issues that are in themselves an entry point into the mystery of the saving God.

From the outset, it is to be noted here that it is not merely a matter of reversing a logical deductive movement but rather of making a case in favor of a solid hermeneutical circle—or better, a hermeneutical spiral. When considering theological expressions of faith, ethical discernment, and practices, there are constant interactions among the three. Faith convictions and theological elaborations can prompt actions through the mediation of ethics. In return, however, practices captured in ethical guidelines can reshape our ways of expressing our beliefs. By focusing on how ethics, and CST specifically, contributes to theology, we attend to the part of the circle that is too often missing without, at the same time, downplaying the well-acknowledged fact that theology is a source for Christian ethics.

This book, therefore, will highlight the contribution post–Vatican II Catholic Social Teaching—more specifically, the papal social magisterium—has made to theology. By addressing various social, political, and economic issues from an ethical or moral point of view, and by promoting some practices and denouncing others, this teaching brings insights to the theological endeavor. The magisterial concern with social issues stresses certain dimensions of the mystery of "God for us" that otherwise could be forgotten, and it also challenges other forms of theological discourse and helps to reorient them. As case studies, we will focus on four encyclicals that take up the challenge of integral development in a globalized world: Paul VI's *Populorum progressio* (PP), John Paul II's *Sollicitudo rei socialis*, Benedict XVI's *Caritas in veritate* (CiV), and Francis's *Laudato si'* (LS). This will lead us to deal more specifically with three theological themes:

methodology and style as theologically significant, theological anthropology, and Christology.

THEOLOGY

Now, what do we mean by "theological" when we intend to investigate the *theological* dimension of some social encyclicals and attempt to engage their *theological* contribution? Theology, broadly speaking, refers to past and contemporary reflections that interpret Scripture and have God and the Christian faith as their object. Etymologically, *theology* means discourse or reasoning (*logos*) about God (*theos*). Theology refers to a "reasoned mode of understanding according to revelation";[2] it can be thought of as "an intellectual discipline, that is, an ordered body of knowledge about God."[3] Because the church has the mission to proclaim the good news of God's salvation in Jesus Christ, it must testify, in all that it teaches, social teaching included, to the mystery of God. In other words, there ought to be a theological dimension to CST in that it contributes to a reasoned discourse about God and about things considered in their relation to God.

Nonetheless, by envisioning this theological dimension of CST, a shift takes place in the understanding of theology from a purely intellectual discipline to an articulation of theory and praxis. The social encyclicals are an elaborate discourse reflecting something of the perennial and universal truth of the Christian faith. They do this, however, by relying on an analysis of historical situations and by offering practical orientations as well. They are a speculative moment in a reflection on human experiences, but they also offer a theology that is not purely speculative and is rather strongly articulated with practices.

Moreover, the object of the theological endeavor is certainly God, but more precisely, it is "God for us," or God as "God in relation with human beings," God loving us, and God saving us. Theology, especially when it is approached from the perspective of social ethics, which deals with concrete human life, is necessarily soteriology. It deals not so much with who God is per se but with who God is *for us*, how God interacts with us and how God saves us.

Last, there is certainly not merely one theology developed in CST. We cannot speak of "the" theology of CST, even if we limit our study to the post–Vatican II papal magisterium. This is because of the nature of the documents, the diversity of their authors, and the diversity of their contexts. Moreover, it is certainly not the case that these documents provide a comprehensive or systematic theology; rather they provide hints and pointers on some aspects of the question of "God for us," and they leave the door open to different schools of thought. In brief, whatever theology we find in them is marked by a sense of plurality.

Consequently, Karl Rahner's notion of mystery is a useful guideline to defining a *theological* endeavor.[4] For the German theologian, theology is "the science of mystery."[5] Mystery in the theological sense is not something that remains hidden to human reason and is impossible to apprehend. On the contrary, it is the reality that we must always try to apprehend more deeply with our reason and more broadly with all our being, while what we try to apprehend remains beyond any complete comprehensibility. God, and subsequently Jesus Christ, humanity, the church, and so on, are mysteries or various aspects of the one mystery of God's loving self-communication to and in humanity. Theology is the endeavor to apprehend these mysteries while recognizing that it is a matter of letting oneself be drawn into the one mystery. Therefore, many ways and approaches—many theologies and many different theological questions—are possible. Far from exhausting the mystery, they are paths to entering it.

In summary, to explore what social encyclicals offer us regarding several theological themes is to recognize some contributions, among many others, to a very wide theological endeavor of entering the mystery of "God for us."

FRAMEWORKS

Sensitive to the reality of theological pluralism, this book will use a typology of theological frameworks. A theological framework is a certain way of articulating a vision of God and a vision of the human world that emphasizes certain aspects of the mystery, uses a certain set of categories, and privileges certain theological questions. There are four theological frameworks relevant for the analysis of the social encyclicals.

The first two are developed by Joseph Komonchak in his description of the various currents of interpretation of Vatican II.[6] He sees two theological trends at work: one is closer to Aquinas (the neo-Thomist), the other to Augustine (the Augustinian). The first is more incarnational, the second more eschatological. The first views the world primarily as the place of God's revelation in the creation, accessible by human reason participating in the eternal law. The second stresses the dimension of sin that is at work in the world and darkens human reason in need of redemption. The first highlights the autonomy of the created world and the intelligibility of nature, humanity, and history. The second stresses the necessity of grace, seeing true wisdom—as opposed to mere scientific knowledge—and true freedom as results of the redemption accomplished in Christ.

To these two theological frameworks is a third, the liberationist, which is exemplified in Latin American liberation theology. In this framework, the vision of the world is focused on the social and communal dimensions of human life and on the fact that God interacts with human beings not only as individuals but as collectives. Salvation is envisioned in its dimension of bringing about the kingdom of God, which implies changes at the level of institutions and structures. Sin is also named and approached in its social and structural aspect.

Finally, a fourth framework will be useful in examining *Laudato si'*, the last encyclical of our study. This framework is Franciscan, referring to Saint Francis of Assisi and the Franciscan theological tradition. Here, attention is paid to the category of creation. God is Creator and the world is God's creation. As creatures, human beings are part of this creation and in relation with all other creatures. Moreover, in the Franciscan tradition, as distinct from the Dominican and Thomist tradition but not in opposition to it, a greater stress is put on the faculty of love than on that of knowledge and on the category of freedom than of that of truth.

Of course, these four theological frameworks are not exclusive of one another. In the social encyclicals, sometimes one is favored over the others, for example, the neo-Thomist in *PP*, or the Augustinian in *CiV*. Sometimes, they balance each other in the same document as in *SRS*, or *LS*. Each framework highlights an important aspect of the mystery of "God for us." Nonetheless, we will see that the theological frameworks cannot be merely juxtaposed. From the perspective of CST and of social ethical challenges, theology is better developed within the neo-Thomist framework, completed by the liberationist and

Franciscan frameworks, and corrected, or balanced, by the Augustinian framework.

As a caveat, this typology is useful in capturing the theological insights of CST and articulating both their complementarities and their tensions. However, it should not be absolutized. First, in naming the framework, the reference to a theological tradition associated with a key figure helps to identify specific accents, but it does not reduce the traditions to the few characteristics listed. Augustine's thought cannot be reduced to the Augustinian framework! The same applies to the other frameworks. They are named merely as an indicator of a certain proximity to the principal tenets of these theological traditions. Second, associating any of the encyclicals with one or another framework is never meant to be exclusive of other theological readings. Finally, as for every typology, the shaping of the four frameworks is open to discussion. Using the four frameworks simply allows us to highlight specific theological insights in the various encyclicals. The specific typology is not the central outcome of the reflection. It is merely a tool.

SOME FOUNDATIONS

In addition to the typology, some foundational remarks are needed before engaging the theological reading of the encyclicals. Why is it theologically sound to make the journey from ethical reflection to theology, to consider social ethics a possible *locus theologicus*, to read social encyclicals as contributing to theology?

Vatican II shows us the way by enshrining in the magisterium the dimension of historicity at work in revelation. With its pastoral approach, as intended by Pope John XXIII, the council itself is an example of developing a historically embedded theology. Christoph Theobald speaks of a "principle of pastorality," which is a key to interpret the council and to continue to receive it creatively:

> There can be no proclamation of the gospel without taking into account its recipients; and, to define the position of the latter more clearly, we should add that "what" is at stake in the proclamation is already at work in them, in such a way that they accede to it in all freedom.[7]

In its four years of debates and its sixteen documents, the council became more aware of what it means to consider the recipients in the formulation of the good news and to recognize God at work within them.[8]

According to *Dei verbum*, revelation is not the transmission of a set of truths but God's salvific self-communication to humankind. This means that the truth of faith is not expressed by the mere repetition of ahistorical dogmas but through a pastoral approach that considers what is at work in various contexts and in the challenges of the current time. *Gaudium et spes* (GS), through its dialogical engagement with the current world, is the council's best attempt to put this understanding of revelation into practice. The constitution affirms the necessity for the church to read the "signs of the times,"[9] and it does just this.

Social encyclicals should be read following the lead initiated by Vatican II's turn to history. It is a way of receiving this turn, not by merely "implementing" it, but by reenacting creatively its mode of producing a new kind of theology conscious of its historicity.

In keeping with the council, Karl Rahner is also a useful resource in interpreting the social encyclicals theologically. He points to fundamental questions relevant to the articulation of ethics and theology, or praxis and theology. As already noted, his understanding of theology as the science of mystery is a solid base for envisioning a plurality of theologies and of *loci theologici*.

Moreover, Rahner stresses the fundamental ties uniting anthropology, Christology, and theology, thus supporting the theological nature of the anthropological reflections we encounter in social encyclicals. Reflecting on the meaning of "God became man," Rahner concludes that "Christology is the beginning and the end of anthropology and this anthropology in its most radical actualization is for all eternity theology."[10]

The German theologian also affirms the unity of love of God and love of neighbor. For him, love of God and love of neighbor are two names given "to the same reality if we are to summon up its one mystery which cannot be abrogated."[11] Christian social ethics, and CST in particular, are concerned with putting into practice the commandment of the love of neighbor. Rahner shows us the theological implication at work here: through the love of neighbor it is really God who is encountered.

Finally, for Rahner, the world is the place of God's salvific self-revelation.[12] Although remaining the absolute other of the world and of human beings, God is not distant. The mystery of God is a mystery of a salvific closeness, an inner presence in the movement of the world toward its fulfillment and of human beings toward theirs. In a striking formulation of God's presence in the world, Rahner explains,

> There is only one question, whether this God wanted to be merely the eternally distant one, or whether beyond that he wanted to be the innermost center of our existence in free grace and in self-communication. But our whole existence, borne by this question, calls for the affirmation of this second possibility as actually realized.[13]

All these themes, developed systematically by one of the great theologians of the council, support a theology embedded in human experience and historical realities, which is the path we will be taking through our study of some documents of CST.

READING SOCIAL ENCYCLICALS THEOLOGICALLY

How and what do social encyclicals concerned with integral human development contribute to entering the mystery of "God for us"?

Chapter 1 begins the theological reading of the encyclicals with *Populorum progressio*. Promulgated in 1967, less than two years after the closing of the council, *PP* pursues the dynamism of *GS*. It offers a theology very much in line with the neo-Thomist framework, a theology that highlights the possibility of a positive, dialogue-oriented, transformationist relation of the church and the gospel to the world. In a context full of hope due to the recent independence of many countries in the Global South, but also with a growing awareness of the North-South inequalities, Paul VI offers a vibrant plea in favor of authentic development, a development not reduced to the economic sphere, but requiring a global commitment to justice, solidarity, and peace.

The see-judge-act methodology and the explicitly dialogical approach adopted by the encyclical reflect a theological insistence on the mystery of the incarnation as God's grace at work in this world. By reflecting on integral human development for everyone, *PP* stresses the vocation of human beings to grow in all their dimensions—material, intellectual, and spiritual—and recognizes their legitimate aspiration to freedom, but it also highlights their being called to solidarity as an expression of their social nature. Through dealing with concrete issues such as hunger, unjust international trade relations, scandalous waste of money in the arms race, or land reform, the encyclical also points to Jesus Christ as leading the way. He is shown as involved in the world and in proximity with the poor. He is also the full realization of the human vocation.

Chapter 2 turns to John Paul II and *Sollicitudo rei socialis* (1987). Twenty years after *PP*, John Paul II revisited the theme of development in his second major social encyclical. The context had changed. Many hopes prompted by the question of development raised in the 1950s and 1960s had not been fulfilled. Inequalities both between and within countries were increasing. Many nations in the Global South were still struggling from poverty and a lack of real economic and political independence amid various forms of neocolonialism. The Cold War between the two ideological blocs of liberal capitalism and Marxist collectivism, of which the first pope from Eastern Europe had firsthand experience, had dreadful consequences in terms of local wars, arms trafficking, and impediments to proper development. This encyclical takes a more critical and confrontational stance vis-à-vis the world in its current state. It also affirms more strongly its theological nature in its desire to offer a theological reading of the situation and to shed the light of the gospel on it. These are features of the Augustinian framework. However, in *SRS*, the two other theological frameworks of our typology are also at work: the neo-Thomist and the liberationist.

Concerning methodology and style, *SRS* reframes the see-judge-act approach and tempers the dimension of dialogue championed in *PP*. There is still an engagement with secular sciences and concrete realities, some dimension of induction and of dialogue akin to the neo-Thomist framework. However, there is a greater emphasis on the authority of the magisterium and on some more deductive forms of reasoning that reflect the influence of the Augustinian framework. The encyclical also bears the mark of the recent developments in the Latin American church and of the emergence of liberation theology. *Sollicitudo rei socialis* incorporates, with nuances, their notions of structural sin, the option for the poor, and liberation. As in *PP*, transcendent humanism and the social dimension of being human are the basis of the anthropology developed, but the dimension of sin is much more present. Strikingly, the pope denounces "the structures of sin" at work in the world and offers the virtue of solidarity as the antidote to promote an authentic development. In a descending movement, Christ appears as the Redeemer and the Revealer in this world marked by sin, but in a more ascending movement, he is also the one who leads to the poor and who is encountered in them.

Chapter 3 analyzes *Caritas in veritate* (2009). In his sole social encyclical, Benedict XVI chose to pursue the series initiated by Paul VI and to update the message of *PP*. The Cold War is over but the challenges concerning integral human development are still present. Inequalities continue to grow. The whole world is affected by an economic crisis that has started in the financial markets. Environmental issues are on the front page as well. What shapes Benedict's approach to these challenges is his concern for growing secularization in Europe and what he sees as the dangers of individualism and relativism spreading out of Western cultures. His favored theological framework is Augustinian. The stress is on the dimension of conflict between the world marked by sin and God's promise of salvation and on the necessity to bring back a sense of transcendence. The church offers its contribution by presenting the resources of revelation and proclaiming "charity in truth" as the driving force for authentic development.

In this context, deductive forms of reasoning from principles to applications and an insistence on the asymmetry of the dialogue between church and world are characteristic of the style of *CiV*. Beyond the contextual explanation of what appears as drawbacks on the path opened by *GS*, this shift also emphasizes a specific aspect of God's mystery. God's grace is a gift freely given on the part of God; and the church, especially in its teaching office, rather than the world too scarred by sin, mediates the true image of God. Developing reflections on categories like vocation, gift and gratuitousness, or relation and communion, through practical considerations about the economy, the environment, or technology, *CiV* offers a vision of being human that is characterized by transcendence and openness to God. The encyclical also presents various expressions of a Word Christology, which begins with the affirmation of the divinity of the second person of the Trinity and envisions salvation as primarily participation in divine life through union with Christ. Undoubtedly, all these theological notes reflect the Augustinian framework.

Nonetheless, Benedict's concern for global justice, apparent in his addressing concrete social, economic, and political issues, prompts a rebalancing of his theology. This rebalancing is an expression, at least implicitly, of the neo-Thomist and liberationist frameworks. Changes are called for at the level of structures, for example, those of financial institutions, corporate businesses, or international organizations, and not merely at the level of personal morality. This awareness of the role of structures affects the overall anthropological vision and suggests that another type of Christology is possible, a Spirit Christology more sensible to the historical Jesus and to the presence of God in the world through the work of the Spirit.

Chapter 4 turns to Pope Francis's *Laudato si'* (2015). The promotion of integral human development takes the path of integral ecology. Issued only a few years after *CiV*, the global world context has not changed so much. Two world summits of the United Nations (held in the same year) on climate change and on the sustainable development goals, are symbolic of the connection made by *LS* between the social and the ecological questions: "Everything is connected!" In the church, the election of the first pope from Latin America changes the focuses significantly. The name of Francis—referring to Saint Francis of Assisi—that was chosen by the pope illustrates very well his special attention to care for what is most fragile in the world: both the poor and the earth. Although the neo-Thomist framework of openness to the world and the liberationist stress on the social dimension of salvation are still present in the teaching of a pope who likes to refer to his predecessor Paul VI and who comes from the continent that saw the birth of liberation theology, it is the fourth theological framework, the Franciscan, that better helps to capture the theological contribution of *LS*.

Laudato si' returns us to the inductive see-judge-act methodology and embraces resolutely a dialogical approach promoted as the path to integral ecology. As in *PP*, this style carries an insistence on the incarnational dimension of the Christian faith. *Laudato si'* is an instance of a "theology of the signs of the times" for which historical events and the current situation of the world are places for God's revelation. The anthropology developed in *LS* insists on the dynamism and the social dimension of being human as in previous encyclicals, but there is a major shift in focus that considers human beings in their kinship relations with the whole creation and invites us to move from a problematic deviated anthropocentrism to a relational anthropology.

Finally, *LS* offers an invitation to take Saint Francis of Assisi as a model in his following of Jesus Christ in poverty, fully inserted in the created world; the encyclical also presents some pointers, still to be worked out, toward a cosmic Christology that would fully express the impact of Christ's birth, death, and resurrection on the whole creation.

The final chapter gathers the theological insights collected while reading the encyclicals and uses them to reflect on three broad theological questions: (1) How do we understand the role and centrality of historicity for theology? Any discourse about God necessarily begins with human experience and within history, but theology does not originate here and needs always to manifest its transcendent source. (2) How do we articulate within a theological anthropology the individual and social dimensions of the human person or the call for personal conversion and for structural changes? The only truly Christian path is to work out a profound unity between the two. The development of a trinitarian anthropology suggested by some passages of the social encyclicals is a possible clue or pointer in this direction. (3) How do we balance different approaches to the mystery of Jesus Christ from above and from below in Christology? The path suggested by the social encyclicals is to strongly articulate the two while insisting on the inescapable role of the latter. Consequently, it should be stressed that the option for the poor has crucial christological implications.

CST is theological. Hopefully, this book will shed greater light on this theological nature so that ethicists may become more aware of the theological echoes of the ethical reflections developed here, that theologians may gain a greater sense that, far from being merely a pastoral application of theological principles, CST is an essential theological source, and finally, that all those who find inspiration in CST for their commitment to social justice may be enriched in their spiritual journey.

DEVELOPMENT, JUSTICE, AND PEACE

ON MARCH 26, 1967, sixteen months after the end of the Second Vatican Council and in the middle of the first United Nations Development Decade, Pope Paul VI published his first social encyclical and dedicated it to the topic of the development of peoples. *Populorum progessio (PP)*[1] has as its starting point the pastoral concern of the church for and its solidarity with the peoples seeking material development, health, and educational resources, but also political freedom and cultural flourishing. The encyclical demonstrates the church's contribution to the issue of development through a conceptual reflection grounded in its tradition, but also through concrete appeals to actions and reforms addressed to all the faithful Catholics, and more broadly to all people of good will.

The first part deals with the notion of complete human development. The situation of a predominantly postcolonial world is that of growing inequalities between rich and poor people, in material possessions but also in power. The Christian vision of development is the personal development of everyone and the development of all. It demands fostering a transition from less human conditions to more human conditions, materially, culturally, and spiritually. Consequently, action needs to be undertaken in developing countries regarding issues as diverse as land reform, industrial development, state planning, or support to family and to societal intermediary bodies.

In a second part, the encyclical addresses more directly the more affluent countries and appeals to solidarity in providing aid, to justice in reforming international trade relations, and to charity in fostering collaboration and brotherhood. In a world marked by the tensions of the Cold War and postcolonial conflicts, development is also the new name for peace. *Populorum progessio* ends with a vibrant appeal for everyone to take on the task of working for integral human development.

To characterize the message of *PP*, one can say that it strongly connects the notion of development with justice and peace. The encyclical was, in fact, the mission statement of the newly created Pontifical Commission for Justice and Peace.[2] The development of peoples is a matter of justice in that it does not concern merely individual commitments to help the destitute but also brings about just structures and institutions at the national and international levels that will foster the flourishing of persons and societies. This development is then the source of a true peace that is not the mere absence of war, but the path toward a universal fraternity in which humanity recognizes itself as truly a family.

How does this magisterial document dealing with the social, political, and economic issues of its epoch help us to enter more deeply into, or be seized more deeply by, the mystery of "God for us"? What insights concerning crucial theological themes, such as Christology and theological anthropology, are particularly highlighted because of the specific concerns, situation, and methodology of the document? Very much in line with the neo-Thomist framework and in contrast to the antimodernist crusades of the pre–Vatican II period that stressed the sinfulness of the world, the theology of *PP* highlights the possibility of a positive, dialogue-oriented, transformationist relation between the church and the gospel to the world.

CONTEXT

First, there is the world context.[3] At the end of World War II, it was still possible to say that the sun never sets on the British Empire. Most of Africa and large parts of Asia and Oceania were under colonial powers, principally French and British. By the middle of the 1960s, decolonization had officially occurred in most of those regions. India gained its independence in 1948, French colonies in Africa and the former Belgian Congo followed in 1960, and British colonies in Africa between 1961 and 1965. Peoples aspired to freedom and independence but also to participation in their own government and respect for their own culture. These aspirations found strong echoes in the encyclical and undoubtedly shaped some of its anthropological vision.

However, national independence does not mean instant removal of all mechanisms of dependence and colonialism. As *PP* highlights, "Peoples who have recently gained national independence experience the need to add to this political freedom a fitting autonomous growth, social as well as economic, in order to assure their citizens of a full human enhancement and to take their rightful place with other nations" (*PP* 6). A striking feature of the decades following World War II was the growing disparity among nations. Western countries of Europe and North America were largely benefitting from "a time of new and exhilarating social, economic, and cultural advances on a global scale,"[4] a time of economic expansion, industrialization, new technologies, and expanding communications media. With the impulse of the Marshall Plan for the reconstruction of Europe after World War II, and with energy available at very low cost, it seemed that economic growth and technical advancement could continue forever. It was "the myth of infinite growth, of the complete conquest of the planet…and of space."[5] Meanwhile, the gap with the "developing countries" was growing. Statistics speak for themselves:

> 30% of the world's people living in the North, particularly in the North Atlantic region, are enjoying 70% of the world's goods and services, 80% of its trade and new investments, over 90% of its industry and nearly 100% of its critical capacities for advanced research.[6]

The question of development was often spoken about. However, for many the idea remained that of a continuous line of progress on which some were more advanced, and others suffered backwardness and needed to be helped to catch up. A debate was emerging about other analyses of the situation, especially the idea that underdevelopment of some countries was structurally connected to the development of others. With an encyclical focusing on the development of peoples, Paul VI engaged the church at the heart of a crucial world issue.

The Cold War was going on between the West and the East and had repercussions on the entire world. The Iron Curtain still strongly divided the two parts of Europe. Various conflicts in the "Third World," such as the Vietnam War, were simply the offshoring of the major confrontation between the two super powers and their competing ideologies. All this fueled a costly arms race that Pope Paul VI constantly denounced, calling instead for using the money "to relieve the more destitute of the world" (*PP* 51).

Second, there is the context of the church. *Populorum progressio* was published less than two years after the end of Vatican II. The church continued to become more aware of being a "world-Church"[7] and the encyclical reflects this by repeating after John XXIII: "The social question has become worldwide" (*PP* 2).[8] The curia became more international under the pontificate of Paul VI. The pope himself began to travel outside of Italy to get some personal experience of the challenges he addressed in his encyclical. This "direct contact with the acute problems pressing continents full of life and hope" and the opportunity to "see and virtually touch the very serious difficulties besetting peoples…at grips with the problem of development" (*PP* 4) are explicitly recognized as a source for the document. Before being elected pope, Cardinal Montini had traveled to Brazil, Zimbabwe (then Southern Rhodesia), Burkina Faso (then Upper Volta), Nigeria, and Ghana. Then, as pope, he made a significant journey to India in December 1964, where he pleaded wholeheartedly for peace and the diversion of the money spent on arms toward the assistance of developing countries.[9]

Finally, three figures particularly inspired *PP*. The first is Fr. Louis Lebret, OP (1897–1966).[10] Although the authorship of papal encyclicals is given to the pope who signs them, he is usually not the main redactor. In the case of *PP*, it is officially recognized that Lebret wrote the first drafts in 1964 and 1965 and is thus the central inspiration of the document, even if he died before its publication.[11] Before World War II, Lebret began his life as a Dominican priest by helping fishermen in the northern coast of Brittany in France to organize in the midst of a deep crisis prompted by the industrialization of their profession. He realized that it was not merely a social crisis but an *economic* and *structural* one that needed to be addressed, first, by careful study to get an appropriate knowledge of the human reality, and second, by actions at various levels, including the political through unions. During the war, Lebret with some economists founded the center *Économie et Humanisme* (Economy and humanism), whose goal is "to bring economy back to the service of humanity." In 1947, he started to travel around the world and to work on the problem of underdevelopment through counseling governments in analyzing needs and resources and elaborating development plans. According to Lebret, already at this time, "development was for a nation the passage from a less human phase to a more human phase."[12] It implied a profound respect for indigenous values but also an integrated vision of the human being who, in all its dimensions, is in a process of ascension or human fulfillment.[13]

French philosopher Jacques Maritain (1882–1973) is another inspiring figure for *PP*, though not an immediate redactor.[14] In *Integral Humanism*, Maritain defines humanism as that which "tends essentially to render man more truly human, and to manifest his original greatness by having him participate in all that which can enrich him in nature and in history."[15] Maritain also advocated for pluralism in the political organization of society, respect for the freedom of persons, and engagement in the realization of a fraternal community.[16] His approach, grounded in the philosophy and theology of Aquinas, resonates with the relation between church and earthly realities articulated in *GS*: distinction and autonomy without separation. Practically, it supports a transformative vision of society under the impulsion of the Christian values at work in the faithful engaged in various aspects of the social life. *Populorum progressio* incarnates this vision, and the notion of integral development that it promotes obviously has some roots in Maritain's concept of integral humanism.[17]

A final inspirational figure worth mentioning is the Belgian priest Fr. Joseph Cardijn (1882–1967).[18] Born into a modest family, after entering a seminary for secondary education, Cardijn experienced very quickly the growing gap between church ministers and his former schoolmates who were already at work in factories. He thus decided to devote his life to bridging this gap, swearing by the deathbed of his father, "I will give my life to this thing, to end the scandal which brings death to millions of young workers, separating them from Christ and the Church."[19] This led him to gather groups of young workers to foster mutual support and growth in Christian faith. In 1920, the Jeunesse Ouvrière Chrétienne (JOC or Young Christian Worker, YCW) was founded and very soon became an international movement spreading throughout the world. Cardijn summarized the aim of the YCW: "The action of the YCW is a very simple thing—the action of Christ who continues to live and act in the world now in the person of his young Christians."[20] One methodological key of the YCW is the see-judge-act approach that members practice in their meetings and is adopted by *PP*.

Social encyclicals never arise out of a vacuum. On the contrary, they are embedded in a historical context. The few contextual elements for *PP* just listed, taken from world history but also from the more particular personal histories of those having contributed to the document, constitute the background to begin our analysis of the theological contribution of the encyclical. *PP* is aware of the evils and sufferings of the social life of its time, but its overall context in the world and in the church is also open to possibilities of transformation and full of hopes. This renders more natural the development of a theology that is open and in dialogue with the world in reaction to the confrontational stance of the church in the preceding century.

METHODOLOGY AND STYLE

Being attentive to how something is expressed is crucial to grasping the core of what is being said. Vatican II's change of style was not a mere external wrapping of some old teaching but carried with it a doctrinal renewal. *Populorum progressio* follows in the council's footsteps by implementing an inductive see-judge-act approach and providing a crucial place for dialogue. Both aspects are theologically significant. The first highlights the incarnational dimension of the Christian faith, and the necessity to put the gospel into action against the temptation of a faith focused only on otherworldly life while ignoring worldly mediations. The latter is connected to God's own trinitarian mode of revelation and salvation in history.

See-Judge-Act Approach

In the YCW, Fr. Joseph Cardijn had formalized a way of fostering the apostolic vocation of laypeople that was subsequently adopted by all the Catholic Action Movements. He explained, "Laymen are formed first of all by the discovery of facts, followed by a Christian judgment, resulting in the actions they plan, the plans they carry into effect, the responsibilities they shoulder."[21] And John XXIII fully endorsed this approach in his first social encyclical in 1961:

> There are three stages which should normally be followed in the reduction of social principles into practice. First, one reviews the concrete situation; secondly, one forms a judgment on it in the light of these same principles; thirdly, one decides what in the circumstances can and should be done to implement these principles. These are the three stages that are usually expressed in the three terms: look, judge, act. (*MM* 236)

These three steps of seeing, judging, and acting are the basic structure of the first part of *PP*, in which Paul VI reflects on "Man's Complete Development." He starts with the data of the problem (*PP* 6–11), he continues with offering a vision of development informed by Scripture and various theological and philosophical resources (*PP* 12–21), and finally, he makes recommendations by noting several areas where there is "action to be undertaken," such as the limits in the exercise of the right to property, the challenge of industrialization, the need for planning, or demographic issues and the role of the family (*PP* 22–42). In the second part on "The Development of the Human Race in the Spirit of Solidarity," the focus is more directly on the "act" step: recommendations are addressed to the more affluent nations. However, those recommendations are rooted in the observation of reality and a careful analysis of it through the lens of Christian faith.

Furthermore, concerning the implementation of each step of the see-judge-act approach in the encyclical, seeing reality as it stands and taking it as a starting point is an important feature highlighted by many early commentators. The encyclical stays "close to reality," and does not fly from it in abstract reasoning, but rather deepens the understanding of reality with the awareness of its complexity.[22] As Matías García Gómez notes, "It is without explicit philosophical deductions, without the detour of pure natural law that Paul VI envisions religious hopes also at the concrete level of human life."[23] The tone is set in the introduction when the pope mentions the travels he undertook, which opened his eyes to some dimensions of the reality of development issues. Overall the style of the encyclical is "direct, journalistic, and concrete."[24]

Concerning the step of "judging," the role of the Bible is worth highlighting. It is not so much the number of biblical quotations in the encyclical that is significant but the way they are used. They appear to be far less prooftexts, as had been in previous magisterial documents, and much more inspirational or challenging scriptural sources. Notably, several parables concerning riches are mentioned.[25] A parable does not give an immediate ethical rule but prompts one to change one's vision of the world. Many direct quotes are questions: "If someone who has the riches of this world sees his brother in need and closes his heart to him, how does the love of God abide in him?" (1 John 3:17; *PP* 23); "What does it profit a man to gain the whole world if he suffers the loss of his soul?" (Matt 16:26; *PP* 40). The Bible is a source for raising questions rather than immediately giving answers. There is an evangelical tone in the encyclical, and "the vigor of the appeal is like a prophet calling the attention of everyone to some situations which are no longer bearable."[26]

Concerning the last step of "acting," we can note the sense of urgency that runs through the entire encyclical: "solidarity in action at this turning point in human history is a matter of urgency" (*PP* 1); "the question is urgent for on it depends the future of the civilization of the world" (*PP* 44); "it is time for all men and all peoples to face up to their responsibilities" (*PP* 80). The style and tone of the encyclical is meant to mobilize around the urgency of the action to be taken.[27] Some called it a manifesto, and they emphasize that it is a document that also requires taking action at the political level, the level of global structures of societies and of international relations.[28]

The see-judge-act methodology bears a theological meaning. The encyclical starts by reminding us that the gospel "makes it the duty [of the Church] to put herself at the service of all, to help them grasp their serious problem in all its dimension and to convince them that solidarity in action at this turning point in human history is a matter of urgency" (*PP* 1). The Christian faith and the gospel have concrete and practical implications in the present world. They must be put into practice not simply through the conversion of individuals but through the transformation of the temporal realm. Everything in the encyclical is oriented toward an active commitment for this transformation, "in the name of the evangelical message and of the faith."[29] As the Venezuelan Commission Justice and Peace highlighted in its 1968 commentary,

> The Church is not interested in the technical and political aspects of development in themselves. It is her faith which prompts her to engage with the problems of the temporal city, to engage concretely…to engage not only through a doctrinal statement but through offering a global vision of humanity which compels her to concrete formulations. Theologically the participation of the Church as institution and of Christians themselves in the multiple tasks of the development of peoples is plainly justified.[30]

With its focus on concrete reality and its call for action, the encyclical highlights that the salvation proclaimed by the gospel is not purely otherworldly, but on the contrary is already at work when the church fulfills its mission and contributes to the transformation of the present world.[31] Proclaiming the gospel includes proclaiming the gospel in action and in action at the heart of the most crucial political, economic, and social issues of the time.

This insistence on the implementation of social justice for the proclamation of the gospel is an expression of the deep meaning of the mystery of the incarnation. In 1968, Peter Riga remarked that the theological issue at stake was to take seriously "the law of Incarnation" and to reject any form of Docetism. On the one hand, some Christians "wish to regress to God 'in himself,' to contemplation of the eternal verities. This…is an escape from the reality of man with whom, by the Incarnation, God is forever implicated."[32] In this conception, God remains an illusion. On the other hand, "there are others today for whom God can be found only when man has been found…[they] recall that God has become visible in Jesus Christ the man, just as he has become visible in the extension of his body—all men."[33] *Populorum Progressio* is a strong expression of the latter approach. Paul VI is adamant about social justice, because the church must follow the example of the incarnate Word. We cannot abstract the spiritual in human life because "God has made man as a whole and his total vocation is to be what God has created him. This includes the economic as well as the political, the social as well as the spiritual.…To work for more humane conditions among men is, in reality, to work for the extension of the spirit of Christ, the extension of the Gospel into the world of men" (*PP* 32).[34]

In the North American context, where some of the encyclical's critiques of liberal capitalism were not well received—even among

Catholics—Riga's comments stressed that denying the legitimacy of the church to intervene in temporal issues, such as the development of peoples, challenges the very heart of the Christian faith: God became human. The argument is a good pointer to the theological issue at stake. By engaging the magisterial teaching in the realm of concrete reality, by looking at the issue of development, judging it with the light of faith, and urging everyone to action, Paul VI expresses the Christian belief in the incarnation.

Dialogue

Another methodological and stylistic feature of *PP* is the emphasis given to dialogue. Not only does it encourage dialogue and work in common with those who do not entirely share the Catholic faith, but Paul VI shows that he practices what he preaches. He mentions "the memory of [his] unforgettable encounter in Bombay with [his] non-Christian brethren" (*PP* 82) and notes explicitly that the reflection he offers is nourished by the dialogue with economists, sociologists, philosophers, and contemporary theologians. Previous social encyclicals have always been prepared with the help of specialists, priests, or laypeople, but in the footnotes, only references to the Bible, prior magisterial documents, Saint Thomas, or some fathers of the church appeared. For the first time, several contemporary names are cited: two theologians (de Lubac and Chenu), a philosopher (Maritain), an economist (Colin Clark), a moralist (Nell Breuning), and a specialist of development policies (Lebret). It might appear only symbolic for the reader accustomed to modern academic standards, but for a document of the church, it is a very significant symbol. The "deepening of human knowledge" (*PP* 86) about the question of development called for by the pope implies listening to a variety of voices inside and outside the church, and among secular disciplines.[35]

Dialogue is also evident in the way the encyclical attempts to reach a large audience. Following on from John XXIII's *Pacem in terris*, *PP* is addressed, not only to the bishops, priests, religious, and faithful, but to "all men of good will."[36] The church does not intend to impose its teaching or vision of the world on others but is convinced that many can join their efforts in the fight "to further the progress of poorer people, to encourage social justice among nations, to offer to less developed nations the means whereby they can further their own progress" (*PP* 5). The encyclical ends with a vibrant appeal to various categories of people: other Christians and non-Christian believers (*PP* 82), delegates of international organizations, rulers, journalists, and educators (*PP* 83–84).

Moreover, dialogue between nations and between cultures is fostered as a key component for development and peace. There is a need for more dialogue between developed and developing countries (*PP* 53). There is also a need to foster a dialogue between cultures or civilizations that creates fraternity, a "dialogue based on man and not on commodities or technical skills" (*PP* 73). Dialogue and collaboration are also needed among and within developing countries to overcome tensions and conflicts prompted by excessive nationalism and forms of racism (*PP* 62–64).

This emphasis put on dialogue is theologically meaningful. Three years before *PP*, Paul VI, in *Ecclesiam suam* (*ES*), the first and programmatic encyclical of his pontificate, had reflected at length on the notion of dialogue and highlighted that dialogue has its origin "in the mind of God Himself" (*ES* 70). Indeed, as exemplified in prayer, "religion of its very nature is a certain relationship between God and man." Paul VI presents the doctrine of revelation in terms of dialogue:

> Revelation, too, that supernatural link which God has established with man, can likewise be looked upon as a dialogue. In the Incarnation and in the Gospel it is God's Word that speaks to us. That fatherly, sacred dialogue between God and man, broken off at the time of Adam's unhappy fall, has since, in the course of history, been restored. Indeed, the whole history of man's salvation is one long, varied dialogue, which marvelously begins with God and which He prolongs with men in so many different ways. In Christ's "conversation" with men, God reveals something of Himself, of the mystery of His own life, of His own unique essence and trinity of persons. (*ES* 70)

In those few sentences, the pope connects the attitude of dialogue not only to the way God reveals Godself to humanity, but also to the mystery of salvation that occurs within the dialogue between God and humanity in Christ, and finally to the mystery of the Trinity, which is a mystery of dialogue par excellence. This is how much theological weight Paul VI puts on the promotion of dialogue.

This dialogue, "which God the Father initiated and established with us through Christ in the Holy Spirit" (*ES* 71), serves as a model for the dialogue the pope seeks to foster between the church and the modern world. Just as God takes the initiative, the church ought to make the first move toward others (*ES* 72). Dialogue is induced by love (*ES* 73), is neither limited and self-seeking nor coercive (*ES* 74), but rather universal (*ES* 76) and persevering (*ES* 77). In *PP*, we easily recognize Paul VI's attempt to implement this model. Without explicitly restating the theological foundation of what he does, he still emphasizes that God's relation to humanity is a relation of dialogue. Engaging an explicit dialogue with the world is not merely a strategic move for the church to gain a greater audience, but, rather, the recognition of the divine presence at work in the world.

What Rahner says about interdisciplinary dialogue in science and the relation between science and theology is also enlightening.[37] For him, the truth of human existence is found only in dialogue because truth is present to some degree in all groups and people.[38] Despite their pluralism and often their seemingly irreconcilable conflicts, all sciences have a common ground, which is human knowledge. This human factor is the basis for interdisciplinary dialogue among sciences but also between theology and science.[39] The deepening of knowledge about the human condition offered by science is indispensable to theology in its reaching out to the mystery to which this human condition, in its transcendentality, points.

Theologically, this common ground is supported by Rahner's assertion concerning the history of salvation and revelation, and world history, the former being about what theology is concerned and the latter with what science is concerned. "The history of salvation and revelation [is] coextensive with the whole of world history."[40] All individual histories and the whole collective history of the human race are histories of salvation and of revelation grounded in God's self-communication to human beings in grace. Rahner says about philosophy, "Everything human belongs to God, and only so is truly appropriated to man," and so "in the midst of all philosophy the theologian discerns God revealing himself in his grace."[41] By extension, could we not say that amid all the studies concerning the development of peoples, the theologian can discern "God's revealing himself in his grace"? Certainly, this is what we find at work in *PP*.

Conclusion

Style and methodology are theologically meaningful. In the dynamism initiated by *GS* and the council, *PP* puts into practice an inductive see-judge-act approach and stresses dialogue at multiple levels. Consequently, the encyclical expresses, in a practical way, faith in the incarnation and faith in God's salvific revelation through a dialogical encounter with humanity.

Incarnation is not an abstract dogma but the reality of recognizing God's salvation at work when humanization is fostered, when the conditions for an integral human development are implemented, and when dehumanizing, unjust situations are denounced. Believing that Jesus Christ is truly divine and truly human—that God became human—ought to be expressed through discerning the signs of the kingdom of God in the present world as well as the signs opposing it. This discernment leads to actions that bring about this kingdom. The deepening of the mystery of the incarnation is also present in the recognition of God's self-revelation in everything that is authentically human. Dialoguing and collaborating with others in the search for humanization is a crucial locus for encountering God's salvific love. The promotion of dialogue is not a mere strategic move. More profoundly, it reflects the manifestation of the very self of a triune dialoguing God who is at work in history.

These theological insights are not evident in a systematic way in the encyclical, but thanks to other contributions from the pope himself, and from Rahner, we can highlight them and thus grasp something of the mystery of "God for us." Having reflected on the style and methodology at work in *PP*, we now turn to theological anthropology and Christology of the encyclical.

THEOLOGICAL ANTHROPOLOGY

In addressing the issue of the development of peoples in the context of the 1960s, *PP* offers a rich theological vision of the human person and of humanity. Promoting integral development highlights both the transcendent and the social dimensions of the human being.

Transcendent Humanism

The church promotes a notion of integral human development or the "development of the whole person and of all humankind" (*PP* 14). In *PP*, this notion of integral human development bears with it the promotion of a "complete humanism" (*PP* 42), or "new humanism" (*PP* 20), which one commentator qualified as "an incarnate, real, lucid, exigent and combative humanism."[42] The encyclical speaks also of a "transcendent humanism" (*PP* 16). This qualification encompasses a set of three features in the portrait of the human being. First, the human being is not viewed primarily in terms of a fixed human nature but rather in terms of the fulfillment of a human vocation. "In the design of God, every man is called to develop and fulfill himself, for every life is a vocation" (*PP* 15). The notion of development implies a notion of a constant dynamism. The encyclical begins by evoking "those peoples who are striving to escape hunger, misery, endemic diseases, and ignorance…those who are looking for…a more active improvement of their human qualities" (*PP* 1). It speaks of what people "aspire to" (*PP* 6), and how the church can help them attain "their full flowering" (*PP* 13). Characteristic of human beings is a capacity or potential for development in humanity: "At birth, everyone is granted, in germ, a set of aptitudes and qualities for him to bring to fruition" (*PP* 15). This characteristic is theologically grounded because it is recognized as "God's design" or "the destiny intended by [the] Creator" (*PP* 15).

The crucial issue, therefore, is to examine what sustains and what impedes this dynamism of humanization. Then there is the second feature of transcendent humanism: multidimensionality. Development is "the transition from less human conditions to those which are more human" (*PP* 20), and in describing these conditions, various aspects of human beings that are intended to flourish are articulated. First, there is the material dimension. Human beings have material needs that need to be fulfilled in order to flourish in life. Hunger, misery, lack of medical resources, and lack of material necessities are regarded as "less human conditions" (*PP* 21). Large parts of the encyclical deal with the fight against them. For example, the pope expresses alarm regarding those "countless men and women ravaged by hunger" (*PP* 45).

However, the material dimension cannot be separated from other human dimensions, beginning with the intellectual one, that are called to flourish. Striving to "have more" and "do more" goes hand in hand with seeking to "know more," and all are directed toward "being more" (*PP* 6). The encyclical speaks at length about the development of education and culture: "hunger for education is no less debasing than hunger for food: an illiterate is a person with an undernourished mind" (*PP* 35). "Growth of knowledge and the acquisition of culture" are part of those conditions that are "more human" (*PP* 21). Human beings are called to grow in their rational dimension no less than in their material dimension. The social and moral dimensions must also be mentioned here. On the one hand, "the moral deficiencies of those who are mutilated by selfishness" are among the "less human conditions" as well as the distorted social relationship marked by abuses of power. On the other hand, more human conditions are those where we see "increased esteem for the dignity of others…and cooperation for the common good" (*PP* 21).

Last, human beings have a spiritual dimension, an openness to what is beyond the mere human condition. This is also called to develop in the human vocation:

> Conditions that are still more human: the acknowledgement by man of supreme values, and of God their source and their finality. Conditions that finally and above all, are more human: faith, a gift of God accepted by the good will of man, and unity in the charity of Christ, who calls us all to share as sons in the life of the living God, the Father of all men. (*PP* 21)

There is a fundamental orientation of the human being toward God. "Just as the whole of creation is ordained to its Creator, so spiritual beings of their own accord orient their lives to God, the first truth and the supreme good" (*PP* 16). Therefore, the encyclical stresses that "there is no true humanism but that which is open to the Absolute and is conscious of a vocation which gives human life its true meaning" (*PP* 42). The human being is not the ultimate measure of all things, and *PP* recalls the saying of Pascal: "Man infinitely surpasses man" (*PP* 42). In this sense, this humanism is rightly called *transcendent* humanism.[43]

Because all those dimensions of the human being are interrelated and called to thrive together, true human development cannot be reduced to mere economic growth.[44] The criterion of integral human development, the touchstone constantly repeated for the practical evaluation of issues concerning the development of peoples, bears with it a rich multilayered vision of the human being in a process of humanization ultimately oriented toward God.

A last feature of transcendent humanism portrayed in the encyclical is the centrality of freedom. People aspire to "freedom from misery" as well as "political" freedom (*PP* 6). And indeed, the human being is "endowed with intelligence and freedom" (*PP* 15). Becoming more human means becoming freer. Misery, destitution, and growing inequalities directly negate freedom. The second part of the encyclical insists on the necessity for more affluent countries to come to the aid of less affluent ones. This necessity is rooted in the promotion of human freedom:

> The struggle against destitution, though urgent and necessary, is not enough. It is a question rather of building a world where every man, no matter what his race, religion, or nationality, can live a fully human life, *freed from servitude* imposed on him by other men or by natural forces over which he has not sufficient control; a world where *freedom is not an empty word* and where the poor man Lazarus can sit down at the same table with the rich man. (*PP* 47, emphasis mine.)

Freedom also means freedom from a form of enslavement to material possessions:

> Increased possession is not the ultimate goal of nations nor of individuals. All growth is ambivalent. It is essential if man is to develop as a man, but in a way it imprisons man if he considers it the supreme good, and it restricts his vision. (*PP* 19)

Greed, avarice, and selfishness are opposed to true freedom. Working for integral human development implies genuine resistance to the various forms of these vices.

The importance of freedom is also prompted by using the vocabulary of rights and of responsibility. Following up on John XXIII's full endorsement of human rights in *Pacem in terris* (1963), Paul VI several times mentions respect for the fundamental rights of the person. For example, although planning is crucial, *PP* warns against "the danger of complete collectivization or of arbitrary planning, which, by denying liberty, would prevent the exercise of the fundamental rights of the human person" (*PP* 33).

The notion of responsibility is also omnipresent in *PP*. Persons and peoples ought to be the primary agents of their development and this responsibility ought not to be denied by disguised forms of paternalism and colonialism.[45] The encyclical also praises the leaders of development in education, who are "the primary agents of development, because they render man capable of acting for himself" (*PP* 35).

The portrait of the human being as transcendent, that is, being dynamically called to grow in all her dimensions, oriented toward God, and freeing herself from all forms of enslavement, is connected directly to two theological motifs. First, the human vocation is to realize the image of God in which human beings are created. On the topic of work in the context of industrialization, *PP* suggests that the human person "must cooperate with his Creator in the perfecting of creation….God who has endowed man with intelligence, imagination, and sensitivity, has also given him the means of completing his work in a certain way:…everyone who works is a creator" (*PP* 27). The vocation of the human being is to grow in humanity by continuing the creation and by working at the transformation of this world. Second, the fulfillment of oneself through personal development is also the expression of union with Christ. In this union, one attains "a transcendent humanism which gives [a human person her] greatest possible perfection" (*PP* 16). We will return to this aspect in the next section on Christology.

These two theological notes recall that the transcendent humanism highlighted by the encyclical pertains to a theological anthropology or a theological vision of the mystery of humanity. Turning once again to Rahner, we find a confirmation of the theological weight of such anthropological reflection.

Toward the end of his life, the German theologian reformulates in *Foundations of Christian Faith* what he had already formulated about the human being in his earlier works.[46] Although taking the form of a philosophical inquiry, it is at the same time a theological one because the question is to envision what makes divine revelation and salvation possible in the human being. Rahner asks the question, "What kind of hearer does Christianity anticipate so that its real and ultimate message can even be heard?"[47] Three key features of being human come to the fore, and they echo what we have highlighted in *PP*: subjectivity or personhood; transcendent being; and freedom and responsibility.

Human beings are persons and subjects. We experience ourselves as shaped by what we are not (family, culture, environment, etc.). Specific anthropologies, such as biochemistry, psychology, or sociology, explore this fact by trying to comprehend the wholeness of being human through that discipline's specific viewpoint. However, human beings are always more than this. Being a person is more than being the sum total of empirical data. Being a subject means experiencing oneself as prior and more original than the plurality of empirical data. "Being a person…means the self-possession of a subject as such in a conscious and free relationship to the totality of itself."[48] This personalist approach resonates with *PP*'s insistence that the human being—in her entirety or in all her dimensions—is the criterion of authentic development, and the latter is not to be reduced to mere material or economic growth.

For Rahner, saying that human beings are transcendent beings expands the notion of personhood and subjectivity. This is viewed, first, through the transcendent structure of knowledge. Human beings experience an infinite horizon of questioning about themselves even if they do not always explicitly engage in it. This questioning is openness to an infinity beyond oneself. Because it would make no sense that this be an experience of nothingness, Rahner concludes that it is a positive infinity, an absolute, that later will be recognized as the holy mystery or God. Human beings experience themselves not as *absolute* beings but as necessarily receiving from an Absolute Being and being oriented toward it. However, this experience is not an escape from the reality of being-in the-world. On the contrary, it is lived only through this reality. As Rahner insists, this radical openness constitutive of being human is "present precisely when a person experiences himself as involved in the multiplicity of cares and concerns and fears and hopes of his everyday world."[49]

What is experienced through the transcendentality of knowledge is also experienced in agency. Consequently, Rahner says that personhood and subjectivity are also expressed in freedom and responsibility. Rahner distinguishes the originating transcendental freedom from the categorical manifestations of freedom it originates: "freedom is not the power to be able to do this or that, but the power to decide about oneself and to actualize oneself."[50] The object of freedom is the person as such, not a mere tool in her hands. However, once again, it is only in the world, through everyday actions that are always limited and not entirely free, that the human becomes aware of the "more" of transcendent freedom.[51] There is a similar inherent movement of the human person toward self-realization through acting as there is a movement toward self-consciousness through knowing.

With these features of a human being driven to self-consciousness and self-realization in freedom, Rahner can then offer a Christian understanding of salvation. A theological notion of salvation is not only a concern for a future afterlife but rather "the final and definitive validity of a person's true self-understanding, and true self-realization in freedom."[52] And because human subjectivity and freedom cannot take place anywhere other than in the world, Rahner concludes that the history of salvation is "coextensive" with world history.[53]

In *PP*, the salvific mission of the church is expressed in the promotion of the integral development of humanity. This is a concrete expression of the Rahnerian notion of coextensive histories. As one commentator writing about the encyclical's promotion of a transcendent humanism stated, "To rise above what one is in order to tend toward what one ought to be: in Christian formulation this means to orient oneself toward the Kingdom…and it is the collective walk of the whole of humanity toward divine life."[54]

In brief, the vision of the human being in terms of transcendentality and freedom, which we have seen highlighted through practical considerations in the encyclical and more systematically exposed in Rahner, is a theological vision. It starts from, and therefore also points to, the mystery of God's creation of and salvific encounter with humanity. This vision insists on the grace of God working from within the nature of humanity rather than from without, and it is expressive of the main theological framework—neo-Thomist—that is at work in the encyclical. This, however, is only one aspect of the theological anthropology offered by the encyclical. We now turn to a second one, which is the social dimension of being human.

Social Being

A human being is not an isolated being. On the contrary, the human person can flourish only within a society and in relation to others. The social dimension of being human is constantly emphasized in the encyclical alongside the stress put on personal growth and freedom, and it is done through fostering solidarity. Integral human development is development in human solidarity.

From the outset of the document, the pope affirms that the church is concerned with the development of "peoples," not of mere isolated individuals, and he intends to convince everyone that "solidarity in action…is a matter of urgency" (*PP* 1). Human "complete development," which is the title of part 1, cannot be separated from "the development of the human race in the spirit of solidarity" reflected upon in part 2. In the more theoretical section about a Christian vision of development, the considerations about human self-fulfillment are immediately followed by the statement, "But each man is a member of society. He is part of the whole of mankind. It is not just certain individuals, but all men who are called to this fullness of development" (*PP* 17).

The first thing to recognize is that we have inherited from previous generations, and we are benefitting from our contemporaries. This inherent vertical and horizontal solidarity is a source of duty: "we cannot refuse to interest ourselves in those who will come after us to enlarge the human family" (*PP* 17). The possession of material goods and the desire for what is necessary are legitimate for personal development, but they can become a trap when they turn to greed and avarice, replacing bonds of friendship and solidarity with bonds of mere self-interest. Indeed, "both for nations and for individual men, avarice is the most evident form of moral underdevelopment" (*PP* 19). True solidarity, which implies a duty to work for a fairer distribution of material and immaterial goods, is a never-ending process on the journey of humanization or integral human development.

Solidarity is promoted in a very concrete fashion in the second half of the encyclical, dealing with the aid more wealthy nations ought to provide to less wealthy ones. For example, the duty of solidarity requires acting against the situation of hunger, which still concerns whole continents. Here the pope supports the work done by the Food and Agriculture Organization (FAO) (*PP* 45–46). The director of FAO even declared, "If the FAO did not exist, the encyclical could be the base for its foundation."[55] Further in the same section, the pope advocates for the constitution of a World Fund for development that could be partly fed by the money spent on arms (*PP* 51). Solidarity needs to be expressed at the institutional level and at the level of relations between countries: "the superfluous wealth of rich countries should be placed at the service of poor nations" (*PP* 49). However, the call is also addressed directly to individuals. Recalling the parable of the rich man and Lazarus, the pope challenges the rich man of today:

> Is he prepared to support out of his own pocket works and undertakings organized in favor of the most destitute? Is he ready to pay higher taxes so that the authorities can intensify their efforts in favor of development? Is he ready to pay a higher price for imported goods so that the producer may be more justly rewarded? Or to leave his country, if necessary and he is young, in order to assist in this development of the young nations? (*PP* 47)

Solidarity also has to prompt more equitable relationships. It is not simply a matter of a duty of aid from the rich to the poor, but a matter of justice in righting distorted trade relations that are detrimental to the poor nations (see *PP* 56–61). Finally, the spirit of solidarity is present in the promotion of more universal charity fighting against what the pope calls "the lack of brotherhood among individuals and peoples" (*PP* 66). Here, the pope restates the duty of welcoming migrants (*PP* 67–70), the duty for business people to apply the same social sensitivity abroad as in their own industrialized countries (*PP* 71), the importance of fighting racism and avoiding undue nationalist pride (*PP* 72), and the role of dialogue to increase fraternity (*PP* 72).

The expanding movement from solidarity with those closest to us to universal solidarity, from individual charity to universal charity, animates the encyclical. This is prompted by the fact that "the social question has become worldwide" (*PP* 3). So "the rule, which up to now held good for the benefit of those nearest to us, must today be applied to all the needy of this world" (*PP* 49). People living in wealthier countries cannot remain blind and deaf to the struggling of those living in developing ones. This means that what is demanded in terms of solidarity and fraternity between individuals is also valid at a wider level between nations.

Anthropologically, this rich promotion of solidarity in action stresses the social dimension of being human. However, *PP* does not merely restate this "social" feature as a natural characteristic—one of the primary natural law principles[56]—rather, it offers it as a dynamic call to be fulfilled. To become truly human, human beings are called to live their social dimension in developing a true solidarity that extends to all humanity and aims at building a universal fraternity. All the specific concrete recommendations, though embedded in their own context, point to this more fundamental dynamism of becoming brothers and sisters.

As with the transcendent dimension of being human, this pertains to a theological vision of the human being. That human beings are brothers and sisters and therefore ought to work at the realization of this human solidarity is rooted in the affirmation that all are children of God. Paul VI recalls a previous declaration he made at Bombay:

> Man must meet man, nation meet nation, as brothers and sisters, as children of God. In this mutual understanding and friendship, in this sacred communion, we must also begin to work together to build the common future of the human race. (*PP* 43)

Then he mentions that the duty of more affluent nations stems from "a brotherhood that is at once human and supernatural" (*PP* 44). It is in Christ that people are made children of God and therefore brothers and sisters, so in the conclusion of this second part of the encyclical, the whole dynamism of the world striving toward greater fraternity is put in relation to the "building up of the body of Christ in its plenitude: the assembled people of God" (*PP* 79).

Because Rahner clarified the theological meaning of transcendent humanism, it is interesting to return to him concerning the social dimension of being human. Several commentators on the writings of the German theologian point out that, though taking a more explicit form in his later works, the relational and social dimension of being human is central to the theological anthropology of the German theologian from the beginning.[57] Consequently, a vision of the human being that stresses freedom and transcendence is not necessarily in contradiction with the social and relational dimension; nor does this vision downplay it, but, on the contrary, could be foundational for the latter. The two pillars of *PP*'s anthropology are solidly connected when envisioned from a theological perspective.

Gregory Brett argues that Rahner's theological notion of the human person is inherently relational and oriented to being an agent of communion. In his seminal works, *Spirit in the World* and *Hearer of the Word*, Rahner introduces the idea that the core of being human is a dynamic movement of becoming a free subject oriented toward the absolute other, which grounds and directs freedom and subjectivity.[58] However, because the human being is spirit and matter, embedded in world and history, this movement is necessarily realized within the world and through the encounter with others in love. What started as a "subject-other-God" paradigm for the human person becomes a "person-community-God" paradigm. In later reflections on freedom and love, always in the framework of a world "graced" by God—the world as a recipient of God's self-communication—Rahner states more clearly that love is the integrating action that unites persons to each other, and that this same action intimately involves the love of God.[59] Brett notes, "From the time of Vatican II, Rahner's notion of person becomes more clearly interpersonal and more obviously socially aware."[60] Rahner is adamant in showing the unity of the love of God and love of neighbor, and in one of his latest works, he offers the notion of communion as the most realized expression of this love, because "it is communion with others that enables us to enter into communion with the triune God of life."[61] Again in an interview in 1984, he stated,

> The transcendence of man as finite spirit toward God, the absolute being in person, toward mystery in the fullest sense, is necessarily mediated through the (finite) other, through matter, body, the surrounding world of things, the social world, through history and word.[62]

Therefore, in Rahner's theological vision of the human being, starting with reflection on the necessary structure of the human to be a recipient of God's self-communication, transcendence and freedom are inseparable from world and history and relationship with others because the latter are the mediations through which becoming human can be realized. The dynamism of becoming human through knowing oneself and being responsible for oneself, which includes opening oneself to the Absolute Other—in other words, the dynamism of transcendental knowledge and transcendental freedom—is the dynamism of striving in love toward fullness of communion. In *PP*, clearly situated in a historical context where a form of transcendental reasoning with its stress on personal freedom was appealing, this connection between the transcendental and social dimensions of being human is at work. The call to "solidarity and fraternity" is rooted in the aspiration to personal freedom and self-fulfillment.

Conclusion

Populorum Progressio contributes richly to theological anthropology. The issue of the development of peoples and the challenges posed by growing inequalities, enduring poverty, and rising globalization at the dawn of a postcolonial era, are addressed by the church through the encyclical's vision of the human being and humankind. Being human, more than a static natural feature, is a dynamic process of becoming more human or fulfilling a vocation to be human. It implies growing in multiple dimensions—material, intellectual and spiritual, personal and social. It requires fostering the conditions for persons to "do more, learn more, and have more" but always in order "to be more" (*PP* 6) and to be more in solidarity and fraternity within the human family (*PP* 43). Being human is fulfilling a vocation to transcendence, freedom, and solidarity. This is a theological vision rooted in the faith that all human beings are created in the image and likeness of God and that they are made children of God, and therefore brothers and sisters, in Christ. Rahner's transcendental approach offers a more systematic grounding of the anthropological accents highlighted in *PP*. This is not to suggest that *PP* provides a full self-contained theology or that it is an expression only of Rahner's theology. Much more modestly, it shows that *some* theology is produced in a document whose main topic is social ethics. It has also confirmed that this theology is principally situated in the theological framework we have earlier qualified as neo-Thomist, a framework that stresses that God's grace is at work in this human world by its very human nature. We now turn to Christology.

CHRISTOLOGY

There are not many direct references to Christ in *PP*, but they are significant, and they will guide us in our attempt to shed light on the christological contribution of the encyclical. Obviously, this contribution is not systematic and comprehensive. It is much thinner compared to what was developed in the previous section regarding anthropology. It consists of hints and leads rather than full arguments. However, it is far from being irrelevant, because the few explicit mentions of Christ allow us to read the document through a christological lens. What elements of Jesus Christ's portrait, of his message, and what aspects of the christological dogmas are brought into focus in addressing the issue of the development of peoples?

Jesus and the Poor

In *PP*, Jesus Christ appears first and foremost as a teacher and an example prompting action in the world (*PP* 12). It was "urged by the love of Christ" that many missionaries committed themselves to economic development, healthcare, or education as part of their mission to bring faith in Christ to people.[63] Now, it is with the same will to "carry forward the work of Christ himself" who "entered this world to give witness to the truth, to rescue and not to sit in judgment, to serve and not to be served" (*PP* 13) that the church addresses the issue at a more global and structural level. It is with a "renewed consciousness of the demands of the Gospel" (*PP* 1) that the church acknowledges its duty to serve humanity by addressing the problem of development in all its dimensions. Throughout the document, as we noted above, Jesus's words and parables challenge the current situation and call for action. To the rich nations accumulating wealth, it reminds them of the parable of the rich man: "Fool, this night do they demand your soul of you" (Luke 12:20; *PP* 49). To youth who are encouraged to consider a time of service abroad, it reminds them of the parable of the last judgment: "I was hungry and you gave me to eat" (Matt 25:35; *PP* 74). To warn of the dangers for developing countries of sacrificing their culture in search of mere economic growth, Jesus's question is recalled: "What does it profit a man to gain the whole world if he suffers the loss of his soul?" (Matt 16:26; *PP* 40).

These references underscore that Jesus was involved in the world and not merely announcing an otherworldly salvation. Although he was not a political leader aiming at conquering an earthly power (the church, likewise, tries to follow him by respecting the distinction of powers), this does not mean that the Christian faith has to remain merely in the personal sphere.[64] The bringing about of the kingdom of heaven, which Jesus announces, calls for involvement in political, social, and economic realms.

The core of Jesus Christ's teaching highlighted in the encyclical concerns the poor, and thus it stresses a second trait of Jesus's portrait: his commitment to the poor. Jesus himself "cited the preaching of the Gospel to the poor as a sign of his mission" (*PP* 12). This is a reference to Jesus using the prophecy of Isaiah to define his own mission: "Go and tell John what you have seen and heard: the blind receive their sight, the lame walk, the lepers are cleansed, the deaf hear, the dead are raised, the poor have good news brought to them" (Luke 7:22). Everything *PP* does in promoting greater solidarity among nations, greater justice in international exchanges, urgent action against hunger, misery, and lack of education and healthcare, or simply in promoting integral human development, is to pursue the mission of Christ to the poor.

Moreover, at one point the encyclical refers explicitly to the image of Jesus having compassion for the crowd:

> No one can remain indifferent to the lot of his brothers who are still buried in wretchedness, and victims of insecurity, slaves of ignorance. Like the heart of Christ, the heart of the Christian must sympathize with this misery: "I have pity on this multitude." (Mark 8:2; *PP* 74)

Jesus's commitment to the poor and marginalized people begins with his looking with compassion at the multitude, and it is the same outlook on the world at work in the church, which, according to GS, shares "the joys and the hopes, the griefs and the anxieties of the men of this age especially those who are poor and afflicted" (GS 1). *Populorum Progressio* sets a similar tone when it speaks of the people "who are striving to escape from hunger, misery, endemic diseases, and ignorance" (*PP* 1). Later, it states, "Today the peoples in hunger are making a dramatic appeal to the peoples blessed with abundance.

The Church shudders at this cry of anguish and calls each one to give a loving response of charity to his brother's cry for help" (*PP* 3). To look at the current situation with a special awareness of the sufferings and the injustices endured by the poor, individually but also (more importantly in *PP*) considered in the collective reality of the developing nations, is to adopt Christ's way of looking at the world.

In all this, we find some basis for the christological foundation of what will soon be called "the preferential option for the poor," first developed in the church of Latin America before being explicitly integrated into the universal magisterium with John Paul II's *SRS*. In the wake of Vatican II, and a few years after *PP*, Latin American liberation theologians developed a systematic "ascending" Christology, a Christology that starts from the concrete historical Jesus and the context of the current human quest for salvation.[65]

For them, there is no neutral Christology, or neutral theology in general, because theologians who attempt to formulate the contents of the faith are always situated somewhere. There is a subjective point of departure for Christology that is the social and ecclesial locus of theological reflection. In Latin America, the need to opt for the poor and to struggle with them against situations of poverty and oppression is this social locus of theological reflection and the church of the poor is the ecclesial locus.[66] Nonetheless, for Christology to be Christology, this subjective point of departure needs to be dialectically connected with another objective point of departure: the search for an access to the totality of Christ. This access is best found through consideration of the historical Jesus. In the context of Latin America, the historical Jesus is less an object of investigation to ascertain a belief than a criterion for true discipleship, sustaining the transformation of the current unjust situations of the world.[67]

With this methodological approach to Christology, embedded in the reality of poverty and oppression and oriented toward transformative action, liberation theologians focus on several key aspects of the mystery of Jesus Christ: Jesus as herald and mediator of the reign of God, which brings about liberation from all oppressions and life in just relationships; the historical dimension of the cross and its significance for the crucified of today; and the resurrection as a response to situations of injustice and oppression and the promise of full liberation.[68]

There is no elaborated Christology in *PP*, which only offers a few christological hints. However, the theoretical framework developed by liberation theologians explains and justifies the reading of the encyclical we have just made. Concern for the situation of so many people around the world aspiring for more integral development prompts one to emphasize those aspects of the mystery of Jesus Christ that are particularly relevant to support transformative actions, namely, his involvement in the world and his mission to the poor.

Nonetheless, this approach to Christology is not exclusive of other approaches. A survey of the mention of Christ in the encyclical signifies the presence of a more transcendental or existential Christology, focusing on union with Christ as the promise and realization of the fullness of humanity.

Union with Christ

Jesus Christ reveals the fullness of humanity. Union with him is the path to its realization. In its exposition of the Christian understanding of development, *PP* affirms that "by reason of his union with Christ, the source of life, man attains to new fulfillment of himself" (*PP* 16), and later, among "the conditions that are more human," we find "unity in the charity of Christ" (*PP* 21). The reflection on work ends with a Pauline reference to the building up of the perfect human being "who realizes the fullness of Christ" (Eph 4:13; *PP* 28). Finally, at the end of the second part about development in solidarity, reference is made to the "building up of the body of Christ in its plenitude: the assembled people of God" (*PP* 79).

Populorum Progressio is written from the theological perspective of "God who says 'yes' to human history through Christ."[69] The encyclical examines the human situation with the help of faith and offers "the irradiation of the Gospel on the humanity of today."[70] Faith in Jesus Christ, human and divine, Savior of the world, sheds light on the current situation of humanity. Through addressing the issue of development, there is a convergence in the encyclical between an "explicit gospel" and an "implicit gospel." From the explicit gospel comes the affirmation that there could not be any integral human development without an openness to God and also the building of a true universal fraternity. However, there is also the sense that the process of integral development to which many people of good will are committed reveals an attitude believers can recognize as "evangelical."[71] The movement toward integral human development is a path to greater union with

Christ; it is a path toward recognizing Christ as revealing the fullness of humanity.

The explicit gospel confirms what is already currently at work in humanity, as when the encyclical, like *GS*, mentions Christ only at the end of reflections expressed in arguments that are not explicitly theological. Christological faith also denounces all that is inhuman in personal behaviors and social structures.[72] Finally, all the reflections, analyses, recommendations, and urgent formulated calls bear the mark of the faith in Christ revealing and realizing the fullness of humanity, and, as such, they testify to this faith.

For a more systematic study of Christ realizing the fullness of humanity, we can recall Rahner's transcendental Christology.[73] Jesus Christ is the "absolute savior" who realizes both the promise of God's self-revelation and the full acceptance of this revelation in freedom. He thus has an "exemplary significance" for the whole of humanity. In Rahner's wording, "The Incarnation of God is the *highest* instance of the actualization of the essence of human reality which consists in this: that man is insofar as he abandons himself to the absolute mystery whom we call God."[74]

Conclusion

Although explicit christological statements are not numerous in *PP*, they are nonetheless significant in that they invite and legitimize a christological reading of the encyclical that highlights some aspects of the mystery of Jesus Christ emerging from the context of development in the 1960s. Jesus is portrayed as calling us in word and by deed to act for the transformation of this world. More specifically, he appears as one missioned first to the poor. Union with Christ is also presented as the path toward realizing the fullness of humanity in freedom and solidarity, and it grounds the vision of human beings called to flourish in all their dimensions. This does not constitute a full portrait of Jesus Christ nor a full deployment of the christological faith, but it does contribute to the expression of the mystery of Jesus Christ and its meaning for us, within a specific historical setting.

This Christology pertains mainly to a basic type of Christology "from below" or a Christology "of saving history."[75] In entering the mystery of Jesus Christ, the starting point is the consideration of human beings encountering him in their quest for salvation. At some moments, the focus is on the historical Jesus and his proximity to the poor. At other moments, the focus is more on the movement of humanization that is transcendental in its aspiration toward the divine and is recognized as a movement of union with Christ. That Christ is God become human, the incarnate Word, is of course implied, but it is not the methodological starter.

THE THEOLOGY OF *POPULORUM PROGRESSIO*

If we gather together the various theological contributions to which our reading of *PP* has called attention, we end with a theology that can be qualified as strongly incarnational. It fits mainly in the framework that we call neo-Thomist, which takes a positive look at the world and humanity, where God's grace is at work since creation. The adoption of an inductive see-judge-act approach stresses the reality of the incarnation still at work in the contemporary world: "the kingdom of God is among you" (Luke 17:21). The signs of the kingdom ought to be recognized positively and negatively, and its realization urges people to act for the integral development of peoples. Humanity is the locus of God's revelation and the recipient of God's grace bearing fruit for the kingdom, and so it is through dialoguing with others inside and outside the church that believers can seek for God. Any process of true humanization bears the mark of God. Created in the image of God and made adoptive children in Christ, human beings have a vocation to become more human by flourishing in all their personal and social dimensions. They are called to an authentic freedom liberated from material and moral servitudes. Ultimately, this is the aim of true integral development. Jesus Christ shows us the way. The encyclical points to his involvement in the world and his proximity with the poor. It also offers him as the full realization of the human vocation, shedding light on the mystery of humanity. This incarnational and neo-Thomist theology is presented by *PP* through its very concrete historical issues like hunger, unjust international trade relations, aspirations to political freedom, the balance of powers, threats of racism and nationalism, scandalous waste of money in the arms race, land reform, state planning, and technical cooperation.

However, Christian theology is not a matter of either/or but rather of both/and. Jesus Christ is *both* human *and* divine. The kingdom of God is *both* already here *and* yet to come. The human being is *both* sinner *and* offered salvation. By focusing on incarnation, *PP* is not dismissing eschatology. The urgency of what must be done, the cry of so many peoples, or the stress on the sickness of a world that lacks fraternity, point to the "not-yet-there" reality of the kingdom. Not everything that human beings do or are reflects their humanly divine vocation. There is greed and thirst for power, selfishness and avarice, disunity and conflicts among peoples. All these negative aspects of humankind appear in the encyclical. They recall the dimension of sin also at work in humanity. Nonetheless, undoubtedly, the incarnational dimension of the mystery of God for us is more strongly emphasized than the eschatological one.

That *PP*'s theology took this path is understandable when we recall the context. The church had just moved out of a long period of confrontation with the modern world. At the council, it engaged in dialoguing with "the world of this time," with other Christian confessions and other religions. The church made a pastoral turn by taking more strongly into account that God is already at work in the world to which salvation in Jesus Christ is to be announced. *Populorum Progressio* is continuing in this direction. Moreover, the global situation of the world was one of strong human hopes despite great anxieties. It is true that the situation of the Cold War and the threat of a nuclear apocalypse were in everyone's mind, but at the same time, the perspective of economic growth, more efficient production of goods to remedy misery, and progress in education and health were sources of great hope. Reflection and action about development were in their early stages, so it was possible to believe that by implementing the right policies, things would very soon change for the better. This rather optimistic framework, which certainly should not be quickly identified with genuine Christian hope, nonetheless made the type of incarnational theology produced by *PP* more easily relevant.

In the next chapter, we move forward twenty years after *PP* with the study of John Paul II's *SRS*. The context is very different, far less optimistic in terms of the capacity of this present world to bring about justice, development, and peace. The theological contributions of

CST will thus shed light for us on still other facets of the mystery of "God for us." As we will note, theological reflections stemming from Latin America play a decisive role in provoking debate but also, in the end, offering some other key categories to be incorporated into the universal magisterium of the church. Elements of a more Augustinian theological framework, with a vision of the world that is more attentive to the presence of sin and the need of a redemption coming from without, will receive greater attention.

2

DEVELOPMENT IN FREEDOM AND SOLIDARITY

"IN ORDER TO BE GENUINE, development must be achieved within the framework of *solidarity* and *freedom*, without ever sacrificing either of them under whatever pretext" (*Sollicitudo rei socialis* [SRS] 33). Twenty years after *PP*, John Paul II dedicated a major social encyclical to the topic of development, spotlighting and updating the reflections offered by his predecessor. In *Sollicitudo rei socialis*, the Polish pope uses solidarity as a major concept to elaborate his vision of full development and the appropriate responses to the challenges of the late twentieth-century world. However, this concept appears in constant articulation with another, often misunderstood, fundamental anthropological characteristic: freedom.[1]

Sollicitudo rei socialis begins by asserting that the social concern of the church is manifested especially through its social teaching. This teaching, as it appears in the body of documents published since Leo XIII's *Rerum novarum*, always bears both continuity in its fundamental principles and renewal prompted by new situations. Commemorating the twentieth anniversary of *PP*, *SRS* highlights three major contributions of Paul VI's encyclical that were still crucial in the late 80s: the issue of development is not a mere economic and social question but

45

a moral one; the social question has become worldwide; and development is "the new name for peace."

In chapter 3, the pope presents a long survey of the current situation of the world. Hopes of development have very often not been fulfilled. The gap between rich countries and poor ones is widening in social and economic but also cultural terms. Unemployment, housing crises, and international debt are among the many signals of failure affecting not only developing countries, but some parts of the population in the richest ones as well. Rights of people are not respected, and in a clear reference to state-controlled communist countries, the right of economic initiative and religious freedom is too often denied. The logic of blocs and the geopolitical opposition between East and West fuel a devastating arms race, many local conflicts, outbursts of the number of refugees around the world, terrorism, and many other plagues. Nonetheless, amid this dark overview, there are positive signs: an increasing awareness of and concern for human dignity, the potential to transform interdependence into true solidarity, a growing concern for ecological challenges, and a commitment of many to work for peace.

In the fourth chapter, *SRS* offers its vision of authentic development rooted in a reading of the first chapters of Genesis, in which humanity is created in the image of God, and in faith in Christ the Redeemer. On the one hand, full development is not unlimited material progress. "Superdevelopment" is even denounced as a danger in Western consumer societies. On the other hand, true development includes the promotion of human rights and respect for the natural environment. In chapter 5, *SRS* provides a theological reading of the problems related to development. Obstacles are seen in terms of structures of sins, rooted in and fueled by the thirst for power and the desire for profit at any price. The path to overcome them is solidarity as a profoundly human and Christian virtue.

A sixth chapter offers some guidelines by stressing the social doctrine of the church as an important resource. It does not offer a third way or an alternative socioeconomic system, but rather some means for moral discernment. This social doctrine thus pertains to *moral theology*. The adoption of an "option or love of preference for the poor" is another crucial guideline. It should orient some necessary reforms of institutions such as international organizations or the international financial, monetary, and trade systems. There is also an accent on the necessity of promoting participative democracy in developing nations.

In a concluding section, the pope associates development with liberation, reasserts the confidence of the church in humanity, and calls everyone, inside and outside the church, to commitment to development in solidarity. The sacrament of the Eucharist is presented as the effective symbol and resource for this task.

Briefly summarized, this encyclical is another opportunity to highlight the theological contribution of CST. How, through addressing the issue of development in the context of the mid-eighties and of Pope John Paul II's church, does the encyclical contribute to approaching the mystery of "God for us"? What new insights are helpful in expressing better the mystery of salvation seizing humanity? Our study of *PP* in the previous chapter has provided a base of theological elements present in the reflection of the church on development. *Sollicitudo rei socialis* has a more explicitly theological tone that confirms many of these previous elements. However, new developments evidence a rebalancing or reshaping of previous magisterial documents. Because of the different context, there are some theological accents in *SRS* that are different from those found in *PP*. The three different theological frameworks presented in the introduction of the book will interact with each other: (1) the neo-Thomist framework, insisting on humanity and the world as the locus and object of God's grace; (2) a more Augustinian vision that stresses the reality of sin at work and the need for redemption; and (3) a third framework developed by Latin American liberation theology where the main characteristics are the social and structural dimensions of the evil at work in the world and the liberating dimension of salvation.

CONTEXT

To understand the context from which *SRS* emerged, let's recall briefly the situation of the world, the conflicting emergence of liberation theology in Latin America, and the personality of the pope.[2]

Situation of the World in the Mid-eighties

Sollicitudo rei socialis begins with a stark statement: "The hopes for development, at the time [of *PP*] so lively, today appear very far from being realized" (*SRS* 12). Indeed, despite a few signs of progress for some countries in Asia such as South Korea, Taiwan, or Singapore, the overall situation was rather bleak. Poverty, wars, disorganization, and corruption in state structures, lack of proper healthcare and education, exploding international debt, denial of human rights: the list of the plagues affecting Third World countries seemed not to have receded much. The gaps between developed and developing countries and between rich and poor inside any one country were still increasing. The world is also marked by the crisis provoked by two oil shocks of the '70s, which signaled the end of the period of rapid economic growth in Western countries. They had to deal with repeated economic crises and rising levels of unemployment. Segments of their populations remained in dire poverty. This reality had begun to be referred to as the "Fourth World" and is mentioned in *SRS*.[3] Addressing the issue of integral development is not merely a matter of helping developing countries but also of challenging the incomplete and flawed notion of development at work in developed countries.

In the overall picture, the Cold War still had a huge impact. This is a blatant manifestation of what the pope referred to as the "logic of blocs."[4] The encyclical was published merely one year before the peaceful overturn of communist regimes in Eastern Europe, yet almost no one had predicted such an outcome, at least in such a short time. Mikhail Gorbachev, the leader of the Soviet Union, had engaged in a process of reform and liberalization of his country, and the threat of an apocalyptic war between the two superpowers seemed to fade. However, the ideological, political, and military clash between the two was by no means over and was continuously waged by proxy in other parts of the world, affecting processes of development.

In brief, *SRS* was written in a context far less optimistic than *PP* and much more aware of the complexities surrounding the question of the development of peoples.

Latin American Liberation Theology

A key element in the context of the church is the emergence of liberation theology in Latin America during the two decades between *PP* and *SRS*.[5] Following the council's invitation to discern the signs of the times in order to proclaim Christ's message of salvation, Latin American bishops gathered in Medellín in 1968 and recognized that the poor and poverty were foundational signs within their continent. The church ought to testify to the love of God by loving the poor, becoming sisters and brothers with and among them, and being committed to work for their cause.[6] Consequently, liberation became the best expression of the Christian doctrine of salvation for the suffering peoples of Latin America.[7]

In 1971, Peruvian theologian Gustavo Gutiérrez published *A Theology of Liberation*,[8] heralding a variety of theological publications ranging from biblical exegesis and systematics to ethics and spirituality, all of which readdressed traditional questions and took up new ones, always from the perspective of the poor in Latin America. In Latin America, in contrast to Europe, the mission of theology in the aftermath of Vatican II was not to respond to the challenge of the non-believer but rather the challenge of how to proclaim God as Father in a context of dehumanization and injustice.[9] Liberation theology challenged the unjust structures of the South American societies but also some of the traditional positions of a church that had been, historically, close to the wealthy elites. It also put the theologians in proximity with various revolutionary movements and Marxist currents of thought. Inside the Latin American church, as well as in the Vatican, opposition to liberation theology grew as it flourished.

At Puebla in 1979, the bishops confirmed the orientation taken at Medellín and affirmed the centrality of "the option for the poor,"[10] even though, during the preparation of the conference, attempts to shift from this line were strong. Significantly, in his opening speech, Pope John Paul II issued warnings but also clearly endorsed the central concern for social justice and the poor and highlighted the reality of human dignity "crushed underfoot" in so many Latin American countries.[11]

The years following Puebla saw growing tensions between the Congregation for the Doctrine of the Faith (CDF) and Latin American liberation theologians. Two instructions were issued by the former in 1984 and 1986, the first very negative and the second more positive.[12] Some theologians, such as Leonardo Boff, had to leave their teaching positions. The tension was also fueled by the nomination of a new generation of bishops unsympathetic to liberation theology. However, Pope John Paul II declared in a letter to the Brazilian bishops in 1986 that liberation theology was "not only timely but useful and necessary."[13]

Because of its focus on development, *SRS* is at the heart of this debate concerning Latin American theology. In the encyclical, not only liberation theology's fundamental concerns but also some key notions such as liberation, the preferential option for the poor, and the structures of sin are endorsed and thus, although with some nuances, incorporated into the Roman magisterium. This is an important contribution from a new voice in the post–Vatican II church.

A Pope from Eastern Europe

The election of John Paul II to the papacy in 1978 marked a significant new step in the development of a world church. At the balcony of Saint Peter's Basilica, he recognized that the cardinals had "called him from a far country."[14] The Polish pope brought a different perspective on the church and the world.

Both during the German occupation and then under the communist regime, Catholic faith and the Catholic Church of Poland were crucial places of resistance and of defense of the Polish identity. In this context, unity and visible fidelity to the institution were primordial. This is a very different situation for the articulation of church-state relations from Western Europe, where growing secularization meant that the church had to struggle to remain relevant in the public sphere. Far different too were the military dictatorships of Latin America, where those exercising oppressive powers were very often still churchgoers causing a political divide across the church.

Paul VI had initiated papal travels outside Italy, but in comparison to John Paul II, he seems not to have seen very much of the world. By 1987, when *SRS* was written, John Paul had already visited all the continents, most of them several times. Some striking images related to the theme of *SRS* are worth recalling. While in Mexico in 1979, he spoke to more than half a million indigenous people from Oaxaca and Chiapas at Cuilapan, declaring that he wanted "to be [their] voice, the voice of those who cannot speak or who are silenced."[15] In 1983, upon his arrival at the airport in Nicaragua, where the whole Sandinista government welcomed him, the pope had words of reproach to Fr. Ernesto Cardenal, the minister of culture: "Regularize your position with the church!"[16] For John Paul II, there was a clear incompatibility in being a priest and holding such a political position in a government. Undoubtedly, such experiences inform *SRS*, which emphasizes the social concern of the church but with a special insistence on the divine root of this concern and on the differentiation of the church's mission from the sociopolitical transformation of the world.

Pope John Paul II followed very closely the evolution of his Polish homeland and took an active part in the process that would lead to democracy in 1989. At the heart of the Polish opposition movement was the trade union Solidarność (Solidarity), whose name both identifies a program and resonates with the central theme of *SRS*. Fighting for freedom of speech and the right to unionize, the strikers of Gdansk who started Solidarność in the early '80s were certainly in the mind of the pope when he offered solidarity as the appropriate tool to overcome structures of sin (*SRS* 37).

Only twenty years separate *SRS* from *PP*, but the points outlined above sketch a very different background for an encyclical about development. It is against this background that older theological insights were confirmed, and new ones emerged.

METHODOLOGY AND STYLE

Regarding the methodology and style of *SRS* and their theological significance, we face two interpretive options.[17] On one hand, there is an inductive approach, which takes the current world situation seriously for the proclamation of the gospel. A dialogical engagement with this world, with philosophical reflections, and with various theories and practices in the fields of politics and economics is also very much at work. On the other hand, in comparison with Paul VI and *PP*, there is a stronger assertion of the authority of the magisterium of the church and of the pope as well as some more deductive forms of reasoning.

Nonetheless, these two interpretive lines can both be articulated when we consider their theological accents. *Sollicitudo rei socialis* confirms Vatican II's turn to the world, its incarnational theology, and its understanding of God's self-revelation in this world. However, in a framework less optimistic than *GS* and *PP*—more Augustinian and less neo-Thomist—the encyclical recognizes that rejection of God is also at work in this world and that human reason can fail to judge it rightly. Expressed bluntly, the world is graced, but it is still in need of grace because sin is still very much at work. The global and ecclesial context of the encyclical and the personality of its author prompt a reshaping of CST with a greater stress on the latter.

Reframing the See-Judge-Act Approach

The discussion about the notion of the social doctrine of the church helps capture the methodological reframing of *SRS*. How does one refer to the body of documents of the church dealing with social, political, and economic issues? In *SRS*, John Paul II makes use several times, though not exclusively, of the term *doctrine* or *social doctrine of the church. Social teaching* occurs also many times. Clearly, in this authoritative document, the pope did not want to decide definitively on the term, which had become for a while an object of controversy directly connected to the methodology at work in social encyclicals.[18]

In the late '70s, the French Dominican Marie-Dominique Chenu criticized the use of the term *social doctrine*. For him, that term referred appropriately to the type of discourse the church had used prior to Vatican II. Then the church was proposing an understanding of the world and society based on natural law reflection and put into fixed and ahistorical principles and directives to be deductively applied to specific, changing situations. However, at Vatican II, the church defined itself as "church-in-the-world-and-in-history"; therefore, according to Chenu, the notion of social doctrine "is no longer operative and has become outdated methodologically and pastorally."[19] He argued that the church is engaged in a constant discernment of the signs of the times in the light of the gospel and of its social dimension. The changing situations are the "theological locus" of this discernment and no longer the mere points of application of a preconceived "doctrine."[20] In fact, in *GS* and for the next two decades, the term *social doctrine* almost disappeared from Roman documents.

John Paul II revived it shortly after his election when, in his address to the Latin American bishops at Puebla, he encouraged them "to place responsible confidence in this social doctrine" and "to teach it and to be loyal to it."[21] Does this mean the return to a form of timeless dogmatism and to what critics of the term *doctrine* feared: social teaching as fixed and unchangeable, deductive, and an all-encompassing ideology meant to replace other current ideologies? Looking at those three points, fears are dismissed by the components of the definition of *Catholic social doctrine* given by SRS and the way this "doctrine" is presented in the encyclical.

First, in the introduction, John Paul II defines social doctrine as having both a dimension of continuity and a dimension of constant renewal. The renewal comes from the "necessary and opportune adaptations suggested by the changes in historical conditions and the unceasing flow of the events which are the setting of the life of people and society," whereas the continuity lies in the "fundamental inspiration [of the social doctrine], in its 'principles of reflections,' in its 'criteria of judgment,' in its 'basic directives for action' and above all in its vital link with the Gospel of the Lord" (SRS 3). Clearly, then, we are not dealing with a fixed corpus of doctrine but with one in constant evolution. Some might object that the stress is on the changing situations to which rather immutable principles are to be applied.[22] However, it is obvious that the formulation of the principles or even what counts as a significant principle for a specific time is changing and evolving. For example, in SRS, solidarity takes a central and integrative role unknown in previous documents of the social magisterium. More importantly, continuity is placed in "the vital link with the Gospel," which suggests that what remains constant is not to be confused with a mere fixed and dead set of principles and rules.

Second, SRS is also not a return to a full deductive approach in which general principles are applied to specific situations. The see-judge-act approach from Catholic Action, which was implemented in PP, is again largely endorsed. After the introduction and a short review of some significant points of PP, chapter 3 is dedicated to a large survey of the contemporary world. Chapters 4 and 5 offer a theological analysis, and finally, chapter 6 and the conclusion lay down some guidelines. Peter Henriot found here confirmation of the methodology he had developed with Joe Holland and coined "the pastoral circle."[23] Latin American liberation theologians also received enthusiastically what they perceived as the adoption of the same methodology used at Medellín. Ricardo Antoncich stresses that it is from the concrete reality of the situation of development, with its positive and negative aspects, that the pope expounds the insufficiencies in certain concepts and enriches them with the perspective of the faith. He also notes an approach that deals with the concrete situations of persons and not abstract statistics.[24]

Finally, in section 41, John Paul II clarifies that the church's social doctrine is "not a 'third way' between *liberal capitalism* and *Marxist collectivism*, nor even a possible alternative to other solutions" (*SRS* 41). It is not a global, all-encompassing ideology offering a unique vision of what society ought to be and of the path to get there. Rather, it belongs to the field of "moral theology": "theology" because it is done from the perspective of faith and "moral" because it aims at "guiding people's behavior." The latter is crucial because it situates social doctrine in the realm of discernment ordered toward decision and action in freedom. Social doctrine is about "careful reflection on the complex realities of human existence." Its aims are "to interpret" these realities in the light of the gospel and "to guide Christian behavior." It gives rise to "a 'commitment to justice,' according to each individual's role, vocation and circumstances" (*SRS* 41).

Clearly, the use of the term *doctrine* by John Paul II in *SRS* cannot be interpreted as returning to a pre–Vatican II understanding of the church's way of teaching. In line with the blurring of the frontiers between pastoral and doctrinal in *GS*, it is the very meaning of *doctrine* that continues to be renewed. Speaking of *doctrine* for CST is a reminder that it deals with core points of faith, but it does not mean a set of unchangeable, ahistorical pronouncements.

There is, however, an element of evolution from Paul VI to John Paul II in matters of methodology that cannot be ignored.[25] This concerns the articulation between the universal and the local in the development of CST and the question of who produces it. Undoubtedly, John Paul II strongly reaffirms the role of the papal magisterium and the necessity of universal pronouncements. In the passage of the introduction already mentioned, the pope speaks of the "principles of reflection," "criteria of judgment," and "directives of action," which are the foundational inspiration of the church's social teaching. He makes a clear, footnoted, reference to paragraph 4 of *Octogesima adveniens* (OA). However, in this document, Paul VI stated that due to the variety of situations around the world, "it was difficult to utter a unified message and to put forward a solution which has a universal validity" (OA 4). Consequently, Pope Paul was urging Christian communities to "analyze with objectivity the situation which is proper to their own countries, to shed the light of the Gospel's unalterable words and to draw principles of reflection, norms of judgment and directives for action from the social teaching of the church" (OA 4). There was a clear recognition of the role played by local communities. Although referring to his predecessor, John Paul II stresses, rather, the role played by the universal magisterium. Contrary to *OA*, there is little emphasis in *SRS* on the local communities contributing to the development of CST through evangelical discernment about their particular situations.

The affirmation of a central authority in the church is an obvious feature of the pontificates of John Paul II and Benedict XVI, and it finds its expression in CST as well as in other aspects of the life of the church. However, it should not hide the fundamental methodological option taken by the social teaching in favor of historicity and a dimension of induction. We are dealing with a reframing rather than a movement backward.

Dialogue Tempered

In *PP*, the church's engagement in dialogue with the world was noticeable in the explicit footnote references made to nonmagisterial documents. Throughout the almost hundred footnotes of *SRS*, except for two documents of the United Nations, only church documents are cited, and they are principally conciliar or recent papal pronouncements.[26] Does this mean that John Paul II's encyclical is written in isolation from the current debates and ignores what secular disciplines or others outside the Vatican bring to the discussion about development? This is far from the case.

Throughout the encyclical, we find signs of a reflection articulated with other lines of thought. *SRS* is engaged in a critical evaluation of the two socioeconomic and political systems of the West and the East and addresses the ideologies that sustain them. Liberal capitalism and Marxist collectivism are analyzed from the perspective of development, and they are both found wanting.[27] Addressing the issue of international debt, the encyclical is not afraid of making an incursion into the field of economics with the support of the work previously made on the topic by some experts in the Pontifical Commission for Justice and Peace.[28] At a more conceptual level, *SRS* uses the concept of solidarity, which, since it is not a biblical concept, could seem foreign to the Catholic tradition. John Paul II is endorsing it in large part out of the experience of Solidarność, the Polish workers' union, and gives it a solid theological grounding.

Moreover, the process of constructing the encyclical implied a level of real dialogue.[29] During the summer of 1987, Pope John Paul II wrote a first schema in Polish with the help of some professors of the

University of Lublin, Poland. "More than a simple outline but much less than a first draft, it laid out the basic ideas of the documents in chunks of prose."[30] It was then developed into a real draft in Spanish by the Pontifical Commission for Justice and Peace under the responsibility of its president, French Cardinal Roger Etchegaray, and its secretary, Argentinian Archbishop Jorge María Mejía. In the following six months, the document went through several rounds of comments by various members of the curia and revisions under the close control of the pope. The Commission for Justice and Peace had also elicited a global survey of bishops about the situation concerning development since *PP*, and the pope had various conversations on the topic with visitors to the Vatican including Michel Camdessus, the director of the International Monetary Fund, and bishops from around the world participating in the 1987 ordinary synod.[31]

Undoubtedly, compared to John Paul II's encyclicals on other topics or even to his first social encyclical *Laborem exercens*, *SRS* is the fruit of much more discussion and consultation. However, this is not a dimension set forth in the final document itself, and clearly, there was no desire to engage a public or widely open debate during the time the encyclical was being written. In this respect, the methodology adopted by the U.S. bishops for writing their two letters on peace and economic justice in 1984 and 1986 stands in stark contrast.

In summary, although the importance of dialogue so emphasized after Vatican II is present in *SRS*, it is tempered and more discreet. A comment made by George Weigel incidentally points to a possible explanation: "Drafting assistance does not compromise the teaching authority of a papal document, which receives its authoritative 'form' from the Pope's signature, an act that completes the project in a definitive way and without which any draft is just that: a draft."[32] That the famous biographer of John Paul II feels that it is necessary to reaffirm the authority of the encyclical shows, paradoxically, that when dialogue, discussion, and multiple contributions are visible, there is a danger, according to some, of downplaying authority. Tempering dialogue in *SRS* is a reaffirmation of authority. Likewise, not making explicit citations of nonmagisterial works may be a way of avoiding the risk of losing authority by taking a side in a debate. This necessity to reaffirm the authority of the church's teaching, already noted concerning a certain reframing of the see-judge-act approach, needs to be interpreted theologically.

Theological Interpretation

John Paul II's first and programmatic encyclical, *Redemptor hominis* (*RH*), offers a good overview of the theological framework in which he develops its subsequent teaching. Its focus is on Jesus Christ, "the redeemer of man" and "the center of the universe and history" (*RH* 1). In Jesus Christ, God entered the world and gave human life its fullness. This movement of the incarnation is the starting point for all the reflections of the pope about the world and the church. Significantly, in the first lines of his encyclical, he also refers to the state of humanity marked by sin and limitations, mentioning "the original sin and the whole history of the sins of humanity" and "the errors of the human intellect, will and heart" (*RH* 1). Further on, the pope evokes the "difficult postconciliar period" and praises his predecessor for leading it in balance "even in the most critical moments, when the Church seemed to be shaken from within" (*RH* 3). In another section, he speaks of the possibilities of human progress offered by modernity, but also of the ambiguities associated with it and the threat of humanity regressing because what human beings are producing ends up being directed against them.[33] It is against this dark background that God's presence in history through the incarnation is understood. Humanity, marked by sin and limitation, needs God's revelation. The coming of Jesus Christ into humanity is "this act of redemption [which] marked the highest point of the history of man within God's loving plan" (*RH* 1). The mission of the church is to be the sign but also the instrument of this redeeming union of Christ with humanity.[34] The church then fulfills its mission in an important way by teaching and professing the truth of faith.[35]

In this theological framework—a rather Augustinian one—what revelation brings *into* the world and humanity is given greater attention than what can be experienced *from* a world and humanity where God's grace is at work. The church brings God's revelation into the world by announcing Jesus Christ, the fulfillment of humanity, and denouncing what opposes this fulfillment. This is the case in social teaching. Antoncich suggests that this teaching pertains to the "prophetic office" of the church that has to point out "human sin and God's grace."[36] This requires a level of authority and the explicit affirmation that what is said is not merely an opinion among others but has the pretention to pertain to truth. Because of his experience of a resisting church facing an oppressive atheist regime in Poland, Pope John Paul II's understanding of fidelity to the church implies a high level of formal submission to the institution and avoidance of visible signs of dissension in it.[37] The stress is more on division as expression of a sinful condition than on diversity of positions as an expression of an ongoing discernment in which the Spirit is at work.

Nevertheless, it is even more striking that the general methodological features of induction and dialogue are still present. They carry the same theological meaning exposed in *PP* in the previous chapter. *Sollicitudo rei socialis* continues to reflect upon the mystery of the incarnation and of the Triune God at work in history, while paying more attention to the dimension of sin also at work and the need for redemption. The neo-Thomist vision of the world is still the primordial foundation for John Paul II's social encyclical, but a more Augustinian vision of the conflict brought about by sin provokes a reframing.

THEOLOGICAL ANTHROPOLOGY

What does *SRS* say about the human being? What is the contribution of the encyclical to theological anthropology? The two main features that were highlighted in the previous study of *PP* remain central. Transcendent humanism and the social dimension of the human being constitute the basis of the anthropology developed.[38] What, however, marks an evolution from *PP* is the more explicitly biblical and theological grounding given to these features. Moreover, tweaks and new accents occur because of a different context and often through the incorporation of more recent theological reflections into the universal magisterium, especially some elements of language coming from Latin American liberation theology. Four themes need to be considered: the vocation to be human, sin and structures of sin, solidarity, and liberation.

The Vocation to Be Human

The transcendent humanism presented in *PP* is assumed by *SRS* with nonetheless a more theological accent. Chapter 4 of the encyclical, which presents an "authentic human development," is constructed around the reading and commentary of biblical passages, especially the first chapters of Genesis, and some letters of Paul.[39] It is easy to retrieve the three characteristics of the transcendent humanism high-lighted in *PP*.

First, being human is not a static condition but a process of becoming human oriented toward fulfilling a divine (or transcendent) vocation. This dynamism is at work in the promotion of an authentic human development and it is that to which the first chapters of Genesis point. *SRS* affirms,

> The fact is that man was not created, so to speak, immo-bile and static. The first portrayal of him, as given in the Bible, certainly presents him as creature and image, defined in his deepest reality by the origin and affinity that consti-tute him. But all this plants within the human being—man and woman—the seed and requirement of a special task to be accomplished by each individually and by them as a couple....The story of the human race described in sacred scripture is, even after the fall into sin, a story of constant achievements, which, although always called into question and threatened by sin, are nonetheless repeated, increased and extended in response to the divine vocation given from the beginning to man and woman (Gen 1:26–28) and inscribed in the image which they received. (*SRS* 30)

The development the church is promoting is the continuation of this movement initiated at the creation. This development "fundamentally corresponds to the first premise" (*SRS* 30). However, the reality of sin threatens the fulfillment of the human vocation to be in the image and likeness of God. Therefore, it is also faith in Christ the Redeemer that sustains this vocation, because he is "the perfect 'image' of the Father" and opens the way toward fullness of humanity. He "prepares us to share in the fullness which 'dwells in the Lord'" (*SRS* 31).

A second characteristic of this transcendent humanism, and a consequence of this fundamental vocation, is that human beings can-not be reduced to a single dimension. There are multiple dimensions to being human and all those dimensions are called to develop. This is what is at stake in denouncing a purely economic or materialistic vision of development. Authentic development must be social, eco-nomic, political, but also cultural, which means conscious also of the spiritual and religious dimension of the human being. This evokes a traditional anthropological feature recalled by *SRS*: human beings are not mere bodies; they are also spiritual.

> In trying to achieve true development we must never lose sight of that dimension which is in the specific nature of man, who has been created by God in his image and likeness (cf. Gen 1:26). It is a bodily and a spiritual nature, symbolized in the second creation account by the two elements: the earth, from which God forms man's body, and the breath of life which he breathes into man's nostrils (cf. Gen 2:7). (*SRS* 29)

The last characteristic of transcendent humanism underscored in both *PP* and *SRS* is the centrality of human freedom, to which we will return at length in the later section on liberation.

Sin and Structures of Sin

In comparison with *PP*, the anthropological elements just recalled are enriched by a substantial reflection about the sinful condition of the human being. Not that Paul VI's encyclical was denying this dimension, but rather, it was simply assumed and not reflected upon.[40] In contrast, the context of *SRS* prompts the usage of the category of sin in the theological reading of the challenges concerning development.[41]

The behavior of individuals is at stake when bad decisions are taken that slow or hinder the course of development, despite the scientific and technical resources available. However, there are also "economic, financial and social *mechanisms* which, although they are manipulated by people, often function almost automatically, thus accentuating the situation of wealth for some and poverty for the rest" (*SRS* 16).[42] Here, the pope speaks of "structures of sin" (*SRS* 36). It is a matter of sin because there is an obstacle to "the will of the triune God, his plan for humanity, his justice and his mercy," but it is not merely personal sin because it deals with "influences and obstacles which go far beyond the actions and brief life span of an individual" (*SRS* 36).

This way of speaking about sin was not new. Latin American liberation theologians had called attention to the reality of unjust and sinful structures at work in the relations between First World and Third

World countries and between the rich and the poor in the latter.[43] At Medellín, the bishops spoke of "the *unjust structures* which characterize the Latin American situation" (*Med* Justice 2, emphasis mine) and of injustice as "those realities that constitute a sinful *situation*" (*Med* Peace 1, emphasis mine). At Puebla, they stated more explicitly that "sin, a force making for breakdown and rupture…will always be operative, both within the hearts of human beings, and within the various structures which they have created and on which they have left the destructive imprint of their sinfulness" (*Pue* 281).

This way of speaking draws attention to the truth that since the gospel's message has an inherent social dimension, sin, as a refusal of this message, has a social dimension as well. But what does it mean exactly to speak of "structures of sin" or of "structural sin," since it is not possible to ascribe agency and freedom—and therefore responsibility—to a structure in the same way it is to a person? And what happens to individual persons and their freedom when they are viewed as entirely trapped within those structures? Social sciences teach us about the dialectical nature of human beings: both free and fated, creating and being created by their culture.[44] However, does the language of "structures" reduce human beings merely to a fated state? In the end, the crucial point is how to articulate personal sin and structures of sin.

In his 1983 exhortation *Reconciliatio et paenitentia* (RP), John Paul II stressed the personal responsibility contained in the notion of sin. "In the proper sense, sin is always a personal act, since it is an act of freedom on the part of an individual person and not properly of a group or community" (*RP* 16). Then he explained that social sin, in an analogous way, can refer to the unjust relationships between groups and societies. In this case, moral responsibility is hard to attribute to one person because the phenomenon has become generalized and almost anonymous, with causes complex and not always identifiable. Nonetheless, "social sin [is] the result of the accumulation and concentration of many personal sins" (*RP* 16). As González-Carvajal points out,

> The intention of the pope was to legitimize (against a privatized and overly personalized Christian faith) the notion of "social sin" but at the same time to make it clear (against structuralist and determinist conceptions) that the ultimate root of evil is not in the structures themselves but in the

hearts of the persons who originated them and maintain them.[45]

This approach to social sin is confirmed in *SRS*. We do not, however, first find a presentation of personal sin and then a derivative reflection about its social dimension. Rather, in *SRS*, it is first recognized that a world divided into blocs and subject to various forms of imperialism is "a world subject to structures of sin." Only then, the connection is made with personal sin by recalling that those structures "are rooted in personal sin, and thus always linked to the concrete acts of individuals who introduce these structures, consolidate them and make them difficult to remove" (*SRS* 36).

The pope denounces two key sinful attitudes at work among individuals and nations that are fueling structures of sin: "thirst for power" and "all-consuming desire for profit...*at any price*" (*SRS* 37). The moral and theological analyses of the obstacles to integral development allow one to see that "behind certain decisions, apparently inspired only by economics or politics, are real forms of idolatry: of money, ideology, class, technology" (*SRS* 37).

The personal sins that need to be considered in relation to the reality of the "structures of sin" are not merely the far distant ones that have produced the actual structures. Not acting against them or remaining voluntarily blind to them is also sinful:

> It must be said that just as one may sin through selfishness and the desire for excessive profit and power, one may also be found wanting with regard to the urgent needs of multitude of human beings submerged in conditions of underdevelopment, through *fear, indecision,* and basically, through *cowardice.* (*SRS* 47)

The encyclical underscores what Armendáriz calls a "new form of radical sin": cowardice and inaction.[46]

In summary, the balanced position of *SRS* articulating structures of sin and personal sin is well captured by Antoncich when he offers two landmarks: "Social sin does not exist as something independent from concrete personal responsibilities, but from this affirmation it cannot be deduced that sin is only to be encountered in private and individual matters."[47]

Of course, in Christian theology, the way one speaks of sin dictates the way one speaks of salvation, and vice versa. The diagnosis made by John Paul II when he points out "the structures of sin" allows him then to suggest "the path to be followed in order to overcome [the evil diagnosed]" (*SRS* 37). This path is conversion and solidarity.

Solidarity

Already present in the anthropological vision offered by *PP*, solidarity becomes the central notion of John Paul II's renewed vision of development.[48] The second part of chapter 5 of *SRS* begins with a greater awareness "of the urgent need to change the spiritual attitudes which define each individual's relationship with self, with neighbor, with even the remotest human communities, and with nature itself" (*SRS* 38). In Christian language, this change in attitudes in response to sin is called "conversion," and it is well evoked by the biblical image of the transformation of "hearts of stone" into "hearts of flesh" that God has promised.[49]

This conversion is at work when solidarity is recognized and fostered. This is the path to overcome the structures of sin. Indeed, solidarity brings attitudes that are diametrically opposed to them, especially to the thirst for power and the all-consuming desire for profit. Solidarity is not "a feeling of vague compassion or shallow distress at the misfortunes of so many people....It is a firm and persevering determination to commit oneself to the common good; that is to say the good of all and each individual, because we are all responsible for all" (*SRS* 38). It is already in development in the growing awareness of interdependence noticeable, for example, in the fact that many people feel personally affected by the injustices and violations of human rights committed elsewhere in the world.

The encyclical calls for solidarity within society through the recognition of all members as persons entitled to rights and not "just some kind of instrument, with work capacity and physical strength to be exploited at low cost and then discarded when no longer useful" (*SRS* 39). Solidarity implies that the more powerful or influential—those who have a greater share of goods—should feel responsible for the weaker, but also that the latter "should not adopt a purely *passive* attitude" (*SRS* 39). The idea that people should be the first actors of their own development but not abandoned to themselves is at the heart of the exercise of solidarity. The same is applicable at the level of international relationships where "every type of imperialism" or "determination to preserve [one's] hegemony" needs to be surmounted so that "a real international system may be established which will rest on the foundation of the equality of all peoples and the necessary respect for their legitimate differences" (*SRS* 39). This is particularly at stake when the principle of the universal destination of the goods of creation is applied. Solidarity, then, is "the path to peace and at the same time to development" (*SRS* 39). Peace will be achieved "through the putting into effect of social and international justice, but also through the practices of the virtues which favor togetherness, and which teach us to live in unity" (*SRS* 39). The transformation of interdependence into solidarity calls for fostering collaboration and abandoning "the politics of blocs" and of "all forms of economic, military, or political imperialism" (*SRS* 39).

All this is founded on and points to a theological vision of the human being, who is in the image of God and redeemed in Christ. It is possible "to identify many points of contact between solidarity and charity, which is the distinguishing mark of Christ's disciples (cf. John 13:35)" (*SRS* 40). What is exposed in concrete appeals for the exercise of solidarity is an expression of the concretization of the commandment of love.

The pope goes further by pointing to the mystery of the Trinity:

> Awareness of the common fatherhood of God, of the brotherhood of all in Christ—"children in the Son"—and of the presence and life-giving action of the Holy Spirit will bring to our vision of the world a new criterion for interpreting it. Beyond human and natural bonds, already so close and strong, there is, discerned in the light of faith, a new *model* of the *unity* of the human race, which must ultimately inspire our *solidarity*. This supreme *model of unity*, which is a reflection of the intimate life of God, one God in three Persons, is what we Christians mean by the word *communion*. (*SRS* 40)

Images of a Triune God,[50] human beings are called to realize true solidarity and communion of which the unity in God and the loving relationships between the divine persons is the ultimate inspiration.

The trinitarian model of unity is both the source and the end. By making this connection between human solidarity and the Trinity, *SRS* enriches a theological vision of the human being and also contributes to the apprehension of the mystery of a Triune God.

Liberation

Having identified the obstacles to integral development as "structures of sin," *SRS* sets the ground for speaking of this development as liberation in the seventh and conclusive chapter.[51] Once again, a category central to Latin American liberation theology is adopted by the universal magisterium, with qualifications.[52] It enriches the theological anthropology offered by the encyclical with a dynamic approach of human freedom as a process rather than a mere state.

In his *Theology of Liberation*, G. Gutiérrez offers important insights about the notion of liberation and its theological meaning.[53] He distinguishes three reciprocally interpenetrating levels of meaning. First, it "expresses the aspirations of oppressed peoples and social classes, emphasizing the conflictual aspect of the economic, social, and political process which puts them at odds with wealthy nations and oppressive classes."[54] Second, it can be applied to an understanding of history in which human beings are assuming their own destiny. The aim of liberation is "the creation of a new humankind and a qualitatively different society."[55] Third, from a biblical and theological perspective, it can be recognized that salvation in Christ from sin is actually liberation from "the ultimate root of all disruption of friendship and of all injustice and oppression."[56] In the context of poverty, oppression, and violence characterizing the Latin American continent, the concept of liberation becomes the most appropriate means to express the reality of salvation offered by God in Jesus Christ.

In this context, this term *liberation* also replaces the terminology of development, which is often referred to pejoratively as "developmentalism." Here, development is reduced to its economic component and viewed in terms of catching up a delay in modernization, while ignoring the reality of dependency in which the development of some is dependent on the continuous underdevelopment of others. However, most Latin American liberation theologians recognize that the notion of integral development exposed in *PP* and *SRS* is compatible with what they intend in pushing forward the concept of liberation.[57]

Reciprocally, in the context of the tense relations between Latin American liberation theology and Rome, the section of *SRS* that speaks of liberation reads like a solid recognition of the validity of such language. The encyclical states,

> Peoples and individuals aspire to be free: their search for full development signals their desire to overcome the many obstacles preventing them from enjoying a "more human life."...
>
> It is fitting to add that the aspiration to freedom from all forms of slavery affecting the individual and society is something *noble* and *legitimate*. This in fact is the purpose of development or rather liberation and development, taking into account the intimate connection between the two. (*SRS* 46)

Development and liberation have very similar meanings, as they become defined "in the exercise of solidarity, that is to say, in the love and the service of neighbor, especially the poorest" (*SRS* 46).

Mere economic development—in the sense of catching up to the material development of Western countries—cannot bring freedom. On the contrary, it will enslave more. But neither should liberation be reduced to a mere social, economic, and political process of structural change. It concerns the "cultural, transcendent and religious dimension" of the human being and society as well. "Human beings are totally free only when they are completely *themselves*, in the fullness of their rights and duties" (*SRS* 46). Authentic liberation is the overcoming of sin and the structures of sin, and it is Christ who sets us free.

Freedom appears here as a continuous process oriented to an end. "[This] freedom with which Christ has set us free (cf. Gal 5:1) encourages us to become the *servants* of all" (*SRS* 46). It is the freedom to exercise solidarity, to be committed to the common good. It is not a purely individual freedom and certainly not the mere absence of constraints and limits allowing one to do whatever he or she wishes. Elsewhere in the encyclical, this distinction between two freedoms—freedom *for* the common good *versus* unlimited freedom *from* any constraints—is already at work. Considering the relation of humanity to its natural environment, *SRS* reminds us that "the dominion granted to man by the Creator is not an absolute power, nor can one speak of a freedom to 'use and misuse,' or to dispose of things as one pleases" (*SRS* 34). The danger of "superdevelopment" faced by a "civilization of 'consumption' or 'consumerism'" (*SRS* 28) is also connected with a distorted sense of freedom generated by the almost unlimited access to material goods. An often-noticed call of *SRS* is the respect for economic freedom or "right of economic initiative" (*SRS* 15). In the context of state-controlled economies where it is obviously denied, this is a crucial locus for affirming human freedom and "the creative subjectivity of the citizen" (*SRS* 15). However, this should not be mistaken as the consecration of the economic system (liberal capitalism) at work in Western countries. The exercise of economic initiative is subject to some limiting criteria. At least two are underscored: profit should never be the unique criterion and solidarity should be an active principle in the exercise of economic initiative.[58]

In this insistence on human freedom *for* the common good, one can recognize the personalism at work in John Paul II's thought.[59] The combination of this philosophical influence with the notion of liberation inherited from liberation theology brings a rich understanding of human freedom. It is a freedom that knows the limits of being a creature and not the Creator. It is also never an individualistic freedom, nor is it to be confused with pure autonomy, because it is oriented toward fulfilling the social nature of being human and is aware of the structural dimensions of the obstacles to it. It is a freedom in constant need of liberation.

Conclusion

Sollicitudo rei socialis offers a rich theological reflection on the human being through the encounter with and mixing of various theological frameworks. First, the neo-Thomist vision of the world very much at work in *PP* continues to be present through the fundamental anthropological features that Paul VI's encyclical emphasized and are confirmed by *SRS*. Being human is not a static state but a continuous process of fulfilling a vocation to be free and in a just and loving relationship with others, a vocation to be individually and collectively in the image and likeness of God. Transcendent humanism and the social dimension of the human condition cannot be separated. Second, the historical context of *SRS* and the personality of Pope John Paul II introduced a more Augustinian perspective. The world is the place of God's transformative grace at work, but it is also the place of sin and of a conflict between the love of God and the refusal of this love. Sin is part of the human condition, and ultimately only God can liberate human beings from sin. In this framework, the explicit affirmation of the theological grounding of the human vocation, not only through the creation motif but also through the redemption brought by Christ, bears more weight. The Trinity is also an ultimate inspiration for authentic human solidarity. And, of course, a thorough reflection on sin cannot be avoided. This prompts the significant development about the structures of sin and their articulation with personal sin. Finally, a third theological framework is also at work through the adoption by *SRS* of the categories that come to the fore in South American liberation theology. The evil at work in the world has a social and structural dimension and God's salvation is liberation from it. For anthropology, this reminds us that the social dimension of being human is not merely a matter of interpersonal relations but really of social realities, of structures and institutions, in which sin and grace ought to be revealed.

To recognize these three theological frameworks at work in the contribution of *SRS* to theological anthropology is not to ignore the tensions or elements of contradiction that exist among them. This opens us to a variety of interpretations depending on that which is stressed. This section prioritizes the basis already given by *PP* (and *GS*), and adopts the evolution of other frameworks in terms of "reframing" or "rebalancing," like the interpretation of the evolutions in methodology and style in the previous section.

CHRISTOLOGY

When considering the contribution of *SRS* to approaching the mystery of Christ—or rather being seized by it—it is possible to highlight two complementary movements. The first is akin to a descending Christology: Christ reveals God and redeems humanity and a world marked by sin. However, the specificity of producing a social encyclical prompts John Paul II to complement this christological approach with other aspects induced especially by the reflection on the poor, and thus contributes to a more ascending Christology. What is at stake here with the articulation of the two movements is not just a matter of knowledge about Christ or of various complementary ways of apprehending Christ's mystery. It is also a question of soteriology or of understanding the ways in which God saves humanity and brings about the kingdom.

Christ the Redeemer and the Revealer

As seen previously, *SRS* interprets the reality of the obstacles to full development in terms of sin. It is, therefore, only logical that the dimension of redemption brought about by Christ would be highlighted. Throughout the encyclical, there is a strong sense that this world needs the saving revelation that comes with Christ. The movement of Christ bringing salvation, in a certain sense *from without*, is particularly striking when considering the mentions of "Christ," "Jesus," and "Lord," which can be gathered around four points.

First, Christ is associated with the fullness of the revelation of humanity. Christ reveals the Father and thereby reveals and fulfills true humanity. Already in the introduction, Jesus Christ is mentioned as the one who reveals the "fullness of the word" (*SRS* 1). Christ is "the perfect image of the Father" and the history of humanity—created to be in the image of God—is part of the divine plan that begins and culminates in him, and "thus prepares us to share in the fullness which 'dwells in the Lord'" (*SRS* 31). Therefore, "faith in Christ the Redeemer, while it illuminates from within the nature of development, also guides us in the task of collaboration" (*SRS* 31). For example, the notion of development, distorted when conceived as a mere automatic and limitless progress of technological and economic nature,[60] can be recovered. The encyclical asserts,

> The dream of "unlimited progress" reappears, radically transformed by the new outlook created by Christian faith, assuring us that progress is possible only because God the Father has decided from the beginning to make man a sharer of his glory in Jesus Christ risen from the dead, in whom "we have redemption through his blood…the forgiveness of our trespasses" (Eph 1:7). (*SRS* 31)

Second, Christ reconciles and liberates. This is the expression of redemption. "Sin, which is always attempting to trap us, and which jeopardizes our human achievements, is conquered and redeemed by the 'reconciliation' accomplished by Christ (cf. Col 1:20)" (*SRS* 31). This reconciliation finds its expression in the solidarity promoted in response to the challenge of the structures of sin. This solidarity is rooted in "the common fatherhood of God" and in "the brotherhood of all in Christ—'children in the Son'" (*SRS* 40). Christ sets us free to become "the servants of all" (*SRS* 46).

Third, what is at stake is not merely a personal salvation but also the realization of the kingdom with its social and even its all-encompassing cosmological dimension.[61] In section 31, the perspective that each human being becomes a sharer of God's glory in Jesus Christ is completed by the hope of the realization of the kingdom:

> We can say therefore—as we struggle amidst the obscurities and deficiencies of underdevelopment and super-development—that one day this corruptible body will put on incorruptibility, this mortal body immortality (cf. 1 Cor 15:54), when the Lord "delivers the kingdom to God the Father" (v. 24) and all the works and actions that are worthy of man will be redeemed. (*SRS* 31)

Therefore, in concerning itself with the question of integral development, the church places itself "at the service of the divine plan" and recognizes, here, its "fundamental vocation of being a 'sacrament,' that is to say 'a sign and instrument of intimate union with God and the unity of the whole human race" (*SRS* 31).[62] There is a "perennial value of authentic human achievements, inasmuch as they are redeemed by Christ and destined for the promised kingdom" (*SRS* 31).

Finally, Christ is the teacher of the truth about humanity. The church has the proclamation of this truth as its mission and does so by taking up the challenge of integral development.[63] The entire content of the encyclical can be envisioned as teaching the truth of the gospel, but we also find two explicit suggestions that Jesus is directly teaching us. To emphasize that people themselves always ought to be the protagonists of development, *SRS* notes that "indeed, *the Lord Jesus himself,* in the parable of the talents, *emphasizes* the severe treatment given to the man who dared to hide the gift received" (*SRS* 30, emphasis mine). Then, in reference to the danger of forgetting moral, cultural, and spiritual requirements in processes of development, *SRS* writes, "The *Lord clearly says* this in the Gospel, when he calls the attention of all to the true hierarchy of values: 'For what will it profit a man, if he gains the whole world and forfeits his life' (Matt 16:26)" (*SRS* 33, emphasis mine). These quotes stress how much Jesus Christ is a teacher able to project, somehow directly, some truth on present situations.

These christological emphases, which point to Christ bringing salvation into the world, in a certain sense *from without,* resonate with the Christology favored by John Paul II in his programmatic *RH*. What does it mean, in the context of the late twentieth century, that "Christ the redeemer is the center of the universe and of history"? The world is "subject to futility,"[64] and today a great sign of this is given by some terrifying aspects of technical progress, such as the damage done to the environment, the development of nuclear arms, the persistence of armed conflicts, or the lack of respect for the life of the unborn. However, it is "groaning in travail,"[65] longing for the redemption in Christ. Christ the Redeemer penetrates the mystery of humanity through his union with each human being (*RH* 8).[66] The divine dimension of redemption is that Jesus Christ reveals and reconciles us with the Father and reveals the outpouring of the Spirit. This revelation is love (*RH* 9). The human dimension of the redemption, then, is that Christ "fully reveals man to himself." Christ reveals true love and human beings are newly created in him as all in one (Gal 3:28). This is the gospel, the good news to be proclaimed by the church (*RH* 10). The fundamental task of the Church is to enable "the union [of Christ with each human being] to be brought out and renewed continually" (*RH* 13). This is the reason why the way of the church is "the human person" in her entirety, paying attention to human possibilities as well as to threats and oppositions to what make "human life more human" (*RH* 14). Already in this inaugural encyclical, the christological accent on the union between Christ and humanity had concrete consequences, such as a plea for the respect of human rights (*RH* 17) and particularly for freedom of conscience in search for truth (*RH* 12).

In this more general presentation of Christ the Redeemer in *RH*, we find the elements previously highlighted in *SRS*. Christ is the one who reveals humanity to humanity and reconciles the human race (in itself and with the Father). The first paragraphs of *RH* provide a way to qualify this Christology. It is principally a Christology of the incarnate Word. The two first citations from the Bible are from the Gospel of John: "The Word became flesh and lived among us" (John 1:14) and

"God so loved the world that he gave his only Son, so that everyone who believes in him may not perish but have eternal life" (John 3:16). The point of insistence is the movement of God entering the world in order to save it, a movement of incarnation realized in Jesus Christ and which continues to be at work in the world in which we live.

This responds well to the vision of the world put forward by the pope, a rather Augustinian vision that emphasizes many challenges, the reality of sin, and the fragility of human beings. Salvation needs to come, in a certain sense, *from without*. It is less obvious in this context to insist on another dimension of salvation connected with creation, a salvation that comes rather *from within*, a salvation already at work in the creation of human beings called to grow in the image and likeness of God and in the growth of the kingdom "already in our midst."[67] In *SRS*, however, and in contrast with *RH*, this other soteriological dimension, associated with a more ascending Christology, is clearly present through the focus on the human life of Jesus fulfilling the human vocation and on the continuous presence of Christ today, especially in the poor. This is a case of reframing and an important christological contribution offered by the pope's reflection on development.

Jesus Christ and the Poor

For the first time in a document of the universal magisterium, *SRS* explicitly endorses the "preferential option for the poor," the principle central to Latin American liberation theology.[68] This is significant christologically. Jesus Christ is the one to be imitated in his love of preference for the poor. He is also to be encountered in them.

Although the full expression *preferential option for the poor* is not in the final document of the bishops' assembly in Medellín in 1968, the main ingredients are already there.[69] The church is called to denounce "the unjust lack of this world's goods and the sin that begets it," to preach and live in spiritual poverty, and to be itself bound to material poverty.[70] This leads to a "preference" for and "solidarity" with those most in need concerning the pastoral orientations to be taken locally and globally.[71] A decade later, the bishops who were gathered at Puebla solemnly confirmed the centrality of the principle of "a preferential option for the poor" when they stated, "We affirm the need for the conversion on the part of the whole church to a preferential option for the poor, an option aimed at their integral liberation" (*Pue* 1134).

From the beginning, this option did not come merely from social analysis or from human compassion—although they are good motives for a commitment to the poor and oppressed—but is rooted in God. It is really "a theocentric, prophetic option that has its roots in the unmerited love of God and is demanded by this love."[72] In the Old Testament, God appears as taking sides with the indigent, the weak, the bent-over, the wretched, and the defenseless, and sends prophets to denounce injustices. Jesus's mission is also "to bring the Good News to the poor" and "to free the oppressed" (see Luke 4:16–21). He preached that the last shall be first (see Matt 20:1–16).[73]

In *SRS*, despite the polemical context of the relations between Latin American liberation theology and the Vatican, Pope John Paul fully endorses this principle of the "preferential option for the poor," which he also calls "love of preference for the poor."[74] He asserts,

> An option, or a *special form* of primacy in the exercise of Christian charity, to which the whole tradition of the Church bears witness. It affects the life of each Christian inasmuch as he or she seeks to imitate the life of Christ, but it applies equally to our *social responsibilities* and hence our manner of living, and to the logical decisions to be made concerning the ownership and use of goods. (SRS 42)

It must be used as a primary criterion of discernment in our daily life, in the political and economic fields and especially by the leaders of nations. It is given as the root principle for several more practical guidelines that are not new in the social teaching of the church, but that receive here a renewed strength. The goods of this world are originally meant for all. Therefore, private property, which is a valid and necessary right, is always under a "social mortgage," meaning that it has an intrinsically social function and is oriented toward the common good and the benefit of the least advantaged (SRS 42). Concern for the poor must be translated "at all levels into concrete actions" and in what is demanded by the situation of international imbalances. *Sollicitudo rei socialis* highlights the reform of the international trade system and of the world monetary and financial system, the injustices existing in the field of transfers of technology, and the need for a reform of the international organizations to make them more efficient (SRS 43).

Promoting the "love of preference for the poor," in a certain sense, points to some aspects of the mystery of Jesus Christ for us. First, Jesus Christ is the one to be imitated in his relations to the poor. The option for the poor "affects the life of each Christian inasmuch as he or she seeks to imitate the life of Christ" (SRS 42). Indeed, Jesus's mission, as he indicated in the synagogue of Nazareth, is

> to bring good news to the poor…
> to proclaim release to the captives
>   and recovery of sight to the blind,
>   to let the oppressed go free,
> to proclaim the year of the Lord's favor. (Luke 4:18–19)

The faithful are called to be leaders in the commitment to integral development and in working to "implement…the measures inspired by solidarity and love of preference for the poor" in order to be "in conformity with the program announced by Jesus himself" (SRS 47). This imitation even includes the radical love of one's enemy, "with the same love the Lord loves him or her" (SRS 40) and the following of "the example of Christ, who…lays down his life for his friends (cf. John 15:13)" (SRS 48). Jesus is thus a teacher not simply by words but by deeds. His life, in its historicity and concreteness, teaches us to opt first for the poor, the marginalized person, and the outcast.

Second, Jesus Christ is also the one to be encountered in the poor, the one whose presence in them reveals God to us. Significantly, SRS calls the poor "the Lord's poor" and adds, in a footnote, "because the Lord wished to identify himself with them (Matt 25:31–46)" (SRS 43). This same identification is also mentioned earlier in the survey of the situation of the world when SRS asserts that "before these tragedies of total indigence and need, in which so many of our brothers and sisters are living, it is the Lord Jesus himself who comes to question us (cf. Matt 25:31–46)" (SRS 13). The option for the poor is not merely a moral obligation rooted in some commandments of the Lord, or even in his imitation; it is more profoundly the privileged locus to encounter him. Here, the poor acquire a sacramental dimension.

To go a little further than the encyclical in developing this aspect, we can mention the reflection about sacraments made by Latin American liberation theologian Victor Codina in *Mysterium Liberationis*.[75] He points to the kingdom of God as "primordial mystery-sacrament."[76] In this framework "by analogy but truly, the poor can be called sacraments of the kingdom." Not that they are morally superior or perfect or that, per se, they would incarnate better than others the kingdom in their persons, but because their cry is a denunciation of the antiking-dom and their liberation is the manifestation of the kingdom at work. Codina writes,

> In human history, inside and outside the church we find situations of sin that produce victims. These victims of the anti-Kingdom are the poor. They are sacraments of the Kingdom *sub contrario*, precisely to the extent that the privation of life, the sin of the world, and the negation of the Kingdom are manifest in them. Their cry is a cry for the Kingdom....They are a living prophecy of the Kingdom insofar as they denounce the anti-Kingdom, in anticipation of the eschatological judgment of God and proclamation of the mysterious presence of the Crucified One in them.[77]

Consequently, the denunciation of the structures of sin and the promotion of solidarity made in *SRS* participate in the proclamation of the kingdom. The concern for the poor, which is at the root of the encyclical, makes them in some sense "a sacrament of the kingdom" and an inescapable privileged locus for encountering Christ and being seized by his mystery.

Conclusion

Like *PP*, *SRS* does not offer a full, self-contained, systematic Christology. However, the study of its christological references has led us to highlight substantial contributions on the path to approaching the mystery of Jesus Christ for us. In revealing humanity to humanity, Christ reveals the Father. He saves by reconciling and freeing. The truth he teaches and of which the church has the mission to bear witness is crucial for his redeeming work of bringing about the kingdom. Jesus Christ is also the model who, by his life, teaches us to be in solidarity with the poor for the liberation of humanity from all forms of slavery. In a privileged way, he is to be encountered in this solidarity with the poor.

These elements are brought about, once again, through the interplay of three theological frameworks. The Augustinian perspective certainly shapes John Paul II's insistence on a Christology of the incarnate Word and on an understanding of Christ's redeeming work in terms of liberation from sin and reconciliation with the Father. However, the neo-Thomist approach is not entirely absent because of the intrinsic nature of a social encyclical. Social encyclicals promote a substantial transformation of this world and therefore recognize that such a transformation is possible through God's grace. The redeeming work of Christ is operative in history and brings about the kingdom through the mediation of human achievements. Finally, the central notion of the preferential option for the poor as a major contribution of Latin American liberation theology rebalances the incarnate Word Christology with some elements of an ascending Christology that underscores the concrete life of Jesus Christ and his continuous presence in the poor.

THE THEOLOGY OF *SOLLICITUDO REI SOCIALIS*

This chapter's reading of *SRS* has highlighted many theological aspects. The magisterial reflection on the challenges of development offers various ways of approaching the mystery of "God for us" or letting it seize us. Traditional theological themes such as incarnation, redemption and salvation, sin and grace, and Trinity are addressed through offering practical ways of discernment and action on social, political, and economic issues. These themes are not dealt with comprehensively and systematically, but rather by way of suggestive hints complementing and balancing—sometimes even contradicting—each other and always opening various paths for further reflection. Their strength lies in their connection with concrete social issues. If theology is the "science of mystery," as Rahner suggests, then the many theological reflections brought about by the reading of the encyclical, in their diversity and also in their tensions, pertain to this science and are a real contribution for moving deeper into what is always both greater than us and more intimate within us.[78] The very fact that they are not systematic and are sometimes in tension can even be seen as a good antidote against any temptation to "comprehend" the mystery of "God for us," or to enclose it into a single rational system.

At the end of the previous chapter on *PP*, we qualified the theology of Paul VI's encyclical as incarnational and stressed how it was the expression mainly of a neo-Thomist theological framework. This seemed possible even if this theology was not entirely unified. With *SRS*, it is not possible to attribute a unique qualification in the same way. As this chapter has repeatedly underscored, there are constantly at least three theological frameworks at play: the neo-Thomist, the Augustinian, and the liberationist. Some elements of historical context can explain the emergence of the two latter frameworks and why they become relevant. In the aftermath of Vatican II, in a church becoming a world church, the contribution of the South American continent makes its way even if it is not without turbulence. The global political, social, and economic situation of the world, after two decades of development, which have not produced the results hoped for, can justify a more pessimistic view of the world. Additionally, the personality and background of a pope coming from communist Eastern Europe plays its role in reaffirming the divine and transcendent dimension of the church. This diversity of frameworks at play results in an enrichment of the theological insights. The reflection about the structures of sin, the understanding of development as liberation and its soteriological component, or the christological implications of the preferential option for the poor are among the striking examples.

However, a mere juxtaposition of the frameworks and acknowledgment of diversity in theological insights is a minimalist interpretive key. More can be suggested if we adopt a reading in terms of "reframing" and "rebalancing," as was done in this chapter. The neo-Thomist vision of the world as open to transformation under God's grace and of human beings as instruments in this transformation remains the fundamental grounding for CST because it is necessary in order to justify the church's contribution on social, political, and economic issues. The liberationist perspective introduced some correctives as to what could be too individualistic or merely interpersonal in the neo-Thomist, Enlightenment-marked vision. It also recalls the reality of sin at work in a world where the kingdom "is not there yet," and stresses sin's structural and social dimension. The Augustinian vision also offers some correctives in terms of a greater consideration of sin, but without so great an insistence on the social and structural dimension as the liberationist approach. The Augustinian vision's main contribution is to rebalance a neo-Thomist vision and liberationist perspective by insisting on the transcendent dimension of God's salvation. The kingdom of God is never to be reduced to an earthly political and socioeconomic liberation. God's revelation, to which the church testifies, has something substantial to teach to this world marked by sin. This way of articulating the three frameworks guides a certain reading of *SRS* that focuses on the positive elements contributed by each perspective. This is a hermeneutical option. I do not pretend that it resolves all the tensions and the oppositions at work among them and especially between the Augustinian approach and the two others. However, hopefully, this chapter has shown that it is a valid and fruitful hermeneutical option.

Moving to Benedict XVI and *Caritas in veritate*, the Augustinian vision will become predominant. Consequently, the objective of the theological reading of the encyclical will be to show how the social nature of the issues addressed offers some important reframing and rebalancing through which liberationist and neo-Thomist approaches emerge.

3

DEVELOPMENT IN CHARITY AND LOVE

CARITAS IN VERITATE—love or charity in truth—are the initial three words of the Latin version of Pope Benedict XVI's 2009 social encyclical. Importantly, this phrase is the interpretive key and the foundation for the pope's reflection about integral human development in continuing the work of his two predecessors, forty years after Paul VI's *PP* and twenty years after John Paul II's *SRS*. Charity is the "principal driving force behind the authentic development of every human being and of all humanity" (*Caritas in veritate* [*CiV*] 1), but "only in truth does charity shine forth, only in truth can charity be authentically lived" (*CiV* 3). Therefore, it is by proclaiming the truth of God's love and by shedding the light of the gospel on present human situations that the church fulfills its mission in society. The church's social doctrine revolves around the principle of "charity in truth" (*CiV* 6).

The list of social, political, and economic issues addressed in the encyclical is large: markets, financial and economic crises, business enterprises, employment, workers' rights, inequalities, the role of the state, international institutions, migration, and so on. Widely noted is a lengthier treatment of the environment than in previous encyclicals and the incorporation of topics related to the protection of life such as abortion, euthanasia, and bioethics that were not previously developed in social encyclicals. The pope's focus, however, is always to analyze the roots of the issues at an anthropological level by invoking the joint resources of faith and reason.

The encyclical is divided into eight parts. The introduction and conclusion establish solidly the principle of "charity in truth" as revealed by God in Jesus Christ and as the foundation for fostering integral human development in today's world. They insist on the necessary openness of human beings and society to transcendence. Chapter 1 highlights the message of *PP* in connection with other teachings of Paul VI. True development understood in human and Christian terms is the development of the whole person and of humanity. Chapter 2 looks at the present situation and the many challenges to be faced. Chapter 3 stresses gift and gratuitousness as components of a fully human life. From this perspective, the economic life; the role of markets, states, and civil society; and even the notion of globalization are reconsidered. Chapter 4 adopts the perspective of rights and duties to address issues concerning population growth, ethics in the economy, international cooperation, and ecology. Chapter 5 highlights relation as a central anthropological and theological category. It points to the mystery of the Trinity for various reflections about cooperation and solidarity within the human family. This includes themes as varied as international aid, migration, tourism, education, labor unions, employment, financial systems, and international institutions. Chapter 6 looks at the challenge of a world marked more and more by a technological framework and recalls the moral dimension of all human decisions. Specific reflections here concern bioethics, peace building, social communication, and psychology.

The general theological framework in which Benedict XVI deploys his reflections is very Augustinian. In a world marked by sin and the fragility of human reason, the church fulfills its mission of being a "sacrament" of salvation[1] by including the truth of the revelation of God's love. Insistence is placed on what distinguishes the earthly city that we attempt to build and the city of God it prefigures. Focus is placed on the redemption brought by the cross and on the eschatological dimension of the Christian faith. The social teaching of the church is concerned with discerning the signs of the times, but it does so, very significantly, "in the light of the Gospel" and by shedding on them "the light of faith."[2] This is needed because one of the central signs of the times for Benedict XVI is the emergence of modern and postmodern societies marked by relativism, individualism, and the absence of God.[3]

In this framework, the theological insights arising from the reflection of the encyclical on integral human development reinforce the vertical dimension of faith rather than the more horizontal, incarnational one. Nonetheless, the very nature of the topics addressed by the pope prompts some nuancing, even some tweaking and reframing in the direction of a more incarnational or neo-Thomist framework and even sometimes with a liberationist flavor. This is evident when comparing *CiV* with Benedict's first encyclical *Deus caritas est*.

CONTEXT

To understand the context in which *CiV* was produced, we need to recall various phenomena shaking the world at the dawn of the third millennium: continuing globalization and secularization in Western countries. Mention should also be made of the Focolare movement with its promotion of an Economy of Communion, which inspired parts of the encyclical.

Crises

The publication of *CiV* was initially scheduled for the year 2007 to commemorate the fortieth anniversary of *PP*. It had been delayed several times until finally being released on July 7, 2009 (even though it is signed June 29, 2009). The main reason for these delays was the desire to consider the financial and economic crisis affecting the entire world. This does not mean that the crisis is the central theme of the encyclical or that the encyclical is written merely as a response to the then current situation. It has a much broader scope of presenting an articulated faith vision of the world and its challenges. The financial and economic crisis, nevertheless, affected the treatment of all the themes addressed in the encyclical because it works as a revelator of more profound anthropological questions. The crisis was "an opportunity for discernment, in which to shape a new vision for the future" (*CiV* 21) and "to undertake a profound revision of the prevalent model of development in order to correct it."[4]

Although the financial and economic crisis was a major concern from 2007 onward, it is probably more appropriate to speak of crises in the plural to describe the world situation.[5] Indeed, many countries faced a food crisis provoked by an increase of almost 80 percent of the world prices of basic supplies (cereals principally) between 2005 and 2007, which resulted in food riots in several countries in Africa, South America, and Asia. A report of the Food and Alimentation Organization (FAO) stated that in the year 2008, more than 100 million people were added to the category of hungry people, putting the overall number at 1.02 billion, or one in six persons in the world who suffers from hunger.[6]

The constant energy crisis also loomed in the background. During 2008, the price of oil quadrupled before falling again.[7] It raised the question of the limits of the earth's resources since oil is a nonrenewable fossil energy. More generally, in the first decade of the twenty-first century, there was a growing awareness of ecological challenges and especially global warming. Regular yearly meetings of the United Nations Climate Change Conference attempted to push forward agreements among nations about the reduction of greenhouse gases, such as the 1997 Kyoto agreement. However, results did not yet meet the level of urgency of the challenge.

Finally, added to this panorama of crises was the tensions provoked by international terrorism in connection with religious fundamentalism. The shock of the 9/11 attacks against the World Trade Center in New York and the emergence of fundamentalist groups such as Al-Qaeda undoubtedly affected debates concerning the role and place of religion in political and social life.

For Benedict XVI, these crises required actions, especially in favor of those who most immediately suffered from them, but they also needed, more profoundly, moral analysis. Human beings are affected by crises, but they are also largely actors and are responsible for them. Therefore, it is necessary to shed some light, the light of the gospel, on their mechanisms and to reveal some false anthropological assumptions that lie at their roots.

Globalization

John XXIII, Paul VI, and the Second Vatican Council had already highlighted that the social question had become worldwide because of the ongoing process of interconnectedness and "socialization" far beyond national boundaries. However, half a century later, what is now called globalization has taken on proportions unsuspected in the '60s. This is primarily the effect of huge technical progress in the areas of communication and transportation. Consequently, the more people have been able to communicate and interact with each other, even if separated by large distances, the more they have become dependent on each other, whether consciously or not.

At the time of *SRS*, John Paul II noted the logic of how the confrontation between Western capitalist and Eastern communist societies was affecting directly the rest of the world. He denounced it as a structure of sin. Twenty years later, with the collapse of the Soviet Union and Eastern European communist models, the situation looked very different. The Cold War was now history. This explains why *CiV*'s approach to economic activity is not framed by the ideological battle between capitalism and communism. Indeed, these terms are not even mentioned in the encyclical.

The challenge, and the potential localization of a structure of sin (even if Benedict XVI does not use this terminology), is now rather with the dominant position of giant transnational companies. Globalization was seen first in the internationalization of trade and then of the production of goods, but also in an increasingly rapid circulation of capital, the major part of it for speculative purposes. This means an increasing capacity to evade any type of local or national regulation. As the ex-president of a big multinational company expressed it, "For the companies of my group, globalization means freedom to invest when and where they want, to produce whatever they want, to buy and sell wherever they want and to suffer the minimal limitations possible for what refers to labor legislation and the social pact."[8] In 2007, it was estimated that five hundred multinational companies each had a turnover greater than ten billion dollars a year, that is, greater than the annual national GDP in two-thirds of the countries in the world. In other words, each of those companies is larger economically than many of the countries of the world.

It is against this background of a new stage of globalization that *CiV* needs to be read when it deals with the role of entities like the state, international organizations, civil society, and business enterprises.

Secularization, Benedict XVI, and Europe

Crucial to the context shaping *CiV* was the reality of secularization in Europe. In fact, in the last half century, the visibility of religion in Western European societies had changed dramatically. Participation at Sunday Mass had dropped, vocations to the priesthood and religious life had shrunk impressively, and polls were confirming that churches had less and less influence on the lives of most people. For Cardinal Ratzinger, and then as Pope Benedict, this challenge of secularization, which he associated with relativism and individualism, was a major sign of the times for which he had a precise line of interpretation.[9]

In the aftermath of Vatican II, the future pope joined with others, like von Balthasar and de Lubac, in endorsing fully the agenda of *ressourcement* initiated at the council, but expressed concern about the turn taken in the follow-up of GS toward positive dialogue with the world. Whereas someone like Chenu, who played a central role in the elaboration of GS, stressed the need to pay attention to God's liberating presence in the concrete history of humankind and to learn from engaging in dialogue with secular science and with other religions, Ratzinger highlighted the flaws in human thought on which the Christian faith ought to shed light. He was worried about identifying too quickly the "values of the kingdom" with values presented by modern societies.

Ratzinger remained especially critical of a form of radical Enlightenment and of the path taken by modernity visible in various forms of liberalism and Marxism alike. He saw this as leading to the present situation of Europe. The combination of a culture of technological progress and of affirmation of the autonomous subject had led to the rejection of transcendence:

> Europe has developed a culture that, in a way hitherto unknown to humanity, excludes God from public consciousness, whether he is totally denied or whether his existence is judged indemonstrable, uncertain, and so relegated to the domain of subjective choices, as something in any case irrelevant for public life.[10]

Concern about the forms that modernity had taken is not limited to European secularization. In the North American context, discussions about individualism and moral relativism encapsulate it better. In Ratzinger's vision of the world, the response of the church must be the affirmation of the truth of faith. In face of "the dictatorship of relativism that does not recognize anything as definitive and whose ultimate goal consists solely of one's own ego and desires…we have a different goal: the Son of God, the true man. He is the measure of true humanism."[11] Again, Ratzinger insisted, "What we most need at this moment of history are men who make God visible in this world through their enlightened lived faith."[12] This task, so well defined by the then cardinal, would remain central for him as the pope. It shaped the tone and the theological argument of *CiV* even if the encyclical had a broader audience than "the Western World." We recognize here a context and, more precisely, a way of framing this context that fits perfectly with the Augustinian framework characteristic of Ratzinger/Benedict XVI.

Chiara Lubich, Focolare, and the Economy of Communion

A final element of context concerns the way *CiV* adopted insights from the Focolare movement's reflection on the economy. As already highlighted for *PP* with YCW or for *SRS* with Solidarność, it is characteristic of CST that concrete experiences of groups of Christians precede and fuel the universal teaching. In *CiV*, there is no explicit mention of Focolare or Chiara Lubich, its founder, but when there is mention of "civil economy" and "the economy of communion" (*CiV* 46), they are undoubtedly in the background. One of the closest advisers of Benedict XVI on economic issues, Prof. Stefano Zamagni of the University of Bologna, is the inspirer of those parts of the encyclical and is a key contributor to the Economy of Communion Project of Focolare.[13]

The Focolare Movement started during World War II in the city of Trent, in Northern Italy. Chiara Lubich, then a twenty-three-year-old elementary school teacher, gathered regularly with some friends, searching for some ideal to sustain hope amid the hopelessness of war and its destruction. They discovered that God was this ideal, as God is love and God's personal love envelops every aspect of life. The group thus began to focus on living the commandment of love, and experienced it especially in the building of a community in profound unity with God, among themselves, and within the entire human family. After the war, the initial tiny group expanded to encompass all ages and states of life (married people, priests, religious). Focolare houses inspired by Chiara Lubich opened first in various cities of Italy and then throughout the world. When she died in 2008, the movement operated in 182 nations and had over 100,000 adherents.

One of the fruits of Lubich's movement is the Economy of Communion Project, which is a concrete way to foster a culture of communion. It emerged in Brazil in the 1990s when Focolare members started creating for-profit businesses to ensure that the most basic needs of the community would be met. Those businesses would also generate additional jobs and voluntarily allot profits in three directions: (1) for direct aid to people in need; (2) for educational projects to help foster a culture of giving; and (3) for the continued growth and development of the business. As of 2010, over 750 Economy of Communion business initiatives were in operation in more than fifty countries. Central to the project is a reshaping of the notion of for-profit business, but without abandoning it. Central, too, is the idea of the participation of all and the prioritizing of a quality of human relationship marked by love and respect.

Though the weight of these Economy of Communion Projects remains infinitesimal in the scale of the world economy, they are nonetheless useful for inspiring reflection about economy and business because they show that the infusion of a logic of gift and gratuitousness inside, and not only alongside, economic activity is possible. *Caritas in veritate* does not suggest that it is a solution to be generalized, but the very fact that those businesses exist is a prophetic testimony that the path promoted by the encyclical can be taken in concrete situations.[14] Undoubtedly, the concrete realizations of the Focolare movement as much as the spiritual reflections of Chiara Lubich have contributed to this new and rich insight about gift and gratuitousness in CST.

Conclusion

The vision that shaped *CiV* and constitutes the background of its theological contribution is that of a world in crisis—one challenged by globalization and illustrated by the situation of Europe losing a sense of transcendence and foundational truth. In this context, it makes sense to insist that the mission of the church must testify to the truth of salvation in Jesus Christ. And furthermore, the world, which is the place where God's grace is at work, and which has something to contribute to the church in its journey toward God, is not negated, as the mention of the Focolare movement testifies, but is put in perspective. The focus, rather, is on the antithetical relation between church and world: the church must resist the sin at work in the world. This is the mark of what we have called the Augustinian theological framework.

METHODOLOGY AND STYLE

In terms of methodology and style, *CiV* departs from the movement toward induction and dialogue with the world initiated in CST by John XXIII, GS, and Paul VI, and still at work in John Paul II's encyclicals. The approach to social, economic, and political issues is principally deductive, and the dimension of dialogue is principally oriented toward contrasting the Christian faith with secular thinking rather than discerning the seeds of truth in the latter. Beyond the mere contextual explanation of what many see as a drawback in CST, this section will attempt to grasp the theological meaning of *CiV*'s approach. The methodology and style of the encyclical highlight that God's grace is an absolute gift freely given on the part of God, and that the church, especially in its teaching office, rather than the world, too much marked by sin, mediates the true image of God.

Deductive Methodology

Belgian theologian Edouard Herr notes that in the traditional see-judge-act schema, *CiV* is principally focused on the second step without developing very much the step of analysis (see) and the one of action (act). Ultimately, this step of judgment is based on one principle encapsulated in the formula, "charity in truth."[15] Indeed, even from a cursory reading of the encyclical, it is obvious that applying the methodology dear to Fr. Cardijn is not the priority of Benedict XVI. Rather, he favors a deductive approach highlighting that the church has a substantial contribution to make on various issues by shedding the light of the truth of the gospel.

The introduction offers an exposition of the central principle: "Charity in truth, to which Jesus Christ bore witness by his earthly life and especially by his death and resurrection, is the principal driving force behind the authentic development of every person and all humanity" (*CiV* 1). It is a theological principle stressing that God revealed in Jesus Christ is both Love and Truth—*Agape* and *Logos*. In the following paragraphs, explanations and precisions are provided, and more specifically, the ideas that charity without truth risks being reduced to sentimentalism (*CiV* 3) and that the truth about charity takes practical form through justice and the common good (*CiV* 6–7) are highlighted. In its conclusion, the encyclical restates emphatically the centrality of the anthropological principle of openness to God and transcendence (*CiV* 78–79).

Between the introduction and conclusion, every chapter, except the first on *PP*, addresses more concrete issues but always by applying the fundamental principle of "charity in truth." The second chapter offers a large panorama of world situations regarding development, but in the form of an evaluation of what was exposed in the introduction. The next four chapters are all similarly constructed. A first section exposes a theological and philosophical set of concepts: gift and gratuitousness; rights and duties; relationality; and technology. The remainder of the chapter draws consequences about specific situations. That the reasoning goes from principle to application becomes clear in that different theoretical frameworks shed light on the same issue, for example, the financial and economic crisis, appears in various chapters. In other words, the encyclical is organized around those theoretical principles, not around the practical issues.

Of course, this deductive methodology does not dismiss all sense of induction. Because the encyclical deals with concrete historical situations, they inform, at least indirectly, the choice and formulation of the principles presented. For example, the challenge posed by the economic crisis and by a world more and more governed by an economic science disconnected from ethical concerns is certainly not foreign to the promotion of the categories of gift and of relation. Those categories are presented as central to the Christian vision of the human being. Nonetheless, as Drew Christiansen writes, the *via doctrinae* of "moving from the full knowledge of truth to the judgments about experience" is preferred to the *via inventionis* as "a method of discovery from basic needs to our higher satisfactions."[16]

Dialogue?

Certainly, *CiV* seems to draw back from the dialogue between Christian faith and other religions or secular sciences that became prominent at Vatican II and with Paul VI. Throughout the 159 footnotes, there are references only to papal and conciliar documents, except for one citation of a Greek philosopher (Heraclitus of Ephesus), one citation of Saint Augustine, and one of Saint Thomas Aquinas. Of course, the pope did not write the encyclical in isolation; the Pontifical Council for Justice and Peace played an important role. Through this channel, some specialists were consulted and, as noted earlier, the influence of economists close to the Focolare movement is widely recognized. There are also underlying debates with philosophical theories, but nothing is made explicit.

Nonetheless, if not conspicuously practiced, dialogue is advocated at several points in the encyclical. The complexity of the issues related to human development requires "that the various disciplines have to work together through an orderly interdisciplinary exchange" (*CiV* 30). The church's social doctrine is recognized as "having an important interdisciplinary dimension" (*CiV* 31). Benedict XVI also adamantly promotes a fruitful dialogue between reason and faith because "reason always stands in need of being purified by faith" and "religion always needs to be purified by reason" (*CiV* 56). The pope sees in natural law an effective tool for acknowledging "examples of ethical convergence across cultures" in order to ensure "that the multifaceted pluralism of cultural diversity does not detach itself from the common quest for truth, goodness and God" (*CiV* 59).

To make sense of what seems at first a discrepancy between what is said and what is practiced, it is necessary to look at different ways of understanding the notion of dialogue. In GS, a double and reciprocal movement in the dialogical approach of the church to the world was emphasized. The church has something to provide to the world by proclaiming salvation in Jesus Christ and the church receives from the world insights in its quest for God.[17] The notion of "interpreting the signs of the times" includes the task of recognizing the seeds of truth already present in cultures, religions, and human aspirations outside the visible church.

With Benedict XVI, however, the asymmetry remaining in the dialogue between the church and the world is stressed. Dialogue ought to be rooted in truth: *"Truth*, in fact, is *logos* which creates *diá-logos*, and hence communication and communion" (*CiV* 4). No authentic dialogue is possible without this reference to the truth beyond it and without a clear awareness of the specific identity of the various dialogue partners. Otherwise, there is a danger of falling into relativism. This is what happens too often nowadays in the interaction between cultures. *Caritas in veritate* affirms,

> One may observe a *cultural eclecticism* that is often assumed uncritically; cultures are simply placed alongside one another and viewed as substantially equivalent and interchangeable. This easily yields to a relativism that does not serve true intercultural dialogue. (*CiV* 26)

The mission of the church is to give testimony to the truth of Christ, the Logos, in face of a growing relativism. Therefore, the principle of dialogue as understood by Benedict XVI "is not interpreted as a social dialogue between equals but as a way of disclosing already held truth through reason illuminated by faith."[18] Dialoguing with others is not so much a way to reach out to some elements of truth they possess that we are missing, but rather a way of refining and better expressing what the church founded in Christ already possesses. Indeed, it is noticeable that when Benedict XVI mentions explicitly secular thinkers—as he does in his two previous encyclicals—he generally uses them as opportunities to stress what is missing or flawed in their reflection and which the Christian faith is correcting.

Theological Interpretation

The shift in style noticeable in *CiV* in comparison with *PP* and *SRS* is significant of the vision of God, of the world, of the church, and of their relations, at work in the Augustinian framework. It emphasizes an opposing dimension between the world and the church that then Cardinal Ratzinger had described perfectly two decades earlier. He explained,

> It is not Christians who oppose the world, but rather the world which opposes itself to them when the truth about God, about Christ and about man is proclaimed. The

world waxes indignant when sin and grace are called by their names. After the phase of indiscriminate "openness" it is time that the Christian reacquire the consciousness of belonging to a minority and of often being in opposition to what is obvious, plausible and natural for that mentality which the New Testament calls—and certainly not in a positive sense—the "spirit of the world." It is time to find again the courage of non-conformism, the capacity to oppose many of the trends of the surrounding culture renouncing a certain euphoric post-conciliar solidarity.[19]

Stressing the crucial distinction and even a certain level of antithesis between the world and the church is a theological affirmation because, as Ratzinger mentions, it has to do with sin and grace. It offers an important reminder about one aspect of the mystery of God. The world is marked by sin, and grace is a gift freely given from God that the world and human beings cannot generate by themselves. Whereas solidarity with the world and the effort to recognize positive values outside the church underscore the dimension of human cooperation with God's grace, the more oppositional framework highlights the freedom of God's initiative and the creatureliness of the human being.

That grace is a gift is a central theological reminder made throughout *CiV*. Benedict points out that "sometimes modern man is wrongly convinced that he is the sole author of himself, his life, and society…it is a consequence…of *original sin*" (*CiV* 34). This is particularly visible at this moment in history, for example, in the dreadful consequences of considering the economy as entirely autonomous and to be "shielded from 'influences' of a moral character" (*CiV* 34). On the contrary, Benedict continues, "As the absolutely gratuitous gift of God, hope bursts into our lives as something not due to us, something that transcends every law of justice. Gift, by its nature, goes beyond merit, its rule is that of superabundance" (*CiV* 34). Faith, hope, and charity, which grow within authentic human development, are God's gifts beyond any merit on the part of human beings. Grace as gift is not something that human beings can secure by themselves.

By affirming in a rather top-down fashion the teaching office of the church and stressing the asymmetry at work when the church dialogues with the world, *CiV* promotes the dimension of absolute gift, absolute gratuitousness in God's salvation. The retrieval of this category of gift is undoubtedly a crucial contribution in a modern and postmodern world. This, however, runs the risk of downplaying cooperation within God's economy of salvation and its incarnational dimension, which is another aspect of God's grace. Though sinful, the world is also graced, and this grace is already at work in nature through the mystery of Creation. As Rahner states, "Nature is because grace had to be."[20] Furthermore, *CiV*'s approach carries a risk of too quickly identifying the institutional church and its magisterium with the truth of God's salvation. Benedict XVI offers, as Verstraeten writes, "an image of God as exclusively mediated by the Church. And the Church in this view is a distinct socio-linguistic reality that brings God's love-in-truth to the world via truth propositions of the *magisterium*."[21] The qualification "exclusively" is certainly excessive, but the Belgian theologian captures undeniably the main paradigm at work in the encyclical and its implicit limits.

THEOLOGICAL ANTHROPOLOGY

"The social question has become a radically anthropological question" (*CiV* 75). *Caritas in veritate* is adamant in underscoring that the many challenges the world faces in the economic, political, and social areas have their roots in a distorted vision of the human being. For example, it is a mistaken view of the human person that undermines the current economic order. In this view, the person is reduced to a *homo economicus*, driven by self-interest, the pursuit of profit, and the accumulation of wealth.[22] In this context, the mission of the church to testify to charity in truth takes a central form in providing an articulated anthropology rooted in biblical revelation and developed throughout its tradition. At the heart of *CiV*'s argument lies a vision of the human being in the presence of God and in relation to others and the environment. There is much to recover from it in terms of contributions to theological anthropology.

Development as Vocation

Vocation is a preeminent notion in *CiV*'s anthropological vision. There are no less than twenty-six occurrences of the word in the encyclical.

Charity in truth, which is the driving force for authentic development, is a "vocation planted by God in the mind and heart of every human person" (*CiV* 1). The main truth that the encyclical borrows from *PP* is that "integral development," which concerns "the whole of the human person in every single dimension," is "primarily a vocation" (*CiV* 11).[23] This implies a dynamic vision of the human being having the aspiration and desire to develop and to grow humanly in solidarity with others.

Crucially for *CiV*, human development as vocation requires openness to God. The transcendent dimension of the person is essential. The dynamism at work in the development of the human person—and of human societies—has a direction. It is oriented toward and rooted in God. Commenting on *PP*, the encyclical posits,

> Such development requires a transcendent vision of the person, it needs God: without him, development is either denied or entrusted exclusively to man, who falls into the trap of thinking he can bring about his own salvation, and ends up promoting a dehumanized form of development. Only through an encounter with God are we able to see in the other something more than just another creature, to recognize the divine image in the other, thus truly to discover him or her and to mature in a love "that becomes concern and care for the other." (*CiV* 11)

In the conclusion of the encyclical, the pope returns to his fundamental claim that authentic development cannot exclude God. He warns that an "ideological rejection of God and an atheism of indifference, oblivious to the Creator and at risk of becoming equally oblivious to human values, constitute some of the chief obstacles to development today" (*CiV* 75). The reason is that "*a humanism which excludes God is an inhuman humanism*" (*CiV* 75).[24] On the contrary, "awareness of God's undying love sustains us in our laborious and stimulating work for justice and the development of peoples" (*CiV* 75).

Expressing the centrality of human openness to God and transcendence, *CiV* reaffirms the importance of the right to religious freedom. Not only is this right endangered by some forms of religious fanaticism in parts of the world, it is also threatened by the "deliberate promotion of religious indifference or practical atheism" in many others. This deprives the task of authentic development of peoples from necessary spiritual and human resources (*CiV* 29).[25]

Human development as a vocation open to transcendence presupposes also "the responsible freedom of the individual and of people" (*CiV* 17). Individuals and peoples are the first agents of their development and they should not be deprived of this agency. This occurs too often in new forms of colonialism (*CiV* 33) or when subsidiarity is not respected in the implementation of development aid (*CiV* 58, 60). Regarding peace building, the encyclical reminds us that "the voice of the peoples affected must be heard and their situation must be taken into consideration, if their expectations are to be correctly interpreted" (*CiV* 72).

Caritas in veritate is clear in putting freedom as a central feature of being human in connection with the transcendent dimension. Thus, "human rights risk being ignored either because they are robbed of their transcendent foundation or because personal freedom is not acknowledged" (*CiV* 56). This freedom is not pure, unlimited freedom of choice. It is a responsible freedom to do good, to practice charity in truth with and for others. The reflection concerning technology in chapter 6 offers an illustration of this meaning of freedom. Technological progress in such fields as biology and medicine, as well as economics and communications, has considerably extended the range of the possible. But not everything that is technically possible is good for humanity. Technology ought to remain the object of moral choices. Ethics can never be excluded. This is where the authentic meaning of freedom is to be found. Freedom is not the capacity to do whatever technology allows. This would mean falling under the domination of technology in the same way that in previous decades ideologies exercised their domination. On the contrary, *"human freedom is authentic only when it responds to the fascination of technology with decisions that are the fruit of moral responsibility"* (*CiV* 70). Authentic freedom is rooted in the recognition of limits against any Promethean presumption. It is "a response to the call of being, beginning with our own personal being" (*CiV* 70). It requires a constant search for the truth of the moral law "which God has written on our hearts" (*CiV* 68).

Gift and Gratuitousness

A second anthropological motif deployed in *CiV* is the notion of gift and gratuitousness. This motif is the key principle of chapter 3,

"Fraternity, Economic Development, and Civil Society," but it is also at work in what will be said about our relationship to the natural environment in chapter 4.

The recognition of the "astonishing experience of gift" at work in human life runs counter to a "purely consumerist and utilitarian view of life." Making gift and gratuitousness integral parts of various dimensions of social life is an important reminder that the human person is not self-sufficient. Human beings are not the sole authors of their lives. They are not creators of themselves but creatures. They are not "self-generated" (*CiV* 68) or the "product of their own labors" (*CiV* 74). Rather, gift "expresses and makes present [the] transcendent dimension" of the person (*CiV* 34), the fact that he or she depends on God (*CiV* 74). The principle of gratuitousness is also at the base of the building of a community in fraternity (*CiV* 34).

Therefore, *CiV* affirms that the logic of gift, which does not exclude justice, should not be added to it from without, as a second element. On the contrary, "economic, social and political development, if it is to be authentically human, needs to make room for the *principle of gratuitousness* as an expression of fraternity" (*CiV* 34).[26] This is particularly true with economics. The distinction between for-profit companies and nonprofit organizations does not mean that the first cannot be informed by a dimension of gratuitousness. Indeed, any business activity has a human dimension that bears significance "prior to its professional one." Between the world of nonprofit and the world of for-profit there is possible cross-fertilization.[27] In support of this argument lies Focolare's experience of an Economy of Communion. Some commentators have also noticed that, far from being a mere idealistic dream, what is advanced here in the encyclical is already at work in businesses of service where human relations are primary.[28] Other forms of inclusion of the dimension of gratuitousness in economic life evoked in the encyclical include greater awareness of corporate social responsibility (*CiV* 40), ethical investments (*CiV* 40), microfinance (*CiV* 65), and promotion of fair trade and consumer responsibility (*CiV* 66).

Furthermore, considering the importance of bringing the principle of gratuitousness into all dimensions of human life, *CiV* retrieves the distinctions made by John Paul II in *Centesimus annus*, between the market, the state, and civil society. He highlighted the necessity of a balance among the three in the face of the danger of the omnipotence of the market in the post-1989 world. As *CiV* notes, John Paul II "saw civil society as the most natural setting for an *economy of gratuitousness* and fraternity, but did not mean to deny it a place in the other two settings" (*CiV* 38).

When *CiV* deals with the challenge of development in relation to caring for the natural environment, the idea of gift is also central. The pope states,

> The environment is God's gift to everyone, and in our use, we have a responsibility toward the poor, toward future generations, and toward humanity as a whole….*Nature expresses a design of love and truth.* It is prior to us, and it has been given to us by God as the setting for our life. Nature speaks to us of the Creator (cf. Rom 1:20) and his love for humanity. It is destined to be "recapitulated" in Christ at the end of time (cf. Eph 1:9–10; Col 1:19–20)….Nature is at our disposal not as "a heap of scattered refuse" but as a gift of the Creator who has given it an inbuilt order, enabling man to draw from it the principles needed in order to "till it and keep it" (Gen 2:15). (*CiV* 48)

Recognition of nature as gift is recognition of the Creator and of the fact that we, as human beings, are not the Creator. In addressing this issue of environmental crisis, *CiV* reaffirms the traditional teaching of the Catholic Church. It favors the principle of good stewardship.[29] The encyclical insists on the necessity not to make the natural environment more important than the human person, but it also strongly denounces "the opposite position which aims at total technical dominion over nature. The natural environment is more than raw material to be manipulated at our pleasure; it is a wondrous work of the Creator containing a 'grammar' which sets forth ends and criteria for its wise use, not its reckless exploitation" (*CiV* 48).

The recognition of the dimension of gift at the heart of the human condition opens the way for the connection between life and social and environmental issues. *"The way humanity treats the environment influences the way it treats itself and vice versa"* (*CiV* 51). For the pope, whether it is the lack of care for the environment, the lack of care for the unborn or the dying, or the lack of care for the victims of unjust economic and social conditions, the root issue is a moral failure in not recognizing that, as human beings, we receive life, the natural environment, and other human beings as gifts of God. The encyclical speaks of "human ecology" as interrelated with "environmental ecology."[30] The proper consideration of the human person as a creature in relation to the Creator and to the rest of creation is the road toward authentic development, the road of truth in charity (*CiV* 52).

This recognition of the dimension of gift as a central anthropological feature is seen in *CiV* as the path toward building solidarity and cooperation within the human family. It is thus tightly connected to the third anthropological theme to which we now turn: relationality.

Relationality and Communion

In chapter 5, *CiV* deals with various concrete aspects of cooperation and collaboration within the entire human family. Topics range from international aid for development and greater access to education, to tourism, migration, international finance, the role of consumer associations, and finally, the reform of the United Nations. The treatment of these issues reflects one fundamental anthropological assumption. The human being is meant to be in relationship. Isolation is a deep form of poverty. The development of peoples requires the "recognition that the human race is a single family" (*CiV* 53) working toward true communion.

Caritas in veritate offers a metaphysical and theological approach to the category of relation as the grounding for dealing with concrete issues in international cooperation. First, on the negative side, it points to the phenomenon of the isolation affecting modern human beings and highlights its connection with the illusion of self-sufficiency evoked in the previous section. Ignoring the dimension of dependence inherent in a creature leads to alienation and isolation. It is a form of poverty.[31]

Second, on the positive side, *CiV* recalls that "as a spiritual being, the human creature is defined through interpersonal relations" (*CiV* 54). Christian revelation contributes greatly here, especially in stressing how the human community does not absorb the individual, as in various forms of totalitarianism, but values her and allows her to flourish in proper relationship to the totality. As the encyclical affirms, "just as the Church rejoices in each 'new creation' (Gal 6:15; 2 Cor 5:17) incorporated by baptism into her living Body, so too the unity of the human family does not submerge the identities of individuals, peoples and cultures, but makes them more transparent to each other and links them more closely in their legitimate diversity" (*CiV* 53). Therefore, human beings are called to recognize that they constitute one single human family and to work toward ever greater "inclusion-in-relation of all individuals and peoples in the one community." This family is "built on the basis of the fundamental values of justice and peace" (*CiV* 54).

Following on what *GS* 24 and *SRS* 40 had suggested, *CiV* makes even more explicit the connection between this endeavor of realizing the human family and the mystery of the Trinity. The encyclical continues,

> This perspective is illuminated in a striking way by the relationship between the Persons of the Trinity within the one divine Substance. The Trinity is absolute unity insofar as the three divine Persons are pure relationality….God desires to incorporate us into this reality of communion as well: "that they may be one even as we are one" (John 17:22)….*In the light of the revealed mystery of the Trinity,* we understand that true openness does not mean loss of individual identity but profound interpenetration. (*CiV* 54)

A third aspect of the retrieval of a metaphysical and theological understanding of the category of relation is the orientation toward communion. It is true that today humanity appears more and more interconnected with a greater level of interaction among people across the world. Nonetheless, the encyclical insists that "this shared sense of being close to one another must be transformed into true communion" (*CiV* 53). Communion implies the notion of "working together" or "advancing together," and not merely being "a group of subjects who happen to live side by side" (*CiV* 53).

When *CiV* deals with very concrete issues, it implies and points to this vision of the human being in which relationality is essential and where all are called to build the human family in communion according to the trinitarian mode. For example, when subsidiarity is not respected in international aid and when recipients are maintained in a state of dependence (*CiV* 58), it is the dignity of members of the same human family that is not recognized. Or when a blind eye is turned on sex tourism or, in less extreme cases, when "international tourism follows a consumerist and hedonistic pattern, as a form of escapism planned in a manner typical of the countries of origin," this is "not conducive to authentic encounter between persons and cultures," and therefore, it is not fulfilling the human vocation toward authentic communion (*CiV* 61). Conversely, greater consciousness of the specific social responsibility of consumers concerning what they buy, from whom they buy, and how much they pay for it, helps build solidarity and communion (*CiV* 55).

In all of this, what is put forward is the social and interpersonal dimension of being human. This is the basic anthropological feature that we encountered in the two previous encyclicals when dealing with the notion of solidarity. What is more specific with *CiV* is the insistence on the notion of communion to express the central fact that human beings are meant to be in relationship. Here, a quick detour via a reflection from Hans Urs von Balthasar is helpful to capture what is at stake.

When von Balthasar, along with Ratzinger and de Lubac, departed from *Concilium*, the famous international journal of theology founded in the aftermath of Vatican II, they decided to name their new publication *Communio*. In the opening article, von Balthasar reflects on this notion of communion: "*Com-munio* means community in the concrete expressive sense of being brought together into a common fortification…but also into a common achievement, task, administration, which at the same time can mean mutual satisfaction, gift, grace."[32] In a community, with many different freedoms interacting, the struggle is to move forward beyond any crisis of diverging opinions and toward a common and correct decision. For Balthasar, everything then depends on "how solidly the primary foundation is laid on which all the deliberative and critical processes are built."[33] This foundation is to be found in Christian terms. It relies on God as absolute love coming out of the Trinity and on humanity created in the image of God.[34]

Crucial in this approach is, first, the dimension of common work or common activity in the realization of communion. It is an active and dynamic process, not a static state. This is what makes the idea suitable for social ethics that is concerned with building stronger ties within the human family. Second, the notion of communion implies the recognition of the transcendent dimension of the human person. Communion certainly fits well with what Paul VI and John Paul II highlighted when they spoke about solidarity, but there is a strong insistence that communion is founded in God. Bounds of communion are a given and not merely the object of personal initiative. Interpersonal and social relations are always considered in connection with the primordial relationship to the Creator. It is by deepening their common relationship to the Creator that human beings strengthen the unity of the human family. This approach to the social dimension of being human, which stresses a primary transcendent relation with God, is certainly at work in *CiV*.[35] Here appears the connection with the dimension of gratuitousness about which the pope insists so much. Justice as the expression of a reciprocal relationship between equals is fostered and even exceeded by the recognition of its origin beyond human achievements in God's love alone. It fits within the Augustinian framework. On the contrary, more liberationist approaches would be less comfortable with a vision that places the social dimension as second, even if not secondary, to the individual relationship to God.

Personal Conversion and Social Change

All that has been said thus far on the three key anthropological motifs put forward in *CiV* coheres with the Augustinian framework: its insistence on the discrepancy between God's will and the world as it stands and the necessity to make the former heard. There is nonetheless some reframing due to the very nature of a social encyclical. It is evident when considering the articulation between personal conversion and structural or social change.

In the theological approach favored by Benedict XVI, and following on what he wrote in previous encyclicals, one would expect a strong insistence on personal conversion and reluctance vis-à-vis speaking of structural change. In *Deus caritas est* (*DCE*) the pope had drawn on the distinction between charity and justice to stress that, on the one hand, the role of the institutional church was, first, to purify reason and awaken moral forces by its teaching, and second, to practice works of charity oriented toward specific situations of distress. On the other hand, working for a more just ordering of society was the duty of the lay faithful (*DCE* 29). In *Spe salvi* (*SS*), Benedict warned that "the right state of human affairs, the moral well-being of the world can never be guaranteed simply through structures alone, however good they are," even if "such structures are not only important but necessary....The kingdom of God will never be definitively established in this world" (*SS* 24).[36]

Bernard Laurent critiques *CiV* for breaking with the tradition of CST and its denunciation of the ideology of liberalism.[37] For him, the pope does not sufficiently denounce the interplay of structural forces, but rather gives primacy to personal responsibility. It is true that social analysis is not much developed in this encyclical, which wishes to situate itself at the level of a theological and ethical consideration of the issues. In support of Laurent's argument, one notices general statements that seem to ignore the need for structural change, such as the following: "The whole Church, in all her being and acting—when she proclaims, when she celebrates, when she performs works of charity—is engaged in promoting integral human development" (*CiV* 11). Concerning the market and the financial crisis, *CiV* sees the economy and finance as instruments that "can be used badly when those at the helm are motivated by purely selfish ends." Consequently, for the pope, "it is not the instrument that must be called to account, but individuals, their moral conscience and their personal and social responsibility" (*CiV* 36).

Nonetheless, with other commentators, it seems more accurate to highlight that in *CiV* structural change remains very much in the picture. Just a few lines after the previous consideration about finance and the economy, the encyclical posits that the economic sphere "is part and parcel of human activity and precisely because it is human, it must be *structured* and governed in an ethical manner" (*CiV* 36, emphasis mine). And actually, a few years later, the Pontifical Council for Justice and Peace, building on *CiV*'s orientations, issued a more specific document on the reform of the financial world advocating for an international regulatory body.[38]

From the reform of the United Nations to the promotion of fairer international trade relations, changes in migration policies, rebalancing of the relationships between state, private business, and civil society, and many other topics, the encyclical makes it clear that institutions and structures need to be changed. A good illustration is given on the issue of hunger. The encyclical stresses that "hunger is not so much dependent on lack of material things as on shortage of social resources, the most important of which are institutional." And it adds that "the problem of food insecurity needs to be addressed within a long-term perspective, eliminating the structural causes that give rise to it" (*CiV* 27).

Notice also that the promotion of gratuitousness and of communion in various aspects of economic, political, and social life, which we highlighted in the previous sections, has implications at a structural level. The pope invites a profound reshaping of the economy by centering it again on the human person. For example, the relational anthropology he offers informs his plea for redirecting economic activity from "the simple application of *commercial logic*" toward "*the pursuit of the common good*" (*CiV* 35). This implies restructuring the economic sphere by recognizing the need for some regulation and a plurality of actors (profit and nonprofit corporations, the state, mixed entities). The call for greater communion does not downplay but enhances the many specific calls for greater justice.[39]

Even at the level of the principles mentioned in the introduction of the encyclical, the structural aspect is central. Christiansen notes that "for anyone still tempted to think that Benedict does not favor a structural approach to social justice, the encyclical's treatment of the common good is strong evidence to the contrary."[40] Indeed, for the pope, the common good "is the institutional path—we might call it the political path—of charity, no less excellent and effective than the kind of charity which encounters the neighbor directly, outside the institutional mediation of the *pólis*" (*CiV* 7). And here, the pope does not reiterate the distinction he made in *DCE* between the role of the faithful and the role of the institutional church. In *CiV*, the stress is more on consideration of the mission of the entire church.

This greater consideration given to social and structural change is an interesting reframing introduced into the theological framework of Pope Benedict XVI by a more direct confrontation with social, economic, and political issues. It complements the vision of the human being that was mainly focused on the transcendent dimension, the dependence on God, and the vocation to communion. It is an implicit tweaking of the Augustinian framework with a touch of a more liberationist one. The same dynamic is present in the next section on Christology, which we will now examine.

CHRISTOLOGY

In *CiV*, there are far fewer explicit christological references than in *SRS* or even *PP*.[41] This, of course, does not mean that the encyclical has no christological foundations. The opening sentence should be enough to prove the contrary: "Charity in truth, to which *Jesus Christ bore witness by his earthly life and especially his death and resurrection*, is the principal driving force behind the authentic development of every person and of all humanity" (*CiV* 1, emphasis mine). Nonetheless, in our quest for christological contributions in Benedict's social encyclical, we are dealing here with implicit assumptions rather than explicit and fully developed aspects of the mystery of Jesus Christ for us.

At various points in the encyclical, we encounter a Word Christology, favored by Joseph Ratzinger/Pope Benedict. This Christology insists on a strong affirmation of the divinity of the second person of the Trinity and envisions salvation in terms of participation in divine life through union with Christ. Nonetheless, the attention paid to global justice issues suggests a complementary Spirit Christology, which is more attentive to salvation as the inbreaking kingdom of God through Christian discipleship and a reordering of relationships with God, with one's neighbor, and with the community.[42]

Word Christology

In *CiV*, Jesus Christ teaches charity and truth. "According to the teaching of Jesus" (*CiV* 2), charity is the synthesis of the entire law. "Taught by her Lord, the Church examines the signs of the times and interprets them" (*CiV* 18). To feed the hungry is "an ethical imperative for the universal Church, as she responds to the teachings of her Founder, the Lord Jesus, concerning solidarity and the sharing of goods" (*CiV* 27). In the concluding section, the pope reaffirms that, in the face of the enormous challenges concerning development, "we find solace in the sayings of our Lord Jesus Christ who teaches us…and encourages us" (*CiV* 78). Benedict XVI then urges the faithful to pray to the Father "with the words that Jesus himself taught us" (*CiV* 79).

Christ is also the revelation and the perfect manifestation of "truth in love." "In Christ, *charity in truth* becomes the Face of his Person, a vocation for us to love our brothers and sisters in the truth of his plan. Indeed, he himself is the Truth" (*CiV* 1). "Love is revealed and made present by Christ" (*CiV* 5). Therefore, the mission of the church to foster justice and enact charity is inseparable from the proclamation of Christ, or from "making Christ's love visible" (*CiV* 13). The social doctrine of the church is defined as "*caritas in veritate in re sociali*: the proclamation of the truth of Christ's love in society" (*CiV* 5). "Life in Christ is the first and principal factor of development" (*CiV* 8).

Christ teaches love and reveals love in truth but, through union with him, he also empowers human beings to love, and transforms and liberates them for love. Communion with God through union with Christ is the best source for reconciliation among human beings and authentic development. *Caritas in veritate* restates the central affirmation of GS 22: Christ, "in the very revelation of the mystery of the Father and of his love, fully reveals humanity to itself" (*CiV* 18, GS 22). Therefore, "the Gospel is fundamental for development" and ultimately, "every authentic vocation to integral human development must be directed [to Christ]" (*CiV* 18). Later, the encyclical recalls that Jesus said, "Apart from me you can do nothing" (John 15:5); and also encouraged his disciples, "I am with you always, to the close of the age" (Matt 28:20).[43] This union with Christ is possible because in the first place Christ is the one who is united with humanity. He is the Word who became flesh and who unites in his person human and divine natures.

Everything said thus far reflects a Word Christology. As defined by Lisa Cahill,

> Word Christology, derived from the prologue to John's Gospel, provides the basis of a strong affirmation of the divinity of the second person of the Trinity and of Jesus Christ as Word incarnate; it has been in possession from Nicaea onward....Redemption and sanctification are understood as union with the person of Christ, the Word incarnate. Salvation is participation in the life of God (see 2 Pet 1:4), a share in which Christ cannot communicate to us unless he is fully God. Through Christ, one is united with the Father....Word Christology also supports the idea that, sin aside, authentic humanity is possible only in union with Jesus Christ, the perfecter of human nature.[44]

This also agrees with Joseph Ratzinger's favored christological approach as we encounter it in his three books portraying Jesus of Nazareth.[45] Relying greatly on the Gospel of John, he insists on presenting the "real" Jesus as he is presented in Scripture, stressing his divinity from the beginning. As Ratzinger reminds us in his introduction, the

Christ-hymn of the letter to the Philippians (Phil 2:6–11) "offers a fully developed Christology stating that Jesus was equal to God, but emptied himself, became man, and humbled himself to die on the Cross, and that to him now belongs the worship of all creation, the adoration that God, through the Prophet Isaiah, said was due to him alone (cf. Isa 45:23)."[46] For Ratzinger, such an attempt at portraying Jesus implies taking a critical distance from purely historical-critical methodologies in their endeavor to recover a "historical Jesus" disconnected from the "Christ of faith."

It comes as no surprise that in *CiV* the Johannine corpus is cited eight times, whereas there is no explicit reference to Luke–Acts. In addition, direct references to Jesus's concrete life two thousand years ago are almost absent, whereas the notion of personal, concrete, and actual union with Christ appears central.

As pointed out by Cahill, Word Christologies are "successful in affirming the divine origin of Jesus Christ and salvation, of ensuring hope in eternal life, and in conforming the spirituality of believers to the possibility of an elevating and transforming relation to God."[47] They also offer "potential resources for a this-worldly spirituality and an activist Christian political ethic."[48] In insisting on the union of God with humanity, they assert the possibility of communion among human beings because "in the humanity of Christ united with his divine nature, other human beings are also united with God."[49] They also highlight the salvific nature of the incarnation in the face of so many human challenges that could bring us to despair if we were to rely on mere human capacities.[50]

Nonetheless, Cahill adds, "Word Christologies can tend to abstractness or ethereality regarding the specific demands of 'love' and have a proclivity at the ethical level to invoke transcendence, rather than resistant engagement, in the face of the suffering and conflicts of history."[51] There is a danger of downplaying the historical and social dimensions of the incarnation and the significance of the inbreaking of the kingdom of God through the Christian community under the inspiration of the Holy Spirit. Consequently, we need to recognize that the mystery of Christ is not exhausted by a single type of Christology. In the theological tradition, other Christologies, which Cahill calls Spirit Christologies, are present. Although implicitly, this other type is also at work in *CiV*.

Spirit Christology

According to Cahill, "Spirit Christology, rooted in Luke–Acts and some Pauline letters is an alternative (not an opposite) that stresses the reality of the presence of God not only in Jesus Christ, but also in the church, through the risen Christ who sends his Spirit....Spirit Christology works salvation through Christian community as inbreaking kingdom of God and body of Christ, whereas Logos or Word Christology highlights salvation as self-transcendence and contemplation, toward union with the divine."[52]

Key to this approach is the attention paid to concrete models of discipleship drawn on Jesus's earthly life, death, and resurrection, and early church practical ideals. Jesus reached out to the poor and marginalized people and proclaimed the kingdom as the reconciliation and healing of fractured people and communities.[53] This has strong implications in terms of social ethics. When Word Christology carries the risk of evading the present reality, Spirit Christologies "bring us back to history, the humanity of Christ, the concrete texture of the experience of God, and empowerment for God's reign."[54] They encourage attention to social suffering and social change and to how salvation brought by Jesus Christ is at work in history. According to Roger Haight, the "fundamental metaphor" of Spirit Christology is "empowerment."[55] The Spirit of the risen Christ empowers us to bring about the kingdom of God. Moreover, Spirit Christologies are not only motivated by ecclesial or pastoral concerns about living the gospel and bringing about the kingdom of God, they are primarily committed to render more intelligible professing the real humanity of Christ.[56]

As noted, Benedict XVI is greatly concerned with the challenge of secularization in Europe. For him, the crises faced by Western countries are rooted in the modern radical rejection of God. In this context, it makes sense to put forward a Christology with a robust connection between the divine and the human and supporting the recovery of communion with and in God.[57] Nonetheless, this approach appears insufficient when, as in *CiV*, the outlook is turned more broadly toward global justice issues, inequalities at the world level, challenges in the Global South, and the crucial need for social institutional reforms, whether concerning the financial system or the United Nations. As Cahill notes, "The divinity-focused Word Christology, until now favored by Benedict, is necessary but not sufficient to sustain the social role he has begun to envision for the Church and its members since becoming pope in 2005."[58] Implicitly, *CiV* testifies to a diversification in Christologies by developing ethical reflections that are more robustly supported if Spirit Christology is added to the central Word Christology approach.

In the previous section, we concluded that, in contrast with *DCE*, *CiV* sees work for structural change as intrinsic to Christian love and part of the mission of the whole church—not merely the laity. Throughout the encyclical, there is encouragement of structural reforms in social, political, and economic fields. "Love…leads people to opt for courageous and generous engagement in the field of justice and peace" (*CiV* 1). This is much more than an invitation to personal reconciliation and communion with God or the promotion of a spiritual countercultural renewal in a world ignoring the divine. With Cahill, we can conclude that it is a significant, if not entirely achieved, revision of the previous scheme at work in *DCE*.[59]

Fostering work for "Charity in truth" through justice, and the common good (*CiV* 6, 7), would be reinforced by a Christology that stresses the significance of Jesus's earthly life, his commitment to the poor, and the meaning of the kingdom of God. The first sentence of the encyclical opens a path in this direction when it states that Jesus Christ bore witness to charity in truth *"by his earthly life* and especially by his death and resurrection." The remainder of the encyclical makes no further explicit connections with this christological approach. Surprisingly, for example, in *CiV* there is no appeal to the principle of a preferential option for the poor and its theological grounding, which nonetheless was endorsed by Benedict in his opening discourse of the Fifth General Conference of the Bishops of Latin America and the Caribbean, at Aparecida (Brazil) in 2007 and in the World Day of Peace Message in 2009.[60] Overall, we are left simply with an implicit opening toward another christological approach beyond Word Christology.

CONCLUSION

Throughout this chapter, we have seen how *CiV*, addressing the issue of integral human development in the globalized world of the first decade of the twenty-first century, highlights some aspects of the mystery of "God for us." When we discuss the roots of the financial and economic crisis; consider environmental challenges; denounce the scandals of poverty, hunger, inequalities, and denial of basic human rights, beginning with the right to live, we have an opportunity to offer a specific vision of God, of Christ, and of humanity. In a world that is tempted to forget God and where the illusion of self-sufficiency and absolute autonomy grows, *CiV* reminds us that God is the Creator and Savior of humanity, and that grace is a gift freely given from God and mediated by the church. All the insistences on metaphysical foundations for ethical thinking, on openness to God, on the truth to be witnessed by the church and its magisterial teaching, go in this direction. On the contrary, ignorance of the moral dimension of economic life or exclusive reliance on technical solutions for the various crises of the current times are denounced as deadly paths. Crucial for *CiV* is the recovery of an adequate anthropology. It includes the sense of being human as a vocation including a transcendent dimension. Being human implies also recognition of the dimension of gift and gratuitousness inherent in being a creature and not the Creator. Being human implies striving with others toward authentic communion. *Caritas in veritate* points toward Jesus Christ as the incarnate Word of God, uniting the human and the divine, and opening a path for humanity's union with God and humanity's unity in one family.

All these elements fit within an Augustinian framework, which is preponderant in Benedict XVI's thinking. Insistence is placed on the gap remaining between the created world and humanity as marked by sin and God's infinite love. The world needs God's grace and salvation brought about by Christ's death and resurrection. The relation between the church and the world is marked by a dimension of confrontation and opposition. It is the church's mission to testify to the truth through its teaching office. Salvation comes through personal union with the divine. Undeniably, this approach responds well to the world situation, exemplified particularly in the secularization and growing relativism at work in the West. More generally, it has also the merit of connecting solidly the social thought of the church with theological notions. It makes clear for believers that they cannot eschew the social, political, and economic resonances of their faith. It also brings a profound hope, in face of the breadth of the challenges, by reaffirming that God, not mere human capacities, is the source of hope.

Nonetheless, there are obvious limits to this framework if it remains alone. *Caritas in veritate* illustrates them very well. The affirmation of the centrality of faith and union with God for working toward development, especially when it is formulated with a phrase like "a humanism which excludes God is an inhuman humanism" (*CiV* 78), can render rather difficult dialogue and association with men and women from other faiths or with no declared faith. There is also a danger of placing little hope in what can be done in this world, because all the weight is in the "not yet there" of the eschatological hope for the coming of the kingdom rather than in the "already here" of what Jesus Christ announced (cf. Luke 17:21: "the kingdom of God is among you"). The insistence on ontological personal union with God can greatly overshadow the historical dimension of salvation. The Word Christology of the Johannine literature, which tends to focus on knowing Christ as the truth, risks leaving aside the sense that revelation consists in the manifestation of God in action and not merely an "icon" of the divine. The latter is often highlighted better in the Christology of the Synoptic Gospels and Paul. Finally, there is the risk of stressing the personal moral dimension of the issues and downplaying their social and structural aspect.

Therefore, it is very significant that, operating in this Augustinian framework, *CiV* nonetheless continues to offer some openings toward the two other frameworks we have seen more at work in *PP* and *SRS*. The recognition of some aspects of inductive methodology, especially the incorporation of the experience of Focolare, points toward a neo-Thomist vision of the world, a world that is the locus and object of God's grace. The real attention paid by *CiV* to the necessity of structural changes to bring about justice is also an opening in the direction of the liberationist framework. Those openings are prompted by the very nature of the encyclical. Because it deals with issues of global justice, with concrete historical situations, and with social, political, and economic challenges, it cannot stay in the purely Augustinian framework. As we navigate with magisterial CST in these three frameworks, *CiV* seems to go the furthest possible in the Augustinian direction. The limitations of the encyclical suggest rather that CST, to be relevant ethically and theologically, needs to give more priority to theological frameworks where the world is less antithetical to God and the church. Only six years later, Pope Francis will return in this direction with his first social encyclical, *Laudato si'*.

4

DEVELOPMENT AS INTEGRAL ECOLOGY

ONLY SIX YEARS AFTER *Caritas in veritate*, Pope Francis promulgated a new social encyclical. *Laudato si'* (*LS*) is, without a doubt, a major step in the development of CST. Although its publication does not celebrate an anniversary of *PP*, as did the encyclicals we discussed in the previous chapters, one can say that it continues the reflection on development in a globalized world. On the one hand, *LS*'s central concept of integral ecology can be considered an updating—with substantial corrections—of the church's understanding of integral human development. On the other hand, *LS* may be as powerful in initiating new paths in CST as *Rerum novarum* or *PP* were in their times. Time will tell!

In *LS*, the social question is viewed through the lens of ecology or "care for our common home." At stake is not merely the conservation of our natural environment but really an all-encompassing conscientization regarding the damages inflicted by human beings on creation, with the first victims being the poor, the excluded, and the most vulnerable (*LS* 48). Everything is connected, and the ecological and the social questions especially are one and the same challenge posed to humanity (*LS* 139). Hence, the urgent need for a profound ecological conversion at the personal level (*LS* 217) that is also a profound cultural revolution at the institutional level (*LS* 114). Economy, politics, education, spirituality, lifestyles, cultures, sciences; every dimension of human life is of concern and is addressed in the encyclical.

The first words, *Laudato si'*, come from the famous *Canticle of the Creatures* authored by Francis of Assisi. They place the entire document under the inspiration of the thirteenth-century saint and give us a crucial clue for framing the theological contribution of *LS*. Chapter 1 offers an uncompromising overview of the current situation of "our common home": the various pollutions, climate change, loss of biodiversity, scarcity of clean water, as well as the inequalities, the degradation of social life, and the lack of decision-making necessary to tackle real problems. Chapter 2 moves to an analysis of the situation, offering insights from Scripture and from the Christian faith tradition. Human beings are part of God's loving project of creation. In this project, nonhuman creatures have value in themselves, and whatever specific responsibility human beings have in caring for creation does not imply a right to dominate and exploit. Faulty interpretations of biblical narratives—unfortunately not absent from the Christian tradition—need to be challenged. The encyclical underlines God's call for communion among all creatures, human and other than human alike. The third chapter then analyzes the human roots of the ecological crisis. Technological development and scientific progress have brought some major improvements in human life, but they carry with them a challenging increase of power. Human beings have fallen into a deviated anthropocentrism that recognizes no limits to technological and economical possibilities because humans consider everything—natural resources, nonhuman creatures, and even other human beings—merely as disposable objects. In the fourth chapter, we consider the third stage of the encyclical's analysis: the constructive proposal. Considering that everything is closely interrelated, Pope Francis invites us to take the path of integral ecology. Integral ecology, because it is centered on care of the most fragile aspects of the environment and society, considers both the human and social dimensions (e.g., environmental, economic, political, and social concerns) in the search for the common good. It also considers the preservation of the diversity of cultures, including indigenous ones, the challenges of daily life, gender and sexuality, and looks ahead to the generations to come.

The final two chapters provide orientations for actions to be taken. Chapter 5 focuses on the need for dialogue at every level: international, national, and local, between economy and politics, between sciences and religions, and among them all. Chapter 6 deals with education and highlights the spiritual resources that already exist in the Christian tradition and that can foster and inspire the much-needed ecological conversion.

How does all this rich reflection on crucial contemporary ethical issues provide an expression of the mystery of God's saving love? The turn to ecology as the entry point for addressing social, political, and economic questions is certainly a tremendous shift from the previous encyclicals. This shift calls for an additional fourth theological framework alongside the three used in analyzing previous encyclicals. The figure of Saint Francis of Assisi and the Franciscan theological tradition will help us here. In the Franciscan theological tradition, the entire created world manifests God and, although, with some distinctions, all creatures—human beings included—are bound in communion as brothers and sisters. This tradition has specific emphases in its understanding of God, world, humanity, as well as the connections among the three, that are enriching for theology. The following reading of *LS* highlights the presence of some of the frameworks we saw earlier, especially the neo-Thomist and the liberationist, but also underlines the emergence of the Franciscan framework.

CONTEXT

Between the publication of *CiV* in 2009 and that of *LS* in 2015, the overall context of the world had not changed dramatically. What was described in the previous chapter regarding the challenges of the ongoing phenomenon of globalization and the consequences of various crises was still very much at stake. Nonetheless, it is worth pointing out the immediate context that is marked by two crucial world summits, the phenomenon of persistent and worsening global inequalities, and the change of pope.

World Summits and Global Inequality

Laudato si' was released on June 18, 2015, though dated May 24 (Pentecost Sunday). Three months later, the General Assembly of the United Nations adopted seventeen sustainable development goals. In

December of the same year, the twenty-first session of the Conference of the Parties to the United Nations Framework Convention on Climate Change (UNFCCC), or "COP21," was held in Paris. Clearly, the encyclical was not written simply because of these two major events, for its agenda is much broader and more farsighted, but it is significant that the timely release of the encyclical helped to connect and contribute to the debates surrounding these two events.

As hoped, both within and without the church, the voice of the pope amid the debates leading up to the Paris Conference was not disappointing. He states clearly that "climate change is a global problem with grave implications: environmental, social, economic, political and for the distribution of goods" (*LS* 25), adding that "a very solid scientific consensus indicates that we are presently witnessing a disturbing warming of the climatic system," which is the consequence of the raising of the concentration of gases released "mainly as a result of human activity" (*LS* 23). The pope goes further by inserting climate change into a larger set of other environmental challenges that threaten our world: pollution from wastes that make "the earth, our home, is beginning to look more and more like an immense pile of filth" (*LS* 21), depletion of clean water, loss of biodiversity, and so forth. Everything is connected because it is the result of the same patterns of human activity, shortsightedly oriented toward immediate profit and unlimited use of natural resources.

While presenting the encyclical at a conference in the Vatican shortly after its publication, Pietro Parolin, the Cardinal Secretary of State, connected it not only to the Paris Conference, but to the adoption by the United Nations of the new set of development goals the following September. The eight Millennium Development Goals adopted on the eve of the third millennium were set with a target date of 2015. Though significant progress was made in many regions of the world, much more remained to be done, and a new set of seventeen goals was designed, engaging all the nations on a journey, with the goal of achieving them by 2030. Significantly, they are named "Sustainable" Development Goals. The connection between concerns for eradicating poverty and ensuring basic human needs such as universal health care and education, and concern for environmental and climate change are already present in the Millennium Goals, and they are even more visible in the Sustainable Development Goals. This connection is at the heart of *LS*.

Among the key elements to which Pope Francis calls attention in the overview of the state of "our common home" is global inequality. Indeed, though it is not something new in human history, economic inequality is becoming more and more pronounced, both at national and international levels. It is true that extreme poverty in the world (people living on less than $1.90 a day) was cut in half between 1990 and 2010. This is one of the Millennium Development Goals successfully achieved. But, in the meantime, inequalities of income and of wealth continued to rise to astonishing levels. According to a 2014 Oxfam study, the wealthiest 1 percent of the world population owned 50 percent of the wealth, and most of the remaining wealth is owned by the wealthiest 20 percent, which means that 80 percent of the world had only 5 percent to share.[1] Inequalities of wealth generate huge differences when it comes to their impact on the environment. On the one hand, the most vulnerable people are the ones who contribute least to ecological degradation such as greenhouse gases emissions, and on the other hand, those same people are the first to suffer from ecological degradation. For example, the ecological footprint of a citizen in the United States is ten times that of a citizen of Bangladesh, a country already suffering badly from rising sea levels.[2] If we look at just a single country, it is the same. In France, the wealthiest 10 percent of households have an ecological footprint that is three times higher than the poorest 10 percent of households.[3]

Pope Francis calls attention to the fact that "the deterioration of the environment and of society affects the most vulnerable people on the planet" (*LS* 48). He gives the example of fishing communities affected by the depletion of fishing reserves and the example of water pollution that primarily affects those who cannot afford to buy bottled water. Furthermore, "the impact of present imbalances is also seen in the premature death of many of the poor" (*LS* 48). The pope pleads that we always "integrate questions of justice in debates on the environment so as to hear both the cry of the earth and the cry of the poor" (*LS* 49).

The rising inequalities and the more proximate context of important international negotiations are significant aspects of the overall context in which *LS* was written. But it is the change that occurred in the papacy itself, in 2013, that is a crucial key for interpreting this encyclical.

Francis, a Pope from Latin America

At his first appearance on the balcony of Saint Peter's Basilica following his election, Pope John Paul II pointed out that the cardinals had "called him from a far country."[4] In the case of Pope Francis, they went much farther! They "have gone to the end of the earth to get [a bishop for Rome]," the newly elected pope told the crowd from the balcony of Saint Peter's on March 13, 2013.[5] Francis is the first pope from Latin America and the first to be named after the saint of Assisi. Both features are significant.

Unlike his predecessors, Francis did not participate in the Second Vatican Council, but he appears today as a new symbol of the shift, initiated by that council, from a European-centered church to a world church. Being Argentinian and having lived his entire life in Argentina, Francis has been part of the very rich theological and pastoral development of the church in Latin America since the council. He also has firsthand experience of poverty, underdevelopment, and political violence. He had to find his way in the murky waters of the troubled period of military dictatorship in the 1970s, when he was provincial of the Jesuits. As archbishop of Buenos Aires from 1998 to 2013, he showed a special interest in ministering in the slums of this city.[6]

Francis may have shown some reserve toward the more politically engaged, revolutionary forms of liberation theology, but he is firmly linked to one current of it developed in Argentina and known as "theology of the people."[7] The roots are the same. The theology of the people springs from consideration of massive poverty as the key sign of the times for the continent. As Kasper explains, however,

> Different from other forms that are generally better known to us, Argentine liberation theology does not proceed from an analysis of socio-political and economic relations or from antagonisms in society in order then to interpret them with Marxist categories, in the sense of a theory of dependence. Rather it proceeds from an historical analysis of the culture of the people, who are united in a common ethos. It is a theology of the people and of culture.[8]

Francis also played an important role during the fifth General Conference of the Bishops of Latin America and the Caribbean, held in the Sanctuary of Aparecida (Brazil) in May 2007. He chaired the committee charged with writing the final document (*Ap*).[9] Following the earlier gatherings in Medellín, Puebla, and Santo Domingo, Aparecida is an important step in the development of a continent-specific identity within the universal church. Many elements that appear in the final document—its content but also its methodology and style—are present in Francis's teaching. *Laudato si'* has the strong flavor of Latin America. As Brazilian theologian, Leonardo Boff noted,

> Many expressions and ways of speaking refer to what is being thought and written mainly in Latin America. The themes of the "common home," of "Mother Earth," the "cry of the Earth and the cry of the poor," the "care" of the "interdependence of all beings," of the "poor and vulnerable," the "paradigm shift," the "human being as Earth" that feels, thinks, loves and reveres, the "integral ecology" among others, are recurrent among us.[10]

In approaching *LS*, it is also very meaningful to recall why Jorge Bergoglio chose "Francis" as his papal name. A few days after his election, he explained that it was because Francis of Assisi "is the man of poverty, the man of peace, the man who loves and protects creation."[11] The Italian saint gives strong testimony and inspiration for the central message the pope wishes to convey. Attention to the poor, to creation, and to peace cannot be separated and ought to drive the changes necessary in the world. In the introduction, the pope states,

> I believe that Saint Francis is the example par excellence of care for the vulnerable and of an integral ecology lived out joyfully and authentically. He is the patron saint of all who study and work in the area of ecology, and he is also much loved by non-Christians. He was particularly concerned for God's creation and for the poor and outcast. He loved, and was deeply loved for his joy, his generous self-giving, his openheartedness. He was a mystic and a pilgrim who lived in simplicity and in wonderful harmony with God, with others, with nature and with himself. He shows us just how inseparable the bond is between concern for nature, justice for the poor, commitment to society, and interior peace. (*LS* 10)

Clearly, to shed some light on the theological contribution of *LS*, and considering the specific background of Pope Francis, it is useful to return to both Latin American contemporary theology and Franciscan-inspired theology.

METHODOLOGY AND STYLE

From the beginning of his pontificate, Pope Francis has received attention because of the way he exercises his ministry. He teaches as much by words as by signs, such as living in Casa Santa Marta with other people instead of living in the private apartment used by his predecessors, avoiding rich ornamentation for liturgies, choosing to travel in ordinary cars, retaining his custom of calling people directly on the phone, and changing plans during pastoral visits so that he can meet everyday people directly. He chose the island of Lampedusa in the Mediterranean Sea for his first trip out of Rome to show solidarity with the migrants dying in their attempt to reach Europe, and on one Holy Thursday, he went to a prison for minors, where we saw him washing the feet of a young Muslim woman. Attention has been drawn to the simplicity of his homilies, always loaded with stories and images that connect easily with everyday life.

This style, reflected in the man himself, is also characteristic of *LS*, although we are dealing with a very long document (the longest social encyclical so far, four times the length of *PP*) and one that is technical and quite tedious in some parts. The gospel is thus proclaimed with distinctive emphases.[12] We have returned to features that were pushed to the front at Vatican II and in its immediate aftermath: a see-judge-act methodology and dialogue. Theologically, these features emphasize incarnation and the presence of God in the world.

A Return to See-Judge-Act

In his social magisterium, Benedict XVI departed from the see-judge-act methodology that had been largely adopted by his predecessors ever since John XXIII. In *LS*, Francis clearly returns to it. The outline of the encyclical is clear. In the first chapter, the pope looks at "What Is Happening to Our Common Home" (*LS* 17; chapter 1).

Then, he critically analyzes the situation by recalling some principles from the Judeo-Christian tradition (chapter 2), discerning some of the human roots of the ecological crisis (chapter 3), and offering a new integral approach to ecology (chapter 4). Finally, he offers some paths for action through dialogue (chapter 5) and some resources both to inspire and to guide the action (chapter 6).

When the Latin American bishops deliberately returned to this see-judge-act method at Aparecida in 2007, after having dropped it in their previous meeting at Santo Domingo in 1992, they insisted,

> Many voices from the entire continent…stated that this method has been helpful for living our calling and mission in the church with more dedication and intensity. It has enriched theological and pastoral work and in general it has been helpful in motivating us to take on our responsibilities toward the actual situations in our continent. (*Ap* 19)

Francis carries on this line of thought. For him, "Theological and philosophical reflections on the situation of humanity and the world can sound tiresome and abstract, unless they are grounded in a fresh analysis of our present situation" (*LS* 17). The present situation prompts and shapes his teaching, which is inscribed in the church's mission of announcing God's salvation in Jesus Christ. This is not a mere strategic option for writing a document, but it confirms the belief that God is continuously at work in the world. At the beginning of the encyclical, Francis states that "the Creator does not abandon us; he never forsakes his loving plan or repents of having created us" (*LS* 13). In one of the last paragraphs, he writes again, "In the heart of this world, the Lord of life, who loves us so much, is always present. He does not abandon us, he does not leave us alone, for he has united himself definitively to our earth, and his love constantly impels us to find new ways forward" (*LS* 245). The present ecological and social crises are not simply a context in which there is a need to reinterpret the Christian faith, but a place for developing this faith, for encountering God, and experiencing salvation through reconciliation with God, with creation, with others, and with oneself (see *LS* 66, 240). The see-judge-act methodology is the means for welcoming God's revelation today through discerning where the kingdom flourishes and where it is opposed.

Three additional comments should be made about the initial

step of this methodology (see). First, because the way of seeing our present situation is being done by believers, it is already being done through the eyes of faith. Faith does not just play a role in the "judge" step.[13] The whole process is one inspired by the Holy Spirit. *Laudato si'* is addressed to "all people" (*LS* 3). It is, therefore, crucial that, to underscore a large consensus across believers and nonbelievers on the current state of affairs, the approach in chapter 1 avoid too much religion-specific language. Nonetheless, for believers, everything that is said remains within a perspective of faith. This perspective is shaped from the very first words thanks to the *Canticle of the Creatures* by Saint Francis of Assisi. Pope Francis describes the situation of our common home within the global perspective of giving praise to God for "our Sister, Mother Earth" (*LS* 1). He looks at reality as a disciple of Jesus Christ and as a believer in the gospel.[14]

Second, a crucial feature of the first chapter of *LS*, one that is broadly stressed by commentators, is the seriousness and rigor with which the pope reports current scientific research. Although he does not explicitly reference scientific works in footnotes, many commentators have supplied the documentation for his affirmations about climate change, biodiversity, pollutions, clean water, and so forth. Francis thus illustrates both the legitimate autonomy of scientific research as defended by Vatican II,[15] and the duty of pastors, theologians, and all the faithful alike not to ignore it.

Third, what also characterizes the way *LS* draws the state of "our common home" in chapter 1 is the attention paid to the poor, the most fragile in our society, the excluded. On every topic, besides scientific analysis, the encyclical references concrete situations, through examples and images, and they always concern the poor.[16] In this, Francis enacts the preferential option for the poor he had emphasized in his 2013 apostolic exhortation, *Evangelii gaudium* (*EG*). For him, the preferential option for the poor is also an epistemological principle or entry point into reality; "the poor have much to teach us" (*EG* 198).

According to Francis, to look at reality through the lens of the poor has a lot to do with letting one's heart be touched. Contrary to the widespread culture of indifference, Francis repeatedly pleads for developing authentic compassion through "sharing sufferings." In *LS*, where the option for the poor is at the same time an option for the earth, he invites everyone to enter this way of looking at reality. "Our goal," states the pope, "is not to amass information or to satisfy curiosity, but rather to become painfully aware, to dare to turn what is happening to the world into our own personal suffering and thus to discover what each of us can do about it" (*LS* 20).

Multifaceted Dialogue

Dialogue is present throughout the entire encyclical. It is both practiced and encouraged.[17] Once again, one senses a closer identification of Francis with Paul VI than with Benedict XVI.

First, there is dialogue with the sciences. We have already noticed the importance given to the results of scientific research. The encyclical does not merely incorporate scientific results that are taken for granted, it attempts dialogue through discussion, searching for the greater common good. "Given the complexity of the ecological crisis and its multiple causes, we need to realize that solutions will not emerge from just one way of interpreting and transforming reality" (*LS* 63). In other words, every mode of apprehending reality and acting upon it is needed, from scientific data to religious and wisdom texts, poetry and expressions of popular cultures. "If we are truly concerned to develop an ecology capable of remedying the damage we have done, no branch of the sciences and no form of wisdom can be left out" (*LS* 63). Nonetheless, the sciences and other forms of knowledge must also recognize that they are not self-sufficient and not exhaustive. They need each other to remind them of the limits imposed by their specific method (*LS* 199). In *LS*, we see ethical reflection grounded in religious belief offering a necessary critique of economic or political sciences, or even reminding natural sciences that they cannot pretend to elucidate the anthropological question alone. We have not finished saying everything that could be said about the human being when it is—accurately—described as one being among others under the laws of biology. However, by seriously considering the ecological sciences and evolutionary explanations about the world, *LS* recognizes the specific limits of religious discourse.[18] *Laudato si'* also recognizes that not all interpretations of biblical texts are possible, and even that in the past "we Christians have at times incorrectly interpreted the Scriptures" (*LS* 67).

Another key aspect of *LS* is the dialogue within the church. The encyclical incorporates many references to documents produced by local conferences of bishops from all over the world. They are meant to help describe the situation but also analyze it and suggest paths for actions. Local contributions are, therefore, present in every step of the see-judge-act methodology. This reflects the desire of Pope Francis to develop collegiality within the church. As he explained in *EG*, the central structures of the church need to "hear the call to pastoral conversion" and to recognize how, following Vatican II, local episcopal conferences "are in a position to contribute in many and fruitful ways to the concrete realization of the collegial spirit" (*EG* 32). This includes acknowledging their "genuine doctrinal authority" (*EG* 32). In *LS*, Francis leads the way by developing his magisterial teaching through the intertwining of various local reflections and experiences. Noteworthy are the significant references not only from large and powerful conferences of bishops like those of the United States and Germany but also from less known conferences such as in the Dominican Republic and the region of Patagonia. Once again, *LS* paves the way of learning from the margins.

Dialogue also extends to discussions with other Christian churches and even other religions. Strikingly, in a section dedicated to the sacraments, the encyclical refers to a Muslim spiritual master, Alî al-Khawwâç, as an inspiration for better understanding the presence of God in all things (*LS* 233). That a non-Christian reference appears within a reflection of spiritual and theological nature in a document of the magisterium is certainly surprising for many, but it says much about the importance of interreligious dialogue. It is not simply needed for the sake of building peace among people; it is also a possible source for Christian faith.[19]

Dialogue is not merely a matter of intellectual discussion among experts. For Francis, the logic of dialogue is closely connected with his promotion of the "culture of encounter." Dialogue is the fruit of personal and concrete encounters. Individuals and groups are enriched by developing forms of dialogue in which they learn from each other out of their differences. Still, this can only happen if there is a real encounter. Francis laments that too often dialogue within a society is truncated because many voices, including the voices of the poor, are not heard. He says pointedly,

> This is due partly to the fact that many professionals, opinion makers, communications media and centers of power, being located in affluent urban areas, are far removed from

the poor, with little direct contact with their problems. They live and reason from the comfortable position of a high level of development and a quality of life well beyond the reach of the majority of the world's population. (*LS* 49)

Conversely, the simple style of *LS*, typical of Francis, is full of images and allusions to concrete life and reflects his experiences of authentic encounter. For example, when the encyclical refers with admiration to "some places, where the facades of buildings are derelict, [but where] people show great care for the interior of their homes, or find contentment in the kindness and friendliness of others" (*LS* 148) or to "neighborhoods, even those recently built, [which] are congested, chaotic and lacking in sufficient green space" (*LS* 44), or when the pope concludes that "we were not meant to be inundated by cement, asphalt, glass and metal, and deprived of physical contact with nature" (*LS* 44), one can easily perceive the experience of the bishop ministering to the *villas* (slums) of Buenos Aires.

The logic of dialogue at work in *LS* supports its calls for increased dialogue at all levels. Dialogue is indeed the major path proposed by the pope so as "to escape the spiral of self-destruction which currently engulfs us" (*LS* 163). The subtitles of chapter 5 speak for themselves: "Dialogue on the Environment in the International Community," "Dialogue for New National and Local Policies," "Dialogue and Transparency in Decision-Making," "Politics and Economy in Dialogue for Human Fulfillment," "Religions in Dialogue with Science." Clearly, dialogue is not mere polite listening to various opinions but a demanding path of searching for the common good without being prejudiced by particular interests or ideologies (*LS* 188).

Theological Interpretation

What was said in chapter 2 about the theological meaning of methodology and style in *PP* holds true for *LS*. We certainly discover afresh something of the neo-Thomist framework. An inductive methodology underscores the incarnational dimension of Christian faith. God who chose to come into the world through the Son continues to be present in current history through the Holy Spirit. Dialogue practiced and encouraged is also in tune with faith in a trinitarian God who is in dialogue with humanity. Dialogue can become the place for the manifestation of this trinitarian God, along the lines suggested by Paul VI's encyclical, *Ecclesiam suam.*

With the pope's Latin American background, the liberationist framework has also left some traces in *LS* of the see-judge-act methodology, not only because it favors this methodology but because of consideration in the first step of what is contrary to God's will. The tone of *LS*, though not void of joy, is also somber and not at all overly optimistic! The pope himself speaks of a "lengthy reflection that has been both joyful and troubling" (*LS* 246). The denunciation of the damages inflicted on the environment as "a sin against ourselves and a sin against God," according to the words of Patriarch Bartholomew (*LS* 8), is powerful. The description of what goes wrong in our world in terms of structures as much as in personal behaviors is also uncompromising. The criticisms that some raised against *Gaudium et spes* (*GS*) in the '60s because of its optimism are certainly no longer valid for *LS*.

Using current theological reflections from Latin America, one can probably speak of *LS* as an instance of a "theology of history" or a "theology of the signs of the times." Theologians from Chile and Argentina define the notion of the signs of the times and a theology shaped by it:

> The notion of the signs of the times, and its theological development, tries to account for the actual presence and action of God in the life of human beings and in the most diverse historical events recognizing that they are most often fueled with ambiguities and negativities. Jesus Christ, risen Lord, gift of the Father, and fullness of God's revelation is made present and is active in human situations, thanks to Christ's Spirit. First of all, the discernment of his presence or absence within actual events, which requires an historical responsibility, is the fruit of the theological experience of communities of believers. Then, the work of a theology of the signs of the times is to develop this discernment in a systematic way and with a well-founded and consistent argumentation.[20]

History, contexts, and human events are not simply an external help to explain better the mystery of God's saving love. They are a place for experiencing it and a place for developing a theology or scientific discourse about it. Of course, this does not deny the special status of

Sacred Scripture as the fundamental source for theology. Rather, it is a matter of the "book of human history" and "the sacred book," speaking together, the latter being indispensable in deciphering the first, but both viewed as fruits of the single and unique Word of God.[21]

Actual crises, perceived through the lenses of integral ecology and care for "our common home," including all its inhabitants, are important signs to be interpreted in the light of faith. They become paths of the revelation of God who is not far from us; of God whose Spirit at work in our world continues the incarnation; of God who is also rejected and denied in the damage inflicted on creation by sinful human activity; of God who is denied by the persistence of poverty and inequalities; of God who is denied by the lack of responsible engagement to address the situation. As reflected in *LS*, the Christian God is, very concretely, the God of history, the incarnate God, the Triune God.

THEOLOGICAL ANTHROPOLOGY

As with previous social encyclicals, *LS* offers substantial reflection at the anthropological level. Ethical challenges posed by the current state of "our common home" cannot be properly addressed without getting to the fundamental question of "being human." "There can be no renewal of our relationship with nature without a renewal of humanity itself. There can be no ecology without adequate anthropology" (*LS* 118). "What we need is an anthropology that fits our status as creatures and that respects the home for which we were made. This arises only from a theology of creation."[22] Obviously, consideration of human beings in relation to other living creatures in a common environment prompts substantial developments and new accents in the church's discourse. Without pretending to cover the entire anthropological question in *LS*, let us consider two major aspects: (a) shifting paradigms from misguided anthropocentrism to a relational anthropology; (b) human beings as social beings within a multicultural world. Although much will resonate with what was written in earlier encyclicals, it will become clearer that *LS* bears the mark of the Franciscan framework.

From Misguided Anthropocentrism to Relational Anthropology

In chapter 3, *LS* calls for a paradigm shift in the way humanity relates to the rest of creation. Modernity favored the idea that we ought to be "masters and possessors of nature."[23] Nature became an unlimited resource for human needs. Nonhuman reality was considered as entirely external and disposable, knowable and analyzable through the scientific method, and capable of being manipulated through technology. Between human beings and material objects or other beings, "the relationship has become confrontational" (*LS* 106). Francis refers to this as the "technocratic paradigm" rooted in a "deviated anthropocentrism." He recognizes, too, that Christians have, at times, misinterpreted the Genesis account of Creation, which grants "dominion" over the earth (see Gen 1:28), to mean unbridled exploitation. The corrective is crystal clear. "This is not a correct interpretation of the Bible as understood by the Church....We must forcefully reject the notion that our being created in God's image and given dominion over the earth justifies absolute domination over other creatures" (*LS* 67).

Another vision of the relation between human and nonhuman reality needs to be retrieved. Human beings "have to find again their proper place in the universe, renouncing to be absolute dominators."[24] *Laudato si'* grounds this proposed alternative vision in both theological and biblical insights. The very notion of creation implies that God is Creator and human beings are only creatures. To behave as limitless dominators of the rest of creation is to forget our true status and to think that we are God. On the contrary, "we are not God. The earth was here before we were and it has been given to us" (*LS* 67). The notion of creation also implies a connection among all creatures. Like all creatures, "we are dust of the earth (cf. Gen 2:7)" (*LS* 2), and "a good part of our genetic code is shared by many living beings" (*LS* 138). There is even much more. "Called into being by one Father, all of us [creatures] are linked by unseen bonds and together form a kind of universal family, a sublime communion which fills us with a sacred, affectionate and humble respect" (*LS* 89). The poetic expressions of Saint Francis of Assisi in his *Canticle of the Creatures* point to this dimension of kinship.

The earth is "Sister, Mother Earth," the sun is "Brother Sun," water is "Sister Water," and so on. The truth that we are related to the whole of creation as a family has tremendous ethical implications, beginning with a deep sense of compassion. "God has joined us so closely to the world around us that we can feel the desertification of the soil almost as a physical ailment, and the extinction of a species as a painful disfigurement" (*LS* 89). Kinship, then, implies an enormous responsibility to care for creation, to care for this home that is our "common home," and to care for all its inhabitants.

Stressing kinship among all of creation is not to deny real differences and specificities. In denouncing a "misguided anthropocentrism," *LS* is very careful not to endorse an alternative "biocentrism" that would deny any specific role to human beings. For Pope Francis, rejecting a misguided anthropocentrism "is not to put all living beings on the same level nor to deprive human beings of their unique worth and the tremendous responsibility it entails. Nor does it imply a divinization of the earth which would prevent us from working on it and protecting it in its fragility" (*LS* 90). Later, he adds that "when the human person is considered as simply one being among others, the product of chance or physical determinism, then 'our overall sense of responsibility wanes.'…Human beings cannot be expected to feel responsibility for the world unless, at the same time, their unique capacities of knowledge, will, freedom and responsibility are recognized and valued" (*LS* 118).

The crucial point is to retrieve a focus on relationship as fundamental to a proper anthropology. The encyclical goes on to explain,

> If the present ecological crisis is one small sign of the ethical, cultural and spiritual crisis of modernity, we cannot presume to heal our relationship with nature and the environment without healing all fundamental human relationships.…A correct relationship with the created world demands that we not weaken this social dimension of openness to others, much less the transcendent dimension of our openness to the "Thou" of God. Our relationship with the environment can never be isolated from our relationship with others and with God. (*LS* 119)

The way we treat the environment or other living beings is connected to the way we treat other human beings. The sense of kinship, or of "universal communion" and "fraternity," ought to be retrieved for everything and everyone. "Our indifference or cruelty towards fellow creatures of this world sooner or later affects the treatment we mete out to other human beings….Peace, justice and the preservation of creation are three absolutely interconnected themes, which cannot be separated and treated individually" (*LS* 92).

The move from a "misguided anthropocentrism" to a proper relational anthropology takes shape in other important themes that we can mention only briefly. First, all creatures have value in themselves and not merely for what they contribute to human life. "Each organism, as a creature of God, is good and admirable in itself" (*LS* 140).[25] Second, consciousness of relations and interdependency goes hand in hand with an awareness of limits. The earth's resources are not limitless. The idea of unlimited growth, so common in economic, financial, and technological ambits, cannot stand (*LS* 106). Recognition of limits also has something to do with the recognition and acceptance of "one's body as God's gift," whereas "thinking that we enjoy absolute power over our own bodies turns, often subtly, into thinking that we enjoy absolute power over creation" (*LS* 155).

Laudato si' enlarges the anthropological reflection of earlier social encyclicals with aspects not considered before and with profound correctives. Recalling GS's opening statement in its chapter on the dignity of the human person, one cannot help being struck by the change operated by *LS*. Indeed, GS stated, in a very anthropocentric fashion, that "according to the almost unanimous opinion of believers and unbelievers alike, *all things on earth should be related to man as their center and crown*" (GS 12, emphasis mine). If consideration of the universe—including humanity—as "sublime communion" and "universal family" is the new starting point for the social magisterium on the human being, then we face a profound reconfiguration in which the few elements of *LS* mentioned earlier are only the early stages.

More in line with the traditional teaching of the church is the insistence on the social dimension of human beings. Still, it is worth noting some specific emphases of *LS* regarding the union in diversity of all human beings, peoples, and cultures.

Human Beings as Social Beings: Unity and Diversity

CST has always insisted upon the social dimension of being human and its implication for the kind of solidarity that should be fostered within the whole of humanity. *Laudato si'* highlights that "in the present condition of global society, where injustices abound and growing numbers of people are deprived of basic human rights and considered expendable, the principle of the common good immediately becomes, logically and inevitably, a summons to solidarity"; notably, the encyclical adds, the principle summons "to a preferential option for the poorest of our brothers and sisters" (*LS* 158). *Laudato si'* extends this kind of solidarity to future generations and to the entire creation and urges that it be developed primarily with those most in need, most fragile: the forgotten, the discarded, or excluded. We find here the centrality of the option for the poor for Pope Francis.

Solidarity and union within the human family also have a distinctive mark in the Argentinian pope's teaching. He always insists on talking about unity with respect and with due recognition of diversity. One aspect of integral ecology developed in chapter 4 is cultural ecology. The historical, artistic, and cultural patrimony of many peoples is under threat of a globalized economy that subsumes everything in consumerism and "has a levelling effect on cultures, diminishing the immense variety which is the heritage of all humanity" (*LS* 144). Particularly at risk are the cultures of indigenous communities forced to abandon their lands under the pressure of agricultural or mining projects (*LS* 146). The path toward greater solidarity and unity requires us "to respect the rights of peoples and cultures, and to appreciate that the development of a social group presupposes a historical process which takes place within a cultural context and demands the constant and active involvement of local people from within their proper culture" (*LS* 144). Moreover, "the disappearance of a culture can be just as serious, or even more serious, than the disappearance of a species of plant or animal. The imposition of a dominant lifestyle linked to a single form of production can be just as harmful as the altering of ecosystems" (*LS* 145). In chapter 5, where dialogue is encouraged at every level, we also find the idea that creativity in finding solutions will arise from letting local initiatives flourish in their diversity, respecting specific contexts (*LS* 179), while always affirming the unifying goal of caring for our common home.

Although it is not developed as much in *LS* as in *EG*, the framework sustaining Francis's thinking on unity and diversity is his sets of rules for helping to build and guide peoples.[26] That the "whole is greater than the part" (*LS* 141) means that the union of many brings much more than the simple sum of individual contributions. However, it does not mean that the parts disappear within the whole. The image favored by the pope is a polyhedron in contrast to a sphere. In a sphere, "every point is equidistant from the center and there is no difference," whereas the polyhedron "reflects the convergence of all its parts, each of which preserves its distinctiveness" (*EG* 236). That "unity is greater than conflict" (*LS* 198) does not mean that conflicts do not exist, or that they should be minimized, or hidden simply to maintain an artificial and illusory peace. Unity implies that conflict be overcome in "a resolution which takes place on a higher plane and preserves what is valid and useful on both sides" (*EG* 228). In *LS*, Francis adamantly insists that the need to change our model of development should not hide the conflicts at stake. "It is not enough to balance, in the medium term, the protection of nature with financial gain, or the preservation of the environment with progress. Halfway measures simply delay the inevitable disaster" (*LS* 194).

The path to greater unity and solidarity within the human family is a path of growing "awareness of our common origin, of our mutual belonging, and of a future to be shared by everyone" (*LS* 202). This communality of origin and destiny goes hand and hand with the recognition of diversity as a richness. To ground this assertion theologically, *LS* references Aquinas:

> Saint Thomas Aquinas wisely noted that multiplicity and variety "come from the intention of the first agent" who willed that "what was wanting to one in the representation of the divine goodness might be supplied by another," inasmuch as God's goodness "could not be represented fittingly by any one creature." (*LS* 86)

These reflections on unity and diversity highlight that *LS*'s anthropology is dynamic and embedded in history rather than ahistorically essentialist. To be "social" is not so much an essentially static feature of being human, but rather a vocation to develop mutual relationships of solidarity, within and beyond humanity, in the richness of a multifaceted diversity.

Further Theological Considerations

Many of the anthropological aspects in *LS* are aligned with what we found in previous encyclicals. The dynamism of being human or humanity as constant humanization in many dimensions, including the spiritual, is a feature that we highlighted from *PP* onward. The social and relational dimension of being human was also at the heart of the teaching of previous popes. The notion of gift—human life is a gift, the earth is a gift, and so forth—in contradistinction to an attitude of possession and domination was central to the teaching of Benedict XVI. Nonetheless, *LS* offers new emphases and finally a significant reshaping of these themes because it considers more seriously the situation of human beings within the entire creation. For this more holistic approach, theological motives and justifications are also different or corrected. Significantly, *LS* refers three times to the notion of the human being "in the image of God," which has always been central in CST, but the encyclical insists on avoiding misguided interpretations. Our being created in God's image does not justify "absolute domination over other creatures" (*LS* 67) and "should not make us overlook the fact that each creature has its own purpose" (*LS* 84).

What encapsulates the theological grounding of *LS*'s anthropology best is probably the figure of Saint Francis of Assisi and the type of Franciscan theology of creation it represents.[27] First, Francis is a figure of humility in the sense of "being at one's proper place," within creation, and in relation with the Creator. In his *Canticle*, he recognized in the birds, the fish, the trees, and even the water, earth, or sun, who all give praise to the Lord, a reminder of "what it means to be in humble relationship of service with the divine."[28] Pope Francis writes that "the harmony between the Creator, humanity, and creation as a whole was disrupted by our presuming to take the place of God and refusing to acknowledge our creaturely limitations" (*LS* 66). But he adds that "the harmony which Saint Francis of Assisi experienced with all creatures was seen as a healing of that rupture" (*LS* 66).

Second, Francis of Assisi teaches us to envision the whole of creation in terms of familial bonds and communion. This is the world as

God intended it to be, and not how it is currently. The saint's poetic expression of our kinship relations with creation in his *Canticle* manifests an eschatological hope of healing and reconciliation; his behavior in relation to animals and nature gives witness to the "already there" of this hope. As *LS* relates, the Franciscan medieval theologian Saint Bonaventure, half a century later, "held that, through universal reconciliation with every creature, Saint Francis in some way returned to the state of original innocence" where sin has not broken the relationship (*LS* 66). According to Johnson, Saint Francis proposes "a gendered model of familial equality and freedom in which men and women are joined in prayerful ministry by other creatures, who are all brothers and sisters under one Father in heaven."[29] This vision of humanity articulated to the whole of creation offers a solid base for affirming that everything is connected and that care for the environment and care for the poor should be one and a single ethical orientation.

Third, the theology inspired by Saint Francis is a theology of love. Francis experienced Christ's love to the point of choosing to abandon all his material riches and embracing poverty. In responding to Christ's love, Francis showed much love for others, especially the poorest and the most rejected of his time, such as the lepers. "He loved, and was deeply loved" (*LS* 10), and his love extended to all creatures. In the Franciscan spirit, love is what best encapsulates the relationships intended by the Creator within creation. Love and not possession, control, or scientific knowledge! Therefore, Pope Francis highlights in the medieval saint the inspiration for developing an integral ecology:

> Francis helps us to see that an integral ecology calls for openness to categories which transcend the language of mathematics and biology, and take us to the heart of what it is to be human. Just as happens when we fall in love with someone, whenever he would gaze at the sun, the moon or the smallest of animals, he burst into song, drawing all other creatures into his praise....His response to the world around him was so much more than intellectual appreciation or economic calculus, for to him each and every creature was a sister united to him by bonds of affection. (*LS* 11)

Finally, with Saint Francis we gain a profound sense of God's presence in creation. *Laudato si'* says that "Saint Francis, faithful to

Scripture, invites us to see nature as a magnificent book in which God speaks to us and grants us a glimpse of his infinite beauty and goodness" (*LS* 12). All creatures reveal something of God. In a more systematic way, Bonaventure later developed a symbolic theology in which all creatures reflect something of the divine, or more deeply, manifest God's salvific presence.[30] Bonaventure also develops his theology of creation in a trinitarian way. For him "each creature bears in itself a specifically Trinitarian structure, so real that it could be readily contemplated if only the human gaze were not so partial, dark and fragile" (*LS* 239). This implies that "we are created to be relational beings in a universe of creatures in which everything is connected."[31] A contemporary of Bonaventure, the Franciscan mystic Angela of Foligno uses another striking image when she speaks of "a world pregnant of God."[32] The created world is thus not only a book orienting us toward God and prompting praise, but it has a sacramental dimension. *Laudato si'* explains that "the universe unfolds in God, who fills it completely. Hence, there is a mystical meaning to be found in a leaf, in a mountain trail, in a dewdrop, in a poor person's face" (*LS* 233).

All these elements of a Franciscan theology of creation, or as Edwards names it, "a profound theology of the communion of creation,"[33] offer solid grounding and powerful inspiration for the anthropological aspects of *LS* mentioned earlier. They do not constitute a comprehensive theology of creation, nor does what we have singled out in *LS* encompass a full anthropology within an ecological approach. For example, a deeper awareness of the nonharmonious dimensions of our continually evolving world is lacking in *LS*, and these dissonances could probably have been reflected upon theologically if the encyclical had a more explicit theology of the cross.[34] Nevertheless, what is present in *LS* stands as a substantial contribution that both expands and corrects CST's previous teachings thanks to the influence of the Franciscan approach to God and the world. Turning now to Christology, let us call attention to a similar movement.

CHRISTOLOGY

As with the previous encyclicals studied, explicit christological statements are not numerous in *LS*. Nonetheless, it offers significant insights by repeating some traditional aspects and exploring new ways of entering the mystery of Jesus Christ. On the one hand, considering Jesus's relationship to creation in the Gospels, *LS* bears the mark of a Christology "from below" in which the historical Jesus is central and calls for a discipleship that cares for "our common home." On the other hand, *LS* also suggests that the Lordship of Christ, his incarnation, his cross and resurrection, impact all creation. In this respect, the encyclical opens the way for a Christology of the incarnate Word that would be explicitly "cosmic."

Jesus and Creation in the Gospels

Laudato si' makes it clear that Jesus teaches his disciples, and through them all of us, a certain way of relating to other creatures and nature. He proposes "ideals of harmony, justice, fraternity and peace" (*LS* 82) that are at odds with how we live when other living beings are considered as mere objects, when nature is viewed only as a source of profit and gain simply because we have some power over it. "This vision of 'might is right' has engendered immense inequality, injustice and acts of violence against the majority of humanity, since resources end up in the hands of the first comer or the most powerful: the winner takes all" (*LS* 82).

The core of Jesus's teaching is that God is Father. He invites his disciples to recognize "the paternal relationship God has with all his creatures" (*LS* 96) because "they are all important in God's eyes" (*LS* 96). For *LS*, this relation of kinship is fundamental to recovering one's proper place in the creation—as creature and not Creator—but also to understand that the world did not happen by chance, but because of God's love. This teaching about God as Father is a teaching about God's love.

> In the Judeo-Christian tradition, the word "creation" has a broader meaning than "nature" for it has to do with God's loving plan in which every creature has its own value and significance….Creation can only be understood as a gift from the outstretched hand of the Father of all, and as a reality illuminated by the love which calls us together into universal communion. (*LS* 76)

Ethical consequences are obvious, since we should not mistreat what God so painstakingly takes care of. If "not one [sparrow] is forgotten in God's sight " (Luke 12:6), "how then can we possibly mistreat them or cause them harm?" (*LS* 221).

Jesus's very attitudes and practices teach us the proper relationship to creation. *Laudato si'* insists that Jesus "was in constant touch with nature, lending it an attention full of fondness and wonder" (*LS* 97). His contemplative gaze further nourished his teaching in parables, which are full of concrete references to trees, plants, fruits, animals, mountains, sea, and so on. Moreover, "his appearance was not that of an ascetic set apart from the world, nor of an enemy to the pleasant things of life" (*LS* 98). He did not depreciate the body and matter. He "worked with his hands, in daily contact with the matter created by God, to which he gave form by his craftsmanship" (*LS* 98).

Finally, if in *LS* the theme of poverty is not immediately associated with explicit mentions of Jesus Christ, the reaffirmation of the centrality of the option for the poor at the end of chapter 4 bears an implicit christological affirmation. Pope Francis refers to his previous exhortation, *EG*, in which he had extensively developed the christological foundation of this option:

> For the Church, the option for the poor is primarily a theological category rather than a cultural, sociological, political or philosophical one.…This divine preference has consequences for the faith life of all Christians, since we are called to have "this mind…which was in Jesus Christ" (Phil 2:5).…We are called to find Christ in them. (*EG* 198)

Pope Francis also reminded us,

> The Savior was born in a manger, in the midst of animals, like children of poor families.…He was raised in a home of ordinary workers and worked with his own hands to earn his bread. He assured those burdened by sorrow and crushed by poverty that God has a special place for them in his heart: "Blessed are you poor, yours is the kingdom of God" (Luke 6:20); he made himself one of them: "I was hungry and you gave me food to eat" (Matt 25:35). (*EG* 197)

That Jesus leads to the poor and that the poor lead to Christ are christological dimensions at the heart of Francis's teaching.

In everything that we have said thus far, we find a strong affirmation of the humanity of Jesus. These affirmations, taken from the Gospels, are important testimonies against all the temptations of Docetism that would minimize or negate the human nature of the Son of God. Jesus lived on this very planet of ours. He was part of our material world, connected with human and other-than-human creatures, sharing our condition with all its limitations (except sin). In this respect, *LS* points to the historical Jesus, who is remembered in the Gospels, and it offers traces of a Christology "from below" as relevant today as in the time of *PP*. It is a powerful resource for a call to action in this world. *Laudato si'* invites Christians to live fully the consequences of their encounter with Jesus Christ. Becoming disciples, which means listening to Jesus's teaching and taking him as a model as the first disciples did, ought to lead to an ecological conversion (see *LS* 217). The Christology encountered here is very much the same as the one we highlighted in *PP*, where specific references to Jesus's teaching and behavior were meant to inspire us to take action against poverty, inequalities, and injustices.

Something newer appears in other aspects of the Christology offered by the encyclical. Through elements of a Christology much more "from above," we find a development of the salvific role of Christ in relation to the whole cosmos that was not present in previous encyclicals.

Cosmic Christology

As *LS* remarks, there is more in the New Testament about the relationship between Jesus Christ and creation than merely presenting an "earthly Jesus and his tangible and loving relationship with the world" (*LS* 100). The encyclical references the Gospel of John and the Pauline letters (especially the hymns in Paul's Letters) to underscore this relationship.

First, the mystery of Christ is present from the beginning and tied to the whole of creation, for "all things have been created through him and for him" (Col 1:16). The Prologue of John's Gospel speaks of Christ as the Divine Word (*logos*) who is at work in the process of creation: "In the beginning was the Word, and the Word was with God, and the Word was God. He was in the beginning with God. All things came into being through him, and without him not one thing came into being" (John 1:1–3; see *LS* 99).

Second, the mystery of the incarnation has a cosmic dimension. That "the Word became flesh" (John 1:14) means that God enters the cosmos, and this impacts not only humanity but all creation. *Laudato si'* explains that "particularly through the incarnation, the mystery of Christ is at work in a hidden manner in the natural world as a whole, without thereby impinging on its autonomy" (*LS* 99). An extended theology of the incarnation is also found in the section that deals with the sacraments. In their celebration, natural elements and matter are indispensable. We use water, bread, wine, fire, oil, and so on. They mediate God's gift of Godself. Therefore, they call to mind that "for Christians, all the creatures of the material universe find their true meaning in the incarnate Word, for the Son of God has incorporated in his person part of the material world, planting in it a seed of definitive transformation" (*LS* 235).

Third, the paschal mystery of Jesus Christ's death and resurrection also encompasses the whole of creation. The cross is mentioned only twice, without further development, and yet it is crucial. The encyclical states, "One Person of the Trinity entered into the created cosmos, throwing in his lot with it, *even to the cross*" (*LS* 99, emphasis mine). In the next paragraph, *LS* cites Colossians: "For in him all the fullness of God was pleased to dwell, and through him to reconcile to himself all things, whether on earth or in heaven, making peace by *the blood of his cross*" (Col 1:19–20, emphasis mine). As for the resurrection, *LS* reminds us that the New Testament "shows [Jesus Christ] risen and glorious, present throughout creation by his universal Lordship" (*LS* 100).

Finally, there is an eschatological perspective. Directing our gaze to the end of time, we remember that "the Son will deliver all things to the Father, so that 'God may be everything to everyone' (1 Cor 15:28)." It implies that "the creatures of this world no longer appear to us under merely natural guise because the risen One is mysteriously holding them to himself and directing them towards fullness as their end" (*LS* 100). Previously, the encyclical had mentioned that "the ultimate destiny of the universe is in the fullness of God, which has already been attained by the risen Christ, the measure of the maturity of all things," and thus "all creatures are moving forward with us and through us towards a common point of arrival, which is God, in that transcendent fullness where the risen Christ embraces and illumines all things" (*LS* 83).

All these points are made very briefly and not developed in an encyclical whose main objective is an ethical reflection on the socio-environmental crisis. However, they are highly significant because they cover the key dimensions of the salvific mystery of Christ and suggest that considering the entire creation and going beyond humanity requires revisiting all the important christological questions. By opening some doors and directing our attention to them, *LS* is pointing out new fields to be explored.

The suggestion that Christology has a cosmic dimension to be developed does not come in a vacuum, since some theologians have been working on this line of thought for a while. I briefly mention some of them as an illustration of the theological discussions implied by *LS*. This is not to argue in any way that the encyclical is built on these theological propositions, but rather that the encyclical validates a starting point and points to the need to pursue and deepen a theological reflection impacted by an integral ecological consciousness.

Medieval Franciscan theology, which had contributed significant thought and reflection about valuing other than human creatures, was also profoundly christological. Thus, Bonaventure presents Christ as the Master in the symbolic theology that we mentioned earlier. Solignac explains,

> The uncreated Word, as Likeness of the Father and Likeness of all things, is the One who reveals and makes known both the true nature of the Father and true nature of things.... He is master in symbolic theology because he is the way which leads the creature to the Creator, and the Creator to the creature.[35]

For Bonaventure, it is the responsibility of human beings to restore and reconcile all creation to its original vocation. This can be done only by journeying with Christ who is perfectly united with the material, sensible world. Although this medieval theologian has a strongly hierarchical vision of the created world, he still points to the fundamental salvific role of Christ for the whole of creation.

Leonardo Boff, himself a longtime member of the Franciscan order, draws the consequences of an ecological consciousness for

Christology by reflecting on the "Cosmic Christ."[36] He aims at showing "the cosmic relevance of Jesus Christ and how the story of the universe should be interwoven with the story of Christ."[37] Consequently, for him "we must transcend the anthropocentrism that is common in Christologies, for Christ has divinized not only human beings but all beings in the universe."[38] The starting point is an actualized cosmology in accord with current scientific knowledge, one that requires putting aside the static cosmology of the ancient Greek world and adopting resolutely one of evolution. The cosmos is in a process of genesis. Humanity is in a process of genesis. It is from this "cosmogenesis" that Christology should be understood as "Christogenesis." "If Christ has taken shape and consciousness in Jesus, it must be that it already existed in the cosmogenic and anthropogenic process. In nature there is a 'Christic' element, as Teilhard de Chardin called it."[39] Faith prompts the recognition of the crystallization of this Christic element in the person of Jesus Christ. Nonetheless, the Christ of faith rests on the historical Jesus; it is an interpretation of the historical Jesus who, like all human beings, is the product of evolution. We encounter the "cosmic Christ" on the cross because in Jesus "the full force of human and cosmic evil,"[40] suffers, and resurrection means liberation and fulfillment for all creation. Boff explains, "The cosmic Christ emerges as the moving force of evolution; he is its liberator, and the one who brings it to fulfillment."[41] Finally, Boff speaks of "pan-Christism" to express the continuous presence of Christ in the cosmos and all things. "When we embrace the world, delve into matter, feel the force and energy field, or perform the most humble and heavy tasks, like splitting wood and lifting stones, we are in contact with the risen and cosmic Christ."[42]

Such a christological approach is exemplary in accounting fully for evolution—something that remains largely unfinished in *LS*. It broadens our interpretation of the mystery of Christ in relation to creation, and it supports crucial ethical and political consequences. There are, nonetheless, many questions that still need clarification. There is, especially, the question of how this sort of pan-Christic vision, which, for Boff, relates to panentheism (the idea of "God in all and all in God") can be more substantially differentiated from a problematic pantheism (the idea that the material world *is* God).

Recently, there has also surfaced the notion of "deep incarnation." "Incarnation is significant not only for human existential experience but for the natural world as such, for it manifests God as one with material, created being."[43] The first to use the phrase "deep incarnation" is Niels Gregersen, who uses it to understand Christology in evolutionary terms. With the help of Stoic philosophy and some contributions from Arne Naess's "deep ecology," Gregersen interprets John's verse, "the Word became flesh," in the broad sense that it encompasses all creation. Nonetheless, he does not accept the leveling of human moral status that is present in deep ecology. Gregersen says, "Incarnation is 'deep' both in contradistinction to a purely anthropocentric Christology and as opposed to more shallow proposals of a universalist Christology."[44] He defines deep incarnation as

> the view that God's own Logos (Wisdom and Word) was made flesh in Jesus the Christ in such a comprehensive manner that God, by assuming the particular life-story of Jesus the Jew from Nazareth, also conjoined the material conditions of creaturely existence ("all flesh"), shared and ennobled the fate of all biological life-forms ("grass" and "lilies"), and experienced the pains of sensitive creatures ("sparrows" and "foxes").[45]

Elisabeth Johnson has also developed an understanding of deep incarnation, correcting some elements of an excessively Stoic-dependent conception of it by adding ideas of deep ministry, deep crucifixion, and deep resurrection.[46] The idea is to extend and deepen all the key aspects of Christology, not only incarnation. In addition to *Logos*, Johnson emphasizes *Sophia*, or Wisdom, as active in the creation of the world. This is particularly helpful when considering articulation between the universal and the particular.

Celia Deane-Drummond, wary that the theological reflections just mentioned carry the weight of too much detached speculation, turns to Hans Urs von Balthasar's notion of theo-drama as a starting point. *Theo-drama* is a term to speak of God's action in the world, God's action in specific events engaging created freedom, and with the death and resurrection of Christ as central. For Deane Drummond, "theo-drama occupies what might be termed a boundary position between historical and ontological accounts of Christology and, therefore, also of the meaning of deep incarnation."[47] She continues,

While the idea of theo-drama is most developed in the work of Hans Urs von Balthasar, I am critical of those aspects of his work that put stress on divine power in a way that seems to mask the action of other players on the stage. Furthermore, I argue for an extension of an understanding of theo-drama so that it is inclusive in scope, widening out to the universal reach of God's love shown in Christ to all creatures. But that love is only apparent in retrospect in the light of the resurrection, thus bringing in an eschatological element to an understanding of deep incarnation. The profound significance of the incarnation allows human beings to contemplate the fear of what is beyond death, as well as death itself. But this then allows human beings to contemplate more fully not just who they are in the light of the action of the Holy Spirit, but also what they might become through God's grace and their particular vocation in the world. If we are to follow deep incarnation to its limits, then it is associated with an ethical demand to take an active part in the shared drama, a common history of the earth, and therefore to love God and neighbor, acting with sensitivity and responsibly towards the earth and its creatures.[48]

It comes as no surprise then that, when Deane-Drummond comments on *LS*, she writes,

> Towards the end of the encyclical, Pope Francis's interpretation of ecological conversion as both a reference to ecology and ultimately to Christ is in my view an implicit deep incarnation, as is his reference to the Mass on the altar of the world. A clearer more systematic acknowledgement of deep incarnation would have given a stronger basis for environmental and ecological justice.[49]

For this English theologian, deep incarnation is a promising concept for reshaping Christology in an age of integral ecology consciousness.

It is worth connecting this approach to deep incarnation and the reflection on the historical Jesus that was offered in the first section. Deane-Drummond is adamant about not losing sight of the meaning of the concrete, historical accounts of Jesus's life in connection with concrete historical current events. Her use of the concept of theo-drama moves in that direction. Consequently, while the notion of deep incarnation looks at first like a Christology of the incarnated Word "from above," it ends, with Deane-Drummond, as a Christology very much dependent on an approach "from below."

Conclusion

The life of Francis of Assisi and his path of conversion were rooted in following Jesus Christ very concretely. His turn to poverty, to living as a mendicant, and to founding a brotherhood is prompted by the desire to return to the gospel and to follow Jesus Christ poor. It is the same desire that also opened his eyes to the beauty of nature and developed his special awareness of the relationships among all creatures. The figure of Saint Francis thus offers us the inspiration to articulate the christological explorations prompted by *LS*. The concrete elements of Jesus's life as found in the Gospels are a starting point for following him and engaging fully in the ecological conversion required in our time. A deeper understanding of the incarnation, including its cosmic dimension, is also required to make sense that all creation is embraced by redemption. This leads to revisiting the cross and resurrection.

In this christological section, we have encountered once again an articulation of ascending and descending Christologies, and often some concepts not foreign to the theological frameworks used in the previous chapters. In the end, however, it is certainly the more Franciscan vision of the created world and its sense of solidarity with the poor and with other-than-human creatures that is dominant in *LS*. *Laudato si'*'s embryonic Franciscan Christology presents an urgent call for further systematic exploration into the mystery of Jesus Christ.

CONCLUSION

The various theological insights that we have gathered from reading *LS* are largely consonant with the dynamism initiated by Vatican II and as developed by Paul VI in *PP*. The neo-Thomist framework provides a solid base for appreciating *LS*'s contribution to entering the mystery of God. The inductive approach and confidence in dialogue reveal an understanding of God as present in the world, communicating Godself, whose grace operates from within. Reinforcing this theological approach are the anthropological dimensions that point to a multidimensional, relational, and evolutionary human being, and christological hints that value the historical Jesus as an inspiring model for living as disciples.

A liberationist framework, complementing the basic neo-Thomist framework (like what we have seen in *SRS*), is also present in *LS*. The first pope from Latin America brings an acute sense of social, collective, and structural dimensions of the mystery of humanity in relation to God. *Laudato si'* speaks as much about the social structures that need to be transformed as it does about individuals in need of conversion. Moreover, although the theological category of sin is not highly developed, it is clearly affirmed at the very beginning in that the present state of affairs is sinful (see *LS* 8), and the encyclical is uncompromising with its denunciations of situations, personal and structural, that are contrary to the will of God. A noticeable addition to the liberationist framework is the special attention given to cultures and peoples in order to engage the social and collective dimension of the questions. This is not something new in the discourse of the church, but it does carry the specific hallmark of the Argentinian "theology of the people."

In contrast, the Augustinian framework that was helpful to grasp the theological insights of *CiV* is far less evident in *LS*. Francis, of course, situates his teaching in continuity with that of his predecessor, repeating some of the significant points made in *CiV*, for example, regarding God as love, gratuity, and gift, or the need to correct dysfunctional and unjust structures. We could also say that, in insisting on the difference between God the Creator, and human beings, creatures who are not God, or in developing a theology of communion, *LS* has connections with the Augustinian framework. It is not, however, a central interpretive key.

As noted throughout this chapter, the theological contribution of *LS* is better grasped through the lens of the fourth framework, the Franciscan, which is a powerful complement and corrective of the neo-Thomist and liberationist ones. The figure of Saint Francis, and with him aspects of the Franciscan theological tradition, are enlightening. In this Franciscan framework, the focus is on God as Creator who loves all of creation, human beings and creatures other than human, and who is mysteriously present in this creation. The world is viewed as profoundly interconnected and interdependent and its ultimate vocation is a "sublime communion" of kinship relations. The present situation of generalized environmental damage and continuous social fragmentation and exclusion is profoundly contrary to God's plan. Such a vision requires a profound renewal of anthropology and of Christology. The realization that anthropocentrism can easily be misguided and overinflated, and the recovery of a humbler and more responsible situating of human beings within creation, have an impact on theology, opening new areas of research or new ways of entering the mystery of "God for us." In *LS*, we find only the initial traces of this project, but the doors have been opened and the calls that resonate are significant.

5

THEOLOGICAL REFLECTIONS

IN THE PREVIOUS CHAPTERS, we saw how four social encyclicals offer theological insights on the general theme of integral development in a globalized world. They are theological because they provide insight on aspects of the mystery of "God for us." They are a possible path to enter the mystery of God more deeply and to allow the mystery to seize us. This last chapter gathers and develops some of these theological contributions. Taking up three questions that correspond to the three areas explored in the encyclicals—methodology and style, anthropology, and Christology—we demonstrate how theological reflection is enriched by considering the social teaching of the church as it is presented in the papal magisterium.

The first question concerns the relation between theology and history. The challenge of theology is to announce the perennial and universal truth of salvation in Jesus Christ amid a pluralistic and changing world. This challenge is shaped by the central Christian belief that the eternal God entered history. Therefore, theology cannot be the mere repetition of atemporal, unchangeable, metaphysical dogmas. It must consider the current situation and the history of the men and women (and of the world), the object of God's salvation. However, it cannot be reduced to the mere projection onto God of particular and contingent situations. Articulating these two dimensions is fundamental. Because they deal with historical realities, the social encyclicals are useful in considering the role that history and human experience play in developing theological discourse. Significantly, theology necessarily begins with and within historically situated experiences but does not originate in them.

A second question concerns theological anthropology and the articulation between the personal and social dimensions of salvation. Is salvation manifested in personal conversion or structural change? The notion of integral development and integral ecology promoted by the encyclicals points toward maintaining and articulating both aspects. This reflects a theological vision of the mystery of humanity that is fully integrated, refuses all reductionisms, and envisions human beings as both individual *and* social persons. Faithful to this anthropology, any Christian ethical and moral reflection should be concerned with both the personal and structural levels of the issues it addresses. Furthermore, engaging in a resolutely trinitarian anthropology seems a promising path prompted by a theological reading of the social encyclicals.

A third question concerns Christology and the proper balance found in reflecting on the mystery of Jesus Christ "for us"—Jesus Christ truly human and truly God—between both ascending and descending approaches. Reading social encyclicals from a christological perspective supports a plurality of Christologies but gives priority to those adopting a movement from below, and thus highlights the important christological implications in adopting a preferential option for the poor.

On these three questions, the theological frameworks found at work throughout the reading of the encyclicals will be useful, with the necessary ordering already highlighted. The neo-Thomist framework, with its positive vision of the world where God's grace is at work amid contrasted human situations, is the base. It is enriched by the liberationist and Franciscan ones and only corrected by the Augustinian. Along with this epistemological option, reference to Rahner's theology will prove a useful resource.

THEOLOGY AND HISTORICITY

In any attempt to do theology or to express something of the mystery of God's saving revelation, we are confronted with the tension between recognizing the historicity of any discourse, and more profoundly, the historicity of any meaningful salvific encounter of God with humanity, and the absolute otherness of God that grounds salvation and transcends history. In other words, we face the challenge of expressing something in a way both meaningful and true, a way embedded in, coming out of, and directed toward concrete historical situations, which at the same time is not the mere projection of these situations onto the divine. This is a challenge for theology, and for the church's magisterium, which has the mission to express and safeguard doctrine. On the one hand, the repetition of atemporal dogmas is not a solution, since the formulation of these dogmas itself is historically embedded. On the other hand, entirely contextual discourses, if they are not conscious of their limits, fail to testify to the saving God who transcends our human experience. In more trivial words, if God is too distant, I cannot see how God really can save me, but if God is so close that I do not distinguish God from a specific human experience, God can no more save me than I can save myself or, collectively, we can save ourselves.

From a methodological perspective, the question of theology and historicity appears in the appreciation of how and how much inductive approaches, dialogue, contextualization, and constructivism are possible and desirable in a theological endeavor. Our studies of the social encyclicals lead us to formulate a thesis that can work as a guideline for theological reflection. Immanuel Kant said, "Though all our knowledge begins with experience, it does not follow that all arises out of experience."[1] In an analogous way, one could say of theology that *though any discourse about God necessarily begins with experience and within history, it does not follow that theology originates in human experience and history*. God is both the origin and the end of theology, but God entered into history and, for us, God is to be found nowhere else than in this history. This thesis relates to faith in the incarnation and the understanding of revelation. Practically, it implies that any theological reflection should seriously consider historical contexts and human experiences as its starting point and milieu while keeping provision for being challenged by what lies always beyond. God is a *living* mystery whose being and action exceed our comprehension. Entering this mystery of "God for us" is not a mere linear inductive process, going from analyzing concrete experiences to formulating a discourse about God's salvation and the living out of it. Neither is it the mere deductive application of divinely revealed insights to concrete situations. Rather, it is a hermeneutical spiral movement including all of the above.

Vatican II started with the invitation of Pope John XXIII to adopt a pastoral approach in order to present the truth of faith in a way relevant to the current situation of the world. With the progressive reception of what Christoph Theobald calls the "principle of pastorality,"[2] the conciliar fathers became more aware of the importance of historicity for any attempt at theological discourse. Not only does the way truths are expressed change with different historical situations, but it pertains to the very core of the truth of faith to be affected by historicity since, as *Dei verbum* reaffirms, divine revelation is not merely the revelation of a set of truths but the communication of Godself within salvation history culminating in Jesus Christ. Thus, the documents of the council moved away from neo-Scholastic ways of expressing the faith. These ways focused on looking always for more refined, unchangeable formulations of dogmas and then on deductively expounding practical consequences, very often formulated as condemnations of errors, denunciations of deviating behaviors, and a quasi-constant war against the current world. *Gaudium et spes* is the best example of a new discourse that accounts for historicity and emerges from consideration of concrete situations and challenges of the time. The pastoral constitution explicitly adopted a more inductive methodology and a more positive attitude of dialogue with the world.

During the same period, Rahner wrote an article about the historicity of theology.[3] He recognized that "the possibility of uniting absolute truth and the historicity of truth is one of philosophy's most fundamental [and difficult] questions."[4] However, he insisted on viewing historicity as an essential component of theology. This is true because revelation occurs in history and we, ourselves, are in history. Consequently, although theology can and should take a critical look at the "spirit of the age" and confront the prevailing ideologies, it is equally crucial that it should be self-critical and aware of the possibility of error in its midst.

In another essay about practical theology—which, for Rahner, is a better name for what is usually called "pastoral theology"—he defends it as a theological discipline in its own right and not merely the deductive application of systematic theology to particular and concrete realities.[5] Concerned with "the self-actualization of the church *here and now,*[6] practical theology contains a creative and prophetic component that should challenge all other disciplines. Not only does Rahner advocate for the importance of practical theology, which per se begins with practical and historically embedded questions, but he shows that any form of theological endeavor should include such a component. In my opinion, therefore, social moral theology, including the normative magisterial documents of CST, is ideally situated to fulfill this requirement since it concerns itself with social, political, and economic issues at a specific moment in history.

Not surprisingly, since it was published only one and a half years after the closing of the council, *PP* offers a very incarnational theology highlighting how God's revelation and grace is at work in this world while presenting the current struggles of men and women of this time for justice and peace. The see-judge-act methodology is fully endorsed and stresses the necessity of considering appropriately the current situation and listening to the questions and challenges it raises. A positive attitude of openness to dialogue and collaboration with others inside and outside the church is promoted as well. Almost fifty years after *PP*, *LS* explicitly takes the same path of an inductive see-judge-act methodology and of dialogue practiced and promoted as the path for integral ecology. Catalyzed by this dialogical and inductive approach, renewed considerations about the good news of God's salvation in Jesus Christ can emerge.

A dialogical and inductive approach is indeed characteristic of CST. Even in documents like *SRS* and *CiV* in which it is far less enthusiastically embraced, some elements remain. First, the historical context and the questions raised by specific economic, social, and political issues play a stimulating role. They prompt the moral and theological reflection offered by the magisterium.

Second, in social encyclicals, there is always a dimension of listening to and learning from the experiences of various groups of Christians. It is not always explicitly recognized, a fact that is arguably an issue, but it is always significantly present. *Populorum progressio* built on the work of Lebret and Économie et Humanisme. The experience of Solidarność in Poland played a role for some parts of *SRS*, as did Focolare with their notion of the Economy of Communion in *CiV*. In *LS*, the reflections and experiences of local churches are explicitly integrated through various references to documents of conferences of bishops. Because of the nature of the topics addressed, the formulation of social encyclicals usually involves an important contribution of specialists in secular disciplines, for example, through the work of the Pontifical Council for Justice and Peace.

As was repeatedly highlighted in the previous chapters, the dimensions of induction and dialogue in the social encyclicals bear with them a crucial aspect of Christian faith in the incarnation and an important understanding of God's saving revelation. That God entered into history and revealed Godself in Jesus Christ, who lived the fullness of a human life with the exception of sin, shapes definitively the relation of Christians to the world. The present world is not a neutral place that happens to be the place where one lives one's life in the best way in order to gain an eternal reward. Neither is it merely the milieu of evil from which one ought to flee as soon as possible. It is, first, the place and the object of God's grace, of God's offer of a shared divine life, and of the possibility of a free response to this offer. This, of course, includes the possibility of a negative response reflected in the reality of sin and evil at work in the world. This world is not yet the fullness of the "new heavens and a new earth" (Isa 65:17). Nonetheless, it is a central belief of the Christian faith that because of Jesus Christ, God is to be encountered within this world and salvation begins here. As Jesus reminds us, "the kingdom of God is among you" (Luke 17:21).

Already at the council, some worried that, in the dialogical and inductive approach adopted by GS, the term "embracing of the world" was too strong. The risk is to forget the dimension of sin at work in the world and consequently the necessary dimension of conflict that exists between the church's mission to proclaim salvation in Jesus Christ and some aspects of the world. For a theologian like Ratzinger, the desire to come sympathetically to terms with the contemporary situation and with modern thinking was given too much priority over the desire to be more rooted in Scripture and centered on Jesus Christ. The latter inevitably carries with it more confrontation.[7] Faith in the incarnation is also faith in the incarnate Word who brings light into the world.

We are not facing here a refusal of the movement initiated at the council but rather a different inflection within this movement. Theologians like Ratzinger, de Lubac, and von Balthasar agree with others like Rahner, Chenu, and Congar on the need for theology to move away from neo-Scholasticism and to be renewed. But, when the latter theologians foster aggiornamento as entering a positive dialogue with the modern world, the former opt for *ressourcement* as returning, through Scripture and the early tradition of the church, to the centrality of Christ for the whole of human existence. These are the two trends that develop after the council, which we named "neo-Thomist" and "Augustinian" throughout this book.

In SRS, and even more strongly in *CiV*, we have noted some drawbacks in methodology concerning the inductive and dialogical approaches. There we encountered more deductive ways of reasoning, projecting directly the contents of faith onto the current situations of the world in order to denounce sin or structures of sin. The authority of the church in its teaching was also insisted upon and left less room for what can be found as seeds of truth outside of it.

Theologically, these changes in methodology and style express more strongly the Augustinian trend. It is possible to see them not merely negatively as drawbacks but also more positively as reminders of one important aspect of the Christian faith. In a world marked by sin, which also affects the various sciences concerned with bringing about more integral development, it is important to remember that God is not limited by what we experience of God in the world; that salvation and grace at work within this world come fundamentally from without; that the newness that comes with Jesus Christ has a consistency in the tradition of faith borne by the church and its magisterial teaching. In brief, following the establishment of a new type of positive relationship between the church and the world at Vatican II, which is the fundamental ground for a Christian social ethics, the recognition of drawbacks in methodology coming later is a pointer to the transcendence of God in the economy of salvation.

With Rahner, it is interesting to note that, although fully embedded in the neo-Thomist trend and strongly endorsing the move to engage in dialogue with and within the modern world, he never loses sight of the danger of immanentism or reducing God to an internal principle of the world. For example, Rahner warned against the danger of horizontalism regarding the mission of the church.[8] Horizontalism would be the reduction of the church's mission to the humanization of the world and to being responsible for humankind and the world: "'God' is reduced to a mere cipher....It stands for mankind itself."[9]

Of course, Rahner adamantly denounced the mere juxtaposition of vertical and horizontal dimensions. Considering that love of neighbor is a moral duty implied by the love of God is not enough. There is a more intrinsic and essential relationship between the two because "there is no experience of God for pilgrim man on this earth which has not been mediated through an experience of the world."[10]

Rahner concluded that, in current times, we might need a stronger stress on the horizontal dimension, on responsibility for the world and love of neighbor. This can be done—and should be done—without dismissing theology, worship, and other more vertical activities. The mission of the church is to bring salvation. It is to communicate the sign of God, Jesus Christ as God's self-utterance of the truth concerning the ultimate end of the world. The church must preach

> that there is no horizontal dimension which is *entirely whole and complete* in itself without a vertical one; that it is only through God's grace that we are set free in such a way as to be able to use and enjoy the world, and open ourselves unreservedly to our neighbor without becoming enslaved by this social and material environment of ours.[11]

These reflections of Rahner point in the same direction that the theological interpretation of the variations in style and methodology in the encyclicals led us. Theology cannot start elsewhere than in the historicity of human experiences, because that is where God reveals Godself and saves us by offering this revelation as a gift freely given. This, however, does not mean that theology originates here. There is a more fundamental and transcendent source, beyond mere historical embeddedness. Any theological endeavor must reflect this.

PERSONAL CONVERSION AND STRUCTURAL CHANGES

Once historicity is recognized as central for Christian faith, and therefore for theology, then other questions emerge. For example, does salvation, which is the church's mission to make known to the world, entail personal conversion or structural changes? Although formulated here theoretically, this question has concrete implications upon which we touched in our reading of the encyclicals. For example, what should be the main work of the church? Is it to provide sacraments, to proclaim the gospel explicitly, to strengthen the spiritual life of the faithful, to encourage them to practice charity, and, in a nutshell, to foster their personal conversion? Or, is it to transform this world, to prompt change in laws, structures, and institutions, to fight injustice and bring about God's kingdom? Similar questions concern the proper focus of CST. Is it to stress personal values and virtues such as fraternity, solidarity, reconciliation, and charity? Or rather, must it focus on the principles that ought to govern social institutions such as justice and equality, and rights and duties? We can recall that the return of the category of charity in Benedict XVI's encyclicals raised such discussions. Some commentators were concerned that a proper understanding and commitment to justice was weakened.[12] In the opposite direction, some of Pope Francis's gestures and speeches in support of migrants or in fierce criticism of "an economy that kills" (*EG* 53) generates resistance in the church out of fear that the pope steps out of his role of spiritual guide.

The appropriate answer to these questions certainly requires not an either/or approach but rather a solid both/and. Nonetheless, a simple juxtaposition would not suffice. Theological reflection needs to show that there is always a strong interaction between the two aspects of salvation or the two approaches to the church's mission. It is beyond the scope of this section and of this book to envision in detail all the questions raised here. More modestly, the anthropological vision offered by the encyclicals when promoting integral human development or integral ecology constitutes a solid basis for the unity of personal conversion and structural change both in the salvific outpouring of God's grace and in the mission of the church in the world. Personal conversion and structural change strengthen each other, and neither should be ignored. Their unity is essential to the development of CST and Christian social ethics.

In support of this thesis, we will recall some of the key elements of the encyclicals concerning theological anthropology and will conclude with a reflection, supported by the same encyclicals, about trinitarian anthropology, which seems a promising lead in theological anthropology.

Populorum progressio offers a good starting point. We have a workable guideline with Lebret's foundational understanding of integral development as "development of the whole person and of all humanity" that was continuously deployed in the encyclicals that follow it. This understanding allows for multiple aspects of being human, always in a dynamic process and including, importantly, both the personal and social dimensions. To be human is to become more and more human. The encyclical presents an ordered list of conditions that favor humanization, ranging from the material dimension, to the intellectual and cultural, and to the spiritual. Concrete social analyses and recommendations give flesh to this vision. Material misery, lack of food, healthcare, and shelter in many parts of the world are objects of concern, but so too are lack of education and political participation. Ultimately, *PP* highlights openness to God and unity in Christ as the summit of humanization. Freedom, respect for human rights, and stress on the right to be the agent of one's own development are keys in expressing this dynamic transcendent vision of the human being.

This transcendent dimension is immediately and intrinsically linked to the vocation to solidarity. The vocation to be human is the vocation to become children of God, brothers and sisters in Christ. Concretely, the encyclical denounces the obstacles to greater cooperation and mutual aid among peoples. It calls for greater equity in trade relations and a reform of the mechanisms and institutions shaping them. It also points to the intrinsic link between peace and development.

When reading *PP*, there is a strong sense that the aspiration to personal freedom and self-fulfillment is the source for building solidarity and fraternity and for transforming institutions and social structures into better and more just ones. The transcendent dimension of the human person is not in competition with its social dimension but rather finds its realization in the latter.

This movement is highlighted in Rahner's theological anthropology. As he explains, salvation comes through the self-communication of God and its free acceptance by the human person. A key feature of being human is, therefore, the capacity for and openness to the gift of God's own divine life. This is what Rahner expresses by insisting on the dynamism of human freedom as oriented toward union with God and love of neighbor. However, the yes to God's self-communication is always a yes *within* the world, *within* an environment constituted by the created world and society. Rahner affirms,

> The freedom of acceptance or refusal of salvation occurs in
> all the dimensions of human existence, and it occurs always
> in an encounter with the world and not merely in the con-
> fined sector of the sacred or of worship and "religion" in the

narrow sense; it occurs in encounters with one's neighbor, with one's historical task, with the so-called world of every-day life, in and with what we call the history of the individual and of communities.[13]

Because salvation concerns all dimensions of being human, it is not merely a matter of a private, individual union with the divine. Rather, it concerns the entire world in the complexities of human relationships, interpersonal interactions, and social organizations. Rahner adamantly insists on the unity of the love of God and the love of neighbor, which he sees as close to an identity as possible. Love of neighbor is encounter with God and salvation. This love is not reduced to an interpersonal relationship but takes form by transforming sociopolitical structures in view of the kingdom.[14]

It comes as no surprise then that, when Rahner reflects on topics like social work and the mission of the church, or institutions and freedom, he insists on the social dimension of the human person and on salvation concerning the whole of society, even if he does not go into details. This, in fact, will be the task undertaken by Metz's political theology. Rahner says that charity and social work—work for bringing about justice and more human structures in societies and not merely charitable work oriented to lightening the suffering of the poor—are integral to the self-fulfillment of the church. They are part of its mission as a "basic sacrament of unity in the ministry of love."[15]

In *PP*, clearly some social structures, especially those ordering the international economic and political life, are an impediment for integral human development. Social conditions need to change for persons to become more fully human. Therefore, the encyclical is concerned with concrete and practical ways of global organization and cooperation. For example, it is not simply a matter for individuals in the North to provide more aid to the Global South, but for countries to build different types of relationships, for international institutions to be strengthened, and for economic relations to be reoriented beyond the mere logic of profit and toward the benefit of those most in need.

With *SRS* and its incorporation of some of Latin American liberation theology's categories, the role played by structures and the necessity to change them is highlighted and given a theological understanding. Obstacles to integral human development are viewed as structures of sin. In the context of the late 1980s, John Paul II denounces specifically the division of the world into blocs sustained by rigid ideologies and, more generally, he points to various forms of imperialism. As a path to overcome the evil of the structures of sin, the pope then makes a plea in favor of solidarity, which, following his predecessor, includes a dimension of an international system of real cooperation based on equality.

However, reasoning in terms of structures is always articulated with reasoning in terms of personal responsibilities. Structures of sin are originally produced by personal sins, and they are maintained and rendered difficult to remove by other personal sins, such as voluntary blindness or cowardice to act. Two typical attitudes opposed to the will of God and impeding the development of structures of solidarity oriented toward the common good are the thirst for power and the desire for profit.[16] In this anthropological vision offered by *SRS*, there is a very tight articulation uniting the personal and the structural levels. Clearly, what is required are both, personal conversion and structural change, each one nourishing the other.

For Benedict XVI in *CiV*, being human is a vocation to love in openness to God's love and requires recognition of one's creatureliness manifested in the gratuitousness at work in various aspects of human life. It also requires recognition of the centrality of relationality and striving for greater solidarity, and even communion, with one another and with God. All these anthropological features are strongly personalist. They imply both a promotion of individual personal development in freedom and of social development in communion. The more distinct feature is the explicit affirmation of God, God's grace, or God's love, as source and link between the two dimensions of development. Consequently, the refusal to acknowledge transcendence, which is characteristic of Western secularization, is a major impediment to integral development.

It is natural, therefore, that *CiV* would stress mainly the necessity of personal conversion and of a return to God as its central prophetic call. However, as we pointed out in chapter 3, this is far from being the case. The expounding of *CiV*'s theological anthropology takes shape through the consideration of structural issues and the call for structural changes. Individually, those in positions of power and holding greater responsibilities are called to reform themselves and to behave more ethically, but the encyclical also denounces the mechanisms, institutions, and laws that justify, encourage, or simply allow injustices to flourish. To achieve integral human development, personal conversion cannot be separated from structural change.

In *LS*, Pope Francis calls for an "ecological conversion" but insists that it is a "community conversion" (*LS* 219) and speaks also of a "cultural revolution" (*LS* 114). The path toward integral ecology requires lifestyle changes such as greater simplicity and sobriety, compassion with those who suffer including the earth, a contemplative attitude, and a capacity for awe to counter domination tendencies, and so on. *Laudato si'* insists on education. However, these personal changes are intimately connected with the need for structural changes in the economic and political organizations of societies. Moving out of the "technocratic paradigm," out of the supremacy of the technological and economic approach to reality, requires profound changes that are not merely cosmetic. For example,

> It is not enough to balance, in the medium term, the protection of nature with financial gain, or the preservation of the environment with progress. Halfway measures simply delay the inevitable disaster. Put simply, it is a matter of redefining our notion of progress. (*LS* 194)

Laudato si' points to the failures of international World Summits at the global level and the plague of corruption that affects all levels of political and economic life from local to global. Profound reforms are needed; new structures are needed; but this will not occur without a cultural transformation of all, passing from a "throwaway culture" of consumerism to a "culture of encounter."

Theologically, a key and promising path of study for an anthropology uniting personal conversion and structural change is the connection made in several encyclicals between anthropology and the doctrine of the Trinity. In the context of its social teaching, the church has highlighted the notion of being created in the image of God. This is a solid grounding for developing arguments in defense of human dignity for all, no matter the differences of gender, race, or social condition. The idea of being created in the image of God has been central, for example, in the church's appropriation of the human rights agenda since Pope John XXIII. As we have seen, it is a concept very much at work in the encyclicals, although *LS* alerts us of the dangers of misinterpreting it as a problematic supremacy of human beings within creation.

Nonetheless, even prior to *LS*, there was an opening in a new direction. Human beings are created in the image of God, but more precisely, in the image of a *Triune* God. Because this Triune God, while remaining one, is by nature a communion of love among three persons, this immediately focuses on the human person as relational and social. Relationships rather than the individual become the starting point for anthropology.

Gaudium et spes already hinted at finding the communitarian nature of being human in the doctrine of Trinity, with its corollary, the human vocation to solidarity. One section concerned with "the community of mankind," notes that "a certain likeness between the union of the divine Persons, and the union of God's sons in truth and charity. This likeness reveals that man, who is the only creature on earth which God willed for itself, cannot fully find himself except through a sincere gift of himself" (GS 24).

In *SRS*, John Paul II sees a new criterion for looking at the world in the "awareness of the common fatherhood of God, of the brotherhood of all in Christ—'children in the Son'—and of the presence and life-giving action of the Holy Spirit" (*SRS* 40). For him, the Trinity is "a model of unity" that ultimately can inspire human solidarity and overcome the structures of sin. For Benedict XVI, in *CiV*, "the inclusion-in-relation of all individuals and peoples within the one community of the human family…is illuminated in a striking way by the relationship between the Persons of the Trinity within the one divine Substance" (*CiV* 54). The mystery of the Trinity helps to envision how an authentic communion among human beings is not detrimental to their individual identities but, to the contrary, contributes to their full expression.

In *LS*, it is the entire created world, including human beings, that is envisioned as reflecting the Trinity. With reference to the medieval Franciscan theologian Saint Bonaventure, the encyclical writes,

> The divine Persons are subsistent relations, and the world, created according to the divine model, is a web of relationships. Creatures tend towards God, and in turn it is proper to every living being to tend towards other things, so that throughout the universe we can find any number of constant

and secretly interwoven relationships....The human person grows more, matures more and is sanctified more to the extent that he or she enters into relationships, going out from themselves to live in communion with God, with others and with all creatures. In this way, they make their own that Trinitarian dynamism which God imprinted in them when they were created. (*LS* 240)

Laudato si' highlights a relational anthropology that resists a problematic anthropocentrism. This relational anthropology is grounded in this connection with the doctrine of Trinity explicated at the end of the encyclical, even if all the potential of such an affirmation is not deployed.

Of course, recourse to the Trinity as a model for human social interactions and relations is not without difficulties. The most obvious one is that we do not know anything more about the Trinity than what the Trinity reveals in interacting with us. Therefore, it is impossible to take the Trinity as an external model in order to shape, say, human solidarity. We would run the risk of simply reprojecting onto human beings something that, in the first place, we have merely imagined of God from our human experience. In the encyclicals, the language is very cautious, speaking of "a certain likeness," or "inspiration," or "enrichment" to evoke the relationship between the immanent Trinity and human situations. Nonetheless, it remains a noticeable and suggestive move on the part of the magisterium.

Ellen Van Stichel suggests that turning to a more explicitly trinitarian anthropology beyond the mere relational personalist anthropology, traditional in CST, would be a fruitful resource to address some contemporary ethical challenges, especially in the economic area.[17] As she formulates it, the question for theological ethics becomes, "What does a trinitarian *relationship* consist of and how should our (global) society be structured to mirror adequately that series of relations?"[18] Relying on Spanish theologian and *focolarino* Enrique Cambón, she offers a few characteristics of a trinitarian anthropological worldview. Not only relationships, but relationships as *agapic* are fundamental. This means that self-giving is constituent of one's self-realization. Enabling the other to realize oneself is also a path to one's own realization. Finally, "persons act in a trinitarian way when they live *with* others, *for* others, and *thanks* to others,"[19] all three elements being necessary. Concretely, as Van Stichel argues, this leads us to emphasize participation in the work for global justice. A trinitarian perspective, thus, prevents social thought from separating *charity* and *justice* by insisting on reciprocity in love.

Van Stichel's remarks are only tentative insights on a reflection articulating a trinitarian anthropology and social ethics. Much remains to be done to develop it more systematically. Undoubtedly, the evocation of the mystery of the Trinity within social encyclicals is an invitation for theologians and ethicists to do so. It is a good example of how the relationship between theology and social ethics is one of mutual challenge and enrichment rather than a mere linear deductive/application process. It touches the heart of the question of the articulation and unity between the individual and the social dimension of being human. Having a more trinitarian approach in reflecting on the human being as image of God, whatever concrete form it takes, will integrate more strongly the two aspects.

It is also worthwhile to recall Rahner's challenge: "Despite their orthodox confession of the Trinity, Christians are, in their practical life, almost mere 'monotheists.' We must be willing to admit that, should the doctrine of the Trinity have to be dropped as false, the major part of religious literature could well remain virtually unchanged."[20] In response, the German theologian offered his famous axiom: "The 'economic' Trinity is the 'immanent' Trinity and the 'immanent' Trinity is the 'economic' Trinity."[21] Trinity in itself cannot be discussed apart from its revelation as salvation in history. For us, the only access to "God in eternity" is to consider "God for us," but "God for us" is inseparable from "God in eternity." Consequently, consideration of the Trinity in the context of social ethics almost naturally leads us to a closer consideration of God's salvific self-revelation in Jesus Christ. A turn to Christology will also prevent us from the trap of speculative reflection about the Trinity. Whatever insights about relationality we have from reflecting on the mystery of the Trinity—insights that might help us to envision a better realization of human relationships in society—we gain them from contemplating the revelation brought by Jesus Christ of his relationship to the Father in the Spirit. Christology remains the surest path to theological anthropology and to entering into the mystery of a Triune God.

CHRISTOLOGY: FROM ABOVE OR FROM BELOW?

When attempting to reflect and say something about the mystery of Jesus Christ, theologians always face a nagging question: Where to start? Should we begin with Jesus, the Nazarene, whom we know through Scripture and whose life, death, and resurrection had such an impact on his followers that two thousand years later there are more than 2.4 billion Christians around the world? Or, should we begin with the affirmation of faith at the center of the Nicene Creed that Jesus Christ is "God become human"? Should we engage in a Christology from below or from above? Within the perspective of a christological quest, the social encyclicals support approaches that incorporate both movements. However, our study gives a genetic or heuristic priority to the movement from below while not ignoring the classical formulations pertaining to the movement from above. Indeed, being attentive to the challenges of justice in a global world prompts one to highlight some aspects of Jesus's life, such as his proximity to the poor and the social dimension of the salvation brought about by his death and resurrection. This pertains to an ascending Christology. The ethical reflection on social issues offered by the magisterium develops also at length the idea of GS 22 that "only in the mystery of the incarnate Word does the mystery of man take on light." This is an expression of a descending Christology. Although predominant in the encyclical of Benedict XVI, this latter approach could not hide the previous elements that remain implicitly present, even in *CiV*, through the call for structural changes. Furthermore, in *LS*, Francis returned to a more balanced approach, with crucial references to the historical Jesus and to his life and interaction with creation, in order to promote an integral ecology. Therefore, christological insights carried by social encyclicals, because of their objects, highlight a variety of possible approaches to the mystery of Christ both from below and from above, but with a certain priority given to the former.

In an important essay on Christology published in 1972, Rahner reflects on what he considers the two basic types or forms of Christology.[22] On the one hand, there is the form of "saving history" Christology, "a Christology viewed from below." Jesus is seen in the context of the quest of human beings for salvation. He is seen in his fully human reality and in his fate brought to resurrection by God. Faith sees this history as God's "ultimate and irrevocable" utterance of salvation to human beings: "Jesus in his human lot is *the* (not *a*!) address of God to man, and as such eschatologically unsurpassable."[23] If interpreted correctly, it is still possible to arrive from this statement at the Chalcedonian statements about one person and two natures.

On the other hand, there is the "metaphysical" Christology, a "descending Christology" developing downward from above. Here, metaphysical is understood in a broad sense as qualifying merely what goes beyond the initial experience of Jesus by the believer. Two features characterize this type. First, it is a descending approach that considers as self-evident the doctrines of the divine Logos and preexisting Son of God, the second person of the Trinity distinct from the Father. They are *made known*, in a certain sense, by the words of Jesus but do not need to be justified. Christologies of this type proceed from these self-evident axioms and do not need "any further recourse to the experience of Jesus in saving history."[24] Second, metaphysical Christologies imply a doctrine concerning the cosmic and transcendental significance of the incarnation, God's love coming into history. Creation is regarded as the "enabling condition" for the self-communication of God.

For Rahner, even if there are variations, these are *the* two *basic* types. There are no others. They correspond to the two poles of our understanding of humanity, the transcendentality and the historicity of human beings. In the New Testament, the two types are mixed, and Rahner suggests that, possibly, the classic Christology of Chalcedon, which is strongly metaphysical in character, is mixed as well. So, he attempts not so much to classify strictly existing Christologies, but rather to reflect on the types of reasoning at work in producing christological statements. Moreover, he adamantly affirms that both types of Christology can be expressed either in orthodox or unorthodox ways.

However, Rahner also notes that "the second basic type [i.e., the metaphysical type] constantly presupposes that experience of sacred history which is experienced in the first basic type, as its abiding basis and as the necessary criterion of rightly understanding the assertions it contains."[25] And, he adds that "all descending Christology of the second basic type may have a secondary and interpretive character."[26] In other words, Rahner acknowledges a certain genetic or heuristic priority in approaches "from below," especially in the context of modernity for which personal experience is so crucial and dogmatic affirmations are so much put to the test. One cannot but see a convergence of argument with the later claims made by Latin American liberation theologians about the need to begin with the historical Jesus. As Lois states, "We might speak of a theological priority of the Christ of faith and a logical and methodological priority of the historical Jesus."[27]

In his essay, Rahner then concludes that "there is room for a pluralism of Christologies" as far as these "respect the Church's creedal formulae concerning Christ" and include "the essential reference to Jesus as the bringer of eschatological salvation."[28] Indeed, "even the two basic types of Christology, and their mutual interrelationship, render such a pluralism of Christologies both inevitable and legitimate."[29]

What Rahner exposes theoretically is well illustrated by the christological insights highlighted in the social encyclicals we studied. Clearly, we are not considering fully elaborated Christologies but only some sets of significant insights or points of attention relative to the mystery of Jesus Christ. However, they reflect a plurality of approaches and a certain priority given to movements "from below," or from the experience of saving history.

In *PP*, christological insights come clearly out of the human quest for salvation. This quest takes two major forms within the neo-Thomist framework. First, consideration of the current injustices and inequalities in a nascent globalized world prompts an encounter with Jesus in his proximity with the poor. Jesus is the teacher and model urging us to act in favor of the poor. His involvement in the world, his commitment to the poor, and his compassionate gaze for those who are rejected are strongly emphasized. We recognized, here, the premises of the "option for the poor" soon to be developed in the Latin American church.

The quest for salvation is also expressed in a second, more existential, form as the quest for greater or more complete humanization. This is the idea carried out by the notion of integral human development inherited from Lebret and exposed in terms of "the transition from less human conditions to those which are more human" (*PP* 20). Concerning Christology, the reflections about integral human development highlight Christ as realizing the fullness of humanity and the light of Christ's gospel as confirming the humanization present in the processes of authentic development. Therefore, union with Christ is the crowning of integral development, and furthermore, this integral development is viewed as the striving toward solidarity constitutive of the body of Christ.

In *SRS*, we noted that the Augustinian theological framework is more present, yielding insights more clearly of a metaphysical or descending type. John Paul II develops the idea of Christ the Redeemer as central to his ethical reflection and stresses that Christ is "God become human." He brings salvation *into* this world. Christ fully reveals the Father to humanity and humanity to itself. This is what occurs, for example, when the church promotes integral development against the delusions of unlimited progress or the reduction of development to materialistic and economic dimensions alone. Christ teaches the truth. He reconciles and liberates. He brings about the kingdom of God, which is inherently social and not merely a matter of individual salvation. The christological image central in the encyclical is that of the union of Christ with each human being in order to redeem humanity, and it is reflective of a descending Christology of the incarnate Word.

Nonetheless, what shows strikingly the inescapability of christological approaches from below is the incorporation and consecration in *SRS* of the option for the poor, labeled "love of preference for the poor." This is an important contribution brought about by the liberationist framework. Two christological insights come with the affirmation that "the option or love of preference for the poor" (*SRS* 42) is a key guideline in order to address social issues. First, as in *PP*, Jesus Christ is the one to be imitated in his love and concern for the poor, he who was sent

> to bring good news to the poor…
> to proclaim release to the captives
> and recovery of sight to the blind,
> to let the oppressed go free,
> to proclaim the year of the Lord's favor.
>
> (Luke 4:18–19)[30]

Second, Jesus Christ is to be encountered in the poor who are "the Lord's poor" because "the Lord wished to identify himself with them (Matt 25:31–46)" (*SRS* 43 and footnote no. 80). In solidarity with the poor, we are closer to Jesus Christ, sharing in his mission to bring about the kingdom of God.

In *CiV*, the shift toward the predominance of the Augustinian theological framework is complete. The most visible of the christological insights pertains, therefore, to the metaphysical type. Worried about the growing secularization in Europe, Benedict XVI has always adamantly defended a substantial notion of truth that lies beyond full human grasp but can direct human reasoning and action against rampant relativisms of all sorts. It is no surprise, therefore, that, regarding christological claims, he would privilege claims of faith about the incarnate Word of God. Christ teaches love in truth. Christ fully reveals love in truth because indeed, "in Christ, *charity in truth* becomes the Face of his Person, a vocation for us to love our brothers and sisters in the truth of his plan" (*CiV* 1). Through union with him, we are empowered to love in truth. The pope invites everyone to turn to Christ in order to bring about substantive changes in various fields such as financial markets, the distribution of food resources, and care for the environment.

As we suggested, by calling for these structural changes, the encyclical remains open to other Christologies more akin to the "saving history" or "from below" type. Attention to Jesus's earthly life and to the inbreaking of the kingdom of God that is to be realized in this world, and in part *from within,* would support fruitfully the more concrete claims and ethical guidelines offered in the encyclical. This confirms the assumption that attentiveness to christological insights coming out of social encyclicals always leads to recognizing the necessity of "from below" approaches.

In *LS,* christological insights are well captured through the figure of Saint Francis of Assisi, whose solidarity with the poor and with creation was rooted in his desire to follow Jesus Christ in poverty. The call of *LS* is "to hear both the cry of the earth and the cry of the poor" (*LS* 49). In the Gospels, Jesus invites us to a discipleship that cares for "our common home," rejecting relations of domination that damage both the earth and the poor, and proposing "ideals of harmony, justice, fraternity and peace" (*LS* 82). He shows a profound insertion in and connection with the material and natural world, which has such a central place in the parables. By his human life, Jesus gives testimony to the falsity of a dichotomy between spirit and body leading to the depreciation of the latter. In all of this, the encyclical valorizes approaches to the mystery of Jesus Christ "from below." Nonetheless, more "from above" approaches are also present when *LS* suggests that the lordship of Christ, his incarnation, his cross and resurrection, impact all creation. Various forms of "cosmic Christology" or "deep Christology" could further be developed in a direction that is merely suggested as possible by the encyclical.

Now, if approaches "from below" have an inescapable role to play in entering the mystery of Jesus Christ, then, what is probably the most significant contribution to Christology from the encyclicals is the challenge of affirming a "preferential option for the poor." Clearly, this option, which is part of the universal teaching of the church, has a solid grounding in christological faith. As Benedict XVI reminded us at Aparecida, in 2007, "the preferential option for the poor is implicit in the Christological faith in the God who became poor for us, so as to enrich us with his poverty (cf. 2 Cor 8:9)."[31] This option is a commitment to the marginalized people, of a pastoral, ethical, and social nature and is grounded in Christian faith. However, our readings of the encyclicals suggest that their theological nature should be deepened in a direction recently highlighted by Francis. Not only is the option supported by theological claims but "opting for the poor" is in turn a hermeneutical key to elaborate theological claims—christological ones, specifically. "The poor have much to teach us" (*EG* 198). Consequently, the christological insights that come along with the promotion of the preferential option for the poor in the encyclicals, and the images and concepts they favor, surely offer a path into the mystery of Jesus Christ.

Adopting the hermeneutical key of "opting for the poor" is of course the methodological shift instigated by the Latin American liberation theologians. Their writings in Christology are illustrations of a theology elaborated in the context and from the perspective of an option for the poor.[32] It is not within the scope of this work to recall them here. In the following paragraphs, we merely suggest a few threads of thought coming out of the question, What does the preferential option for the poor bring to Christology? An inspiring answer to this question comes from the Chilean theologian Cristián del Campo, who reflects about the Aparecida Conference's concluding document (*Ap*), a few years before the election of pope Francis but very much in line with his more recent teaching.[33]

The fundamental category used at Aparecida is the category of "disciples and missionaries." In the Christian vocation, persons are called to a personal encounter with Jesus Christ in order to follow him and fulfill the mission of proclaiming the good news of God's kingdom. In this dynamism of becoming truly disciples and missionaries, the theme of the preferential option for the poor is dealt with at length.

It is reaffirmed as a confirmation of the teaching of the previous conferences (*Ap* 396), but it is also reactualized within the current context. Following Jesus, all disciples-missionaries are called to translate their vocation into a commitment of solidarity with the poor and marginalized persons (*Ap* 112). The missionary-disciple is also called to recognize Jesus in the encounter with the poor. Without using the terminology of "sacramentality" of the poor, the document offers some openings in this direction:

> If this option [for the poor] is implicit in Christological faith, we Christians, as disciples and missionaries, are called to contemplate, in the suffering faces of our brothers and sisters, the face of Christ who calls us to serve Him in them: "The suffering faces of the poor are suffering faces of Christ." (*Ap* 393)

The encounter with Jesus Christ in the poor is "constitutive" of faith in him (*Ap* 257), and this is the place where personal conversion takes place and social relations are transformed (*Ap* 359).

Despite all these christological citations, which give a theological emphasis to the preferential option for the poor, del Campo notes that the document "does not finish closing the hermeneutical circle because it understands the preferential option for the poor as theological only in one direction."[34] The document shows that the option is rooted in christological faith, but it does not really consider how much "from the poor, Christology, and therefore, discipleship, can be deepened."[35] The implications of the quasi-sacramental affirmation cited above, that the face of Jesus is encountered in the face of the poor, are not taken to their full because, in the implementation of the methodology "see-judge-act," the step of judging is done out of already established theological notions that are not really interrogated or enriched by the "see" and the "act."[36]

Del Campo then suggests three aspects of Christology in which a preferential option for the poor brings a substantial contribution. First, this option helps to improve access to the humanity of Christ. In the face of the ever-resurging danger of various forms of Docetism, the perspective brought by the life of the poor is to rediscover the concrete meaning of the incarnation:

God becomes man, and a man who is poor. This option, which Jesus lived through all his historical existence, is verified in his lifestyle, in his choice of the first recipients of his proclamation, and in the mode of his passion and death. The adjectives qualify the substantive: Jesus lived a simple, poor, and suffering humanity.[37]

Second, if the preferential option for the poor helps us to understand the humanity of Jesus Christ, it also helps us to understand his divinity. As suggested by Juan Luis Segundo, it is Jesus Christ himself who reveals to us what it means to be human and to be divine.[38] Consequently, in order to envision the divinity, it is crucial to look at the cross. Del Campo writes,

> To affirm that the option for the poor is eminently theological implies believing in innocent suffering as a theological reality. This means that we should recognize, not only that the poor are the crucified of today, but that they are the historical body of Jesus Christ on the cross out of which the mystery of a suffering God is enlightened. In Jesus crucified, this God self-appeared as "a lesser God," present in the littles ones and the powerless, a "divinity which hides itself," and in front of which sin seems to triumph.[39]

Third, the preferential option for the poor encourages us to deepen our understanding of God's central project for humanity and Jesus's central mission: the kingdom of God. The poor are the first addressees of the proclamation of the kingdom, a kingdom of justice, peace, and dignity for all. The kingdom of God belongs to them (Matt 5:3). If the poor are those who hope for the kingdom, then "orthopraxis helps to penetrate the mystery of revelation, because it is on the path of transforming reality that the *truth* of the kingdom can be experienced with more clarity."[40] At the same time, history remains open. It is incomplete. The kingdom is "not yet" fully there. The option for the poor nourishes a perception of the eschatological dimension of faith in Christ bringing about the kingdom of God.

The three topics raised by del Campo can be developed in many ways. In fact, many liberation theologians have already done so. In *EG*, Pope Francis confirms the heuristic dimension of the option for the poor. Reaffirming its theological nature and its centrality for the church, he adds,

> This is why I want a Church which is poor and for the poor. They have much to teach us. Not only do they share in the *sensus fidei*, but in their difficulties they know the suffering Christ. We need to let ourselves be evangelized by them. The new evangelization is an invitation to acknowledge the saving power at work in their lives and to put them at the center of the Church's pilgrim way. We are called to find Christ in them, to lend our voice to their causes, but also to be their friends, to listen to them, to speak for them and to embrace the mysterious wisdom which God wishes to share with us through them. (*EG* 198)

In *LS*, this listening to the voice of the poor is obvious and is strongly connected to listening to "our Sister, Mother Earth," who is "among the most abandoned and maltreated of our poor" (*LS* 1–2). Although all the consequences in terms of Christology are not developed in a document whose focus is not Christology, the doors are open.

There are various entries into the mystery of "God for us," many ways of being seized by this mystery of God's love saving us. There are many ways of articulating a reasoned discourse about God or practicing "theo-logy." This book has attempted to show that social ethics in the form taken by CST—and more precisely, papal social encyclicals—is one possible way to do so. With no pretention to be theologically systematic or exhaustive, this teaching, nonetheless, provides significant theological contributions that emerge from particular sets of historical circumstances.

In this last chapter, we have explored how the theological insights gathered throughout our theological reading of the encyclicals could give an orientation for three "meta" theological questions: namely of articulating and uniting (1) theology and history, (2) structural change and personal conversion, and (3) Christology from above and from below. Along the way, some promising paths on more concrete topics raised by the theological reading of the social encyclicals have emerged: trinitarian anthropology and christological implications of a preferential option for the poor.

Within CST, social encyclicals offer a diversity of ethical analyses and political positioning regarding the challenges of bringing greater justice, peace, and solidarity to the world. This diversity is the result of various historical circumstances and the differences of appreciation of these circumstances among the popes. What has been highlighted is that such diversity is reflected in a plurality of theologies. Not only do some theological options better support certain normative and practical responses to the social challenges, but these responses in return also contribute to shape or reshape theological discourse. Greater awareness of this hermeneutic spiral of relations between social ethics and theology enriches any reading of CST, and it should also inform its ongoing development. In this way, entries into the mystery of "God for us" will be multiplied, or rather, we will allow many more ways for the mystery of God's love to seize us.

NOTES

INTRODUCTION

1. John R. Donahue, "The Bible and Catholic Social Teaching," in *Modern Catholic Social Teaching: Commentaries and Interpretations,* ed. Kenneth R. Himes (Washington, DC: Georgetown University Press, 2005), 32; Lisa S. Cahill, *Between the Sexes: Foundations for a Christian Ethics of Sexuality* (Philadelphia: Fortress, 1985), 1–13; James Gustafson, *Protestant and Roman Catholic Ethics: Prospects for Rapprochement* (Chicago: University of Chicago Press, 1978), 142.

2. William J. Hill, "Theology," in *The New Dictionary of Theology*, ed. Joseph A. Komonchak, Mary Collins, and Dermot A. Lane (Wilmington, DE: Michael Glazier, 1987), 1015. Cf. Thomas Aquinas, *Summa theologiae*, I, q.1, a.1.

3. Hill, "Theology," 1011.

4. Karl Rahner, "Mystery," in *Encyclopedia of Theology: The Concise Sacramentum Mundi*, ed. K. Rahner (New York: Crossroad, 1982), 1000–1004; "The Concept of Mystery in Catholic Theology," in *Theological Investigations (TI)*, vol. 4 (Baltimore, MD: Helicon Press, 1966), 36–73.

5. Karl Rahner, "Reflections on Methodology in Theology," in *TI*, vol. 11 (New York: Seabury, 1974), 102.

6. Joseph A. Komonchak, "The Redaction and Reception of Vatican II," available online at http://jakomonchak.files.wordpress.com/2013/04/jak-views-of-gaudium-et-spes.pdf, and first published as "La redazione della *Gaudium et spes*," Il Regno 13 (July 1999): 446–55; Massimo Faggioli, *Vatican II: The Battle for Meaning* (Mahwah, NJ: Paulist Press, 2012), 66–91. I do not pretend to stick always and strictly to Komonchak's typology even if I use his terminology.

7. Christoph Theobald, "The Theological Options of Vatican II: Seeking an 'Internal' Principle of Interpretation," in *Vatican II: A Forgotten Future*, ed. A. Melloni and C. Theobald, *Concilium* 4 (London: SCM, 2005), 94.

8. Christoph Theobald, *La réception du concile Vatican II: Tome 1, accéder à la source* (Paris: Cerf, 2009); "The Principle of Pastorality at Vatican II," in *The Legacy of Vatican II*, ed. M. Faggioli and A. Vicini (New York: Paulist Press, 2015), 26–37.

9. See GS 4, 11.

10. Karl Rahner, *Foundations of Christian Faith: An Introduction to the Idea of Christianity (FCF)* (New York: Crossroad, 1986), 225.

11. Karl Rahner, "Reflections on the Unity of the Love of Neighbor and the Love of God," in *TI*, vol. 6 (Baltimore, MD: Helicon Press, 1969), 232.

12. See Rahner, "The History of Salvation and Revelation," in *FCF*, 138–75.

13. Rahner, *FCF*, 12.

I. DEVELOPMENT, JUSTICE, AND PEACE

1. The English translation used in the subsequent citations is that of *Catholic Social Thought: The Documentary Heritage*, ed. David J. O'Brien and Thomas A. Shannon (Maryknoll, NY: Orbis, 2010), 253–77. This translation is also available at www.newadvent.org.

2. See *PP* 5.

3. For a presentation of the context of *PP*, see Allan Figueroa Deck, "Commentary on *Populorum progressio*," in *Modern Catholic Social Teaching*, ed. Kenneth R. Himes (Washington, DC: Georgetown University Press, 2004), 293–96.

4. Deck, "Commentary on *Populorum progressio*," 293.

5. Paul Poupard, "Le père Lebret, le pape Paul VI et l'encyclique 'Populorum progressio' vingt ans après," *Notiziario* 14 (May 1987): 73.

6. Barbara Ward, "Looking Back on *Populorum Progressio*," in *Readings in Moral Theology No. 5*, ed. C. Curran and R. A. McCormick (Mahwah, NJ: Paulist Press, 1986), 132.

7. Karl Rahner, "Basic Theological Interpretation of the Second Vatican Council," in *TI*, vol. 20 (New York: Crossroad, 1981), 77–89.

8. Cf. *MM* 157.

9. Peter Hebblethwaite, *Paul VI: The First Modern Pope* (Mahwah, NJ: Paulist Press, 1993).

10. François Malley, "Ethics and Economics in Father L. J. Lebret," in *Ethics and Economics: Catholic Thinkers in the 20th Century*, ed. G. Gaburro (Heidelberg: Physica-Verlag, 1997), 53–69; *Le Père Lebret. L'économie au service des hommes* (Paris: Cerf, 1968); Louis Joseph Lebret, *Human Ascent* (Chicago: Fides, 1955); *Dynamique concrète du développement* (Paris: Éditions ouvrières, 1961).

11. Cf. the press conference given by Msgr. (later Cardinal) Poupard for the official presentation of *PP*. Paul Poupard, "Présentation de l'encyclique '*Populorum progressio*,'" *La documentation catholique* 64, no. 1495 (1967): 1015–21.

12. Malley, "Ethics and Economics in Father Lebret," 62.

13. Lebret, *Human Ascent*.

14. Jean-Yves Calvez, "Le retournement: Jacques Maritain," in *Chrétiens penseurs du social (Maritain, Mounier, Fessard, Teilhard de Chardin, de Lubac)*, vol. 1 (Paris: Cerf, 2002), 33–56.

15. Jacques Maritain, *Integral Humanism: Temporal and Spiritual Problems of a New Christendom*, trans. Joseph W. Evans (New York: Scribner, 1968 [French edition, 1936]), 2.

16. Maritain, *Integral Humanism*, 162–210.

17. Deck, "Commentary on *Populorum Progressio*," 298–99.

18. Edmund Arbuthnott, *Joseph Cardijn: Priest and Founder of the Y.C.W.* (London: Darton, Longman and Todd, 1966).

19. Arbuthnott, *Joseph Cardijn*, 10.

20. Arbuthnott, *Joseph Cardijn*, 41.

21. Joseph Cardijn, *Laymen into Action* (London: Geoffrey Chapman, 1964), 150.

22. Matías García Gómez, "Un nuevo tono en el magisterio social de la Iglesia," in *Teología y sociología del desarrollo. Comentario a la* Populorum progressio (Madrid: Razon y Fe, 1968), 3–36. Translation mine.

23. Action Populaire, *Populorum progressio. Introduction et commentaire* (Paris: Spes, 1967), 23. Translation mine.

24. García, "Un nuevo tono," 5.

25. *PP* 47: rich man and Lazarus (Luke 16:19–31; *PP* 49): rich man who does not know where to store his riches (Luke 12:16–21; *PP* 74): the last judgment (Matt 25:35–36).

26. Philippe Laurent, "Introduction à *Populorum progressio*," in CERAS, *Le discours social de l'Église catholique. De Léon XIII à Benoit XVI*, 4th ed. (Paris: Bayard, 2009), 525. Translation mine. Concerning the prophetic tone, see also Vincent Cosmao, "Introduction," in *Le développement des peuples*. Populorum progressio (Paris: Centurion, 1967), 24.

27. García, "Un nuevo tono," 12.

28. Rafael Lopez Jordan, ed., *El manifiesto social de Pablo VI. Comentarios, presupuestos conciliares y repercusión posterior de la encíclica* Populorum progressio (Madrid: Studium, 1967); García, "Un nuevo tono," 9; René Coste, "L'encyclique *Populorum progressio* vingt ans après," *Nouvelle Revue Théologique* 109, no.2 (1987): 179.

29. Action Populaire, *Populorum progressio*, 24.

30. Comisión Venezolana de Justicia y Paz, *Justicia y Paz. El subdesarrollo latinoamericano a la luz de la Populorum progressio* (Caracas, 1968), 1. Translation mine.

31. GS had pointed to this when speaking of the kingdom being already "present in mystery." It is not only our virtues or good intentions that have eternal value but the "fruit of our labors" themselves (see GS 39).

32. Peter Riga, *The Church of the Poor: A Commentary on Paul VI's Encyclical on the Development of Peoples* (Techny, IL: Divine Word Publications, 1968), 4.

33. Riga, *The Church of the Poor*, 4.

34. Riga, *The Church of the Poor*, 5–6.

35. Cf. GS 44, 62.

36. See the title of the encyclical: "Encyclical Letter on the Development of Peoples. His Holiness Pope Paul VI. *To the Bishops, Priests, Religious, the Faithful and to All Men of Good Will.*"

37. Karl Rahner, "A Small Fragment 'On the Collective Finding of the Truth,'" in *TI*, 6:82–88; "The Current Relationship between Philosophy and Theology," in *TI*, vol. 13 (New York: Seabury, 1975), 61–79; "Theology as Engaged in an Interdisciplinary Dialogue with the Sciences," in *TI*, 13:80–93; "On the Relationship between Theology and the Contemporary Sciences," in *TI*, 13:94–102.

38. Rahner, "A Small Fragment," 84.

39. Rahner, "Theology as Engaged in Interdisciplinary Dialogue," 85.

40. Rahner, *FCF*, 142.

41. Rahner, "Current Relationship between Theology and Philosophy," 79.

42. Antonio L. Marzal, "El nuevo humanismo," in *Comentarios de Cuadernos para el dialogo a la* Populorum progressio, ed. Joaquín Ruíz-Giménez (Madrid: Edicusa, 1967), 121. Translation mine.

43. Cf. Maritain, *Integral Humanism*, 4–7.

44. See *PP* 14.

45. See *PP* 15, 54. Donal Dorr, *Option for the Poor and for the Earth* (Maryknoll, NY: Orbis, 2012), 172.

46. Karl Rahner, "The Hearer of the Message," in *FCF*, 24–43. Anne E. Carr, "Starting with the Human," in *A World of Grace*, ed. Leo J. O'Donovan (New York: Seabury Press, 1980), 17–30.

47. Rahner, *FCF*, 24.

48. Rahner, *FCF*, 30.

49. Rahner, *FCF*, 35.

50. Rahner, *FCF*, 38.

51. Karl Rahner, "The Theological Problems Entailed in the Idea of the 'New Earth,'" in *TI*, vol. 10 (New York: Seabury Press, 1977), 260–72; "Immanent and Transcendent Consummation of the World," in *TI*, 10:273–89.

52. Rahner, *FCF*, 39.

53. Rahner, *FCF*, 142. See also, Rahner, "History of the World and Salvation-History," in *TI*, vol. 5 (Baltimore, MD: Helicon Press, 1966), 97–114.

54. Georges Jarlot, "L'Eglise et le développement, l'encyclique 'Populorum progressio,'" *Études* 326, no. 5 (May 1967): 680. Translation mine.

55. Lopez, *El manifiesto de Paulo VI*, 138. Translation mine.

56. Cf. Thomas Aquinas, *Summa theologiae*, I-II, q. 94 a. 2.

57. Andrew Tallon, *Personal Becoming* (Milwaukee: Marquette University Press, 1982); Gregory Brett, *The Theological Notion of the Human Person: A Conversation between the Theology of Karl Rahner and the Philosophy of John McMurray* (New York: Peter Lang, 2013).

58. Karl Rahner, *Spirit in the World*, trans. William Dych (New York: Herder and Herder, 1968); Karl Rahner, *Hearer of the Word: Laying the Foundation for a Philosophy of Religion*, ed. Andrew Tallon (New York: Continuum, 1994).

59. Brett, *Human Person*, 71–92.

60. Brett, *Human Person*, 93.

61. Brett, *Human Person*, 111.

62. Rahner, "Foreword," in Tallon, *Personal Becoming*, 2–3. Rahner adds, "...mediations which I myself certainly neither sufficiently nor thoroughly worked out in their unity and difference." This gives a validity to critiques such as Metz's, but also suggests that a transcendental anthropology, in itself, is not a blindness to those social and historical dimensions but, on the contrary, contains a solid grounding to approach them. The recognition by Metz and some liberation theologians of their indebtedness to Rahner gives a powerful confirmation to this argument.

63. The encyclical recognizes, as well, the ambiguities of the missionary endeavor: "Without doubt [the missionaries'] work, inasmuch as it was human, was not perfect, and sometimes the announcement of the authentic Gospel message was infiltrated by many ways of thinking and acting which were characteristic of their home country" (*PP* 12).

64. Cf. *GS* 4 and *PP* 13.

65. Julio Lois, "Christology in the Theology of Liberation," in *Mysterium Liberationis: Fundamental Concepts of Liberation Theology*, ed. Ignacio Ellacuría and Jon Sobrino (Maryknoll, NY: Orbis, 1993), 168–94. Significant examples of christological investigations in the decade following *PP* include Jon Sobrino, *Christology at the Crossroads*, trans. John Drury (Maryknoll, NY: Orbis, 1978); Leonardo Boff, *Jesus Christ Liberator: A Critical Christology for Our Time*, trans. Patrick Hughes (Maryknoll, NY: Orbis, 1978).

66. Lois, "Christology in the Theology of Liberation," 170–72.

67. Lois, "Christology in the Theology of Liberation," 174.

68. Lois, "Christology in the Theology of Liberation," 175–86.

69. Alfonso Álvarez Bolado, "Evangelio y Desarrollo," in *Teología y sociología del desarrollo*, 82. Translation mine.

70. Álvarez Bolado, "Evangelio y Desarrollo," 76.

71. Álvarez Bolado, "Evangelio y Desarrollo," 78.

72. Álvarez Bolado, "Evangelio y Desarrollo," 79.

73. Rahner, "Jesus Christ," in *FCF*, 176–321.

74. Rahner, *FCF*, 218.

75. According to the distinction established by Rahner between "Christology of saving history" and "metaphysical Christology." Karl Rahner, "The Two Basic Types of Christology," *TI*, 13:213–23.

2. DEVELOPMENT IN FREEDOM AND SOLIDARITY

1. Strikingly, two collections of essays about the encyclical edited in the United States in the immediate aftermath of its publication chose to focus on one or the other of those concepts in their titles. Gregory Baum and Robert Ellsberg, eds., *The Logic of Solidarity: Commentaries on Pope John Paul II's Encyclical on Social Concern* (Maryknoll, NY: Orbis, 1989); Kenneth A. Myers, ed., *Aspiring to Freedom: Commentaries on John Paul II's Encyclical "The Social Concerns of the Church"* (Grand Rapids: Eerdmans, 1988).

2. For an overview of the context of *SRS*: Charles E. Curran, Kenneth R. Himes, and Thomas Shannon, "Commentary on *Sollicitudo rei socialis*," in *Modern Catholic Social Teaching: Commentaries and Interpretations*, ed. Kenneth R. Himes (Washington, DC: Georgetown University Press, 2005), 416–20. See also Fernando Garcia de Cortazar, "Veinte años de historia presente," in *Solidaridad, nuevo nombre de la paz. Comentario interdisciplinar a la encíclica* Sollicitudo rei socialis (Bilbao: Universidad de Deusto, 1989), 71–90; Pierre de Charentenay, "*Sollicitudo rei socialis*. Présentation," in *Discours social de l'Église*, ed. CERAS, 4th ed. (Paris: Bayard, 2009), 755–59; Roberto Suro, "The Writing of an Encyclical," in Myers, *Aspiring to Freedom*, 159–69.

3. See *SRS* 14.

4. See *SRS* 20.

5. Cf. Roberto Oliveros, "History of the Theology of Liberation," in *Mysterium Liberationis: Fundamental Concepts of Liberation Theology*, ed. Ignacio Ellacuría and Jon Sobrino (Maryknoll, NY: Orbis, 1993), 3–32; Peter Hebblethwaite, "Liberation Theology and the Roman Catholic Church," in *The Cambridge Companion to Liberation Theology*, ed. C. Rowland (Cambridge: Cambridge University Press, 2007), 209–28.

6. Oliveros, "History of the Theology of Liberation," 6–8.

7. *Med* Justice, 4.

8. Gustavo Gutiérrez, *A Theology of Liberation: History, Politics and Salvation*, 2nd ed. (Maryknoll, NY: Orbis, 1988).

9. Gustavo Gutiérrez, *The Power of the Poor in History* (Maryknoll, NY: Orbis, 1983), 36–74.

10. *Pue* 1134.

11. John Paul II, "Opening Address at the Puebla Conference," in *Puebla and Beyond: Documentation and Commentary*, ed. J. Eagleson and P. J. Sharper (Maryknoll, NY: Orbis, 1979), 57–76. Hebblethwaite, "Liberation Theology and the Roman Catholic Church," 212–16. Donal Dorr, *Option for the Poor and the Earth* (Maryknoll, NY: Orbis, 2012), 241–44.

12. Congregation for the Doctrine of the Faith, *Libertatis Nuntius: Instruction on Certain Aspects of the Theology of Liberation* (1984); *Libertatis Conscientia: Instruction on Christian Freedom and Liberation* (1986); see www.vatican.va.

13. John Paul II, "Letter to Brazilian Episcopal Conference" (April 9, 1986), in *Liberation Theology: A Documentary History*, ed. Alfred T. Hennelly (Maryknoll, NY: Orbis, 1990), 503.

14. John Paul II, "First Address of Pope John Paul II to Faithful" (October 16, 1978). Quoted by George Weigel, *Witness to Hope* (New York: Harper Collins, 1999), 255.

15. Weigel, *Witness to Hope*, 286.

16. Weigel, *Witness to Hope*, 454.

17. For example, see the positive assessment of Land and Henriot or Antoncich and the critical one of Elsbernd. Peter J. Henriot and Philip S. Land, "Toward a New Methodology in Catholic Social Teaching," and Ricardo Antoncich, "A Latin American Perspective," in Baum and Ellsberg, in *The Logic of Solidarity*, 65–74 and 211–26, respectively; Mary Elsbernd, "What Ever Happened to *Octogesima Adveniens?*" *Theological Studies* 56, no. 1 (1995): 39–60.

18. Henriot and Land, "Toward a New Methodology," 67.

19. M-D Chenu, *La "doctrine sociale" de l'Église comme idéologie* (Paris: Cerf, 1979), 12. Translation mine.

20. M-D Chenu, *La "doctrine sociale" de l'Église comme idéologie*, 80.

21. John Paul II, "Opening Address at Puebla," January 28, 1979, III, 7.

22. Elsbernd, "What Ever Happened to *Octogesima Adveniens?*" 54–56.

23. Henriot and Land, "Toward a New Methodology," 74. Regarding the pastoral circle, see Peter Henriot and Joe Holland, *Social Analysis: Linking Faith and Justice* (Maryknoll, NY: Orbis, 1983).

24. Ricardo Antoncich, *La Preocupación social de la Iglesia. La encíclica* Sollicitudo rei socialis *y sus proyecciones en América Latina*

(Buenos Aires: Latinoamérica Libros, 1988), 6, 9, 25–27; "A Latin American Perspective," in Baum and Ellsberg, *The Logic of Solidarity*, 211–26. See also G. Rodriguez and M. Franco, *La urgencia de transformaciones personales y sociales para la paz. Análisis y comentarios sobre la encíclica* Sollicitudo rei socialis (Bogotá: Cinep, 1989), 200–201.

25. See Elsbernd, "What Ever Happened to *Octogesima Adveniens?*"

26. Not counting the biblical references cited inside the text, which amount to sixty-three, there are twenty citations of GS and five of other Vatican II documents, thirty-three citations of *PP*, and fifteen citations of other encyclicals or speeches of John Paul II.

27. See *SRS* 21.

28. See *SRS* 19. Pontifical Commission for Justice and Peace, *At the Service of the Human Community: An Ethical Approach to the International Debt Question* (December 27, 1986) (Washington, DC: United States Catholic Conference, 1987).

29. On the process of elaboration of the encyclical: Curran et al., "Commentary on *SRS*," 419–420; Suro, "The Writing of an Encyclical"; Charentenay, "Présentation."

30. Suro, "Writing of an Encyclical," 163.

31. Curran et al., "Commentary on *SRS*," 419.

32. Weigel, *Witness to Hope*, 557.

33. See *RH* 15–16.

34. See *RH* 3, 7; *LG* 1.

35. See *RH* 19.

36. Antoncich, *La preocupación social de la Iglesia*, 23.

37. Jon Sobrino, "The Significance of Puebla," in Eagleston and Sharper, *Puebla and Beyond*, 293.

38. See *SRS* 29.

39. Mario Franco Espinal, "Comentario bíblico a la encíclica *Sollicitudo rei socialis*," in Rodriguez and Franco, *La urgencia de transformaciones*, 183–231.

40. Compare fourteen mentions of the term *sin* in *SRS* and only one in *PP*.

41. Gregory Baum, "Structures of Sin," in Baum and Ellsberg, *The Logic of Solidarity*, 110–26. Luis González-Carvajal, "Las estructuras de pecado y su transformación en estructuras de solidaridad mundial," *Sal Terrae* 76, no. 9 (1988): 601–11. Michel Schooyans, "Dérives totalitaires et structures de péché," *Nouvelle Revue Théologique* 110, no. 4 (1988): 481–502. For more global studies about

the social dimension of sin, see Mark O'Keefe, *What Do They Say about Social Sin?* (Mahwah, NJ: Paulist Press, 1990); Mathias Nebel, *La catégorie morale de péché structurel* (Paris: Cerf, 2006).

42. See as well other usages of the terminology of "mechanisms" qualified as "perverse" or "evil": SRS 17, 35, 40.

43. See, e.g., José Ignacio González Faus, "Sin," in Ellacuría and Sobrino, *Mysterium Liberationis*, 532–42.

44. Himes, "Social Sin and the Role of the Individual," *The Annual of the Society of Christian Ethics* (1986): 183–218.

45. González-Carvajal, "Estructuras de pecado," 604. Translation mine.

46. Luis María Armendáriz, "Un proyecto de hombre para un 'plan de desarrollo.' La antropología de la encíclica *Sollicitudo rei socialis*," in *Solidaridad, nuevo nombre de la paz: Comentario interdisciplinar a la encíclica* Sollicitudo rei socialis, ed. Universidad de Deusto (Bilbao, Spain: Mensajero, 1989), 210.

47. Antoncich, *La preocupación social de la Iglesia*, 20. Translation mine.

48. Donal Dorr, "Solidarity and Integral Human Development," in Baum and Ellsberg, *The Logic of Solidarity*, 143–54. Evencio Cofreces Merino, "Nuevo concepto de la 'solidaridad' en la 'Sollicitudo rei socialis,'" in *Comentario a la* Sollicitudo rei socialis (Madrid: Acción Social Empresarial, 1990), 301–30.

49. Cf. Ezek 36:26; SRS 38.

50. See SRS 40.

51. See SRS 46.

52. Armendáriz, "Un Proyecto de hombre," 207.

53. Gutiérrez, A *Theology of Liberation*, 13–25, 83–105.

54. Gutiérrez, A *Theology of Liberation*, 24.

55. Gutiérrez, A *Theology of Liberation*, 25.

56. Gutiérrez, A *Theology of Liberation*, 25.

57. Antoncich, *La preocupación social de la Iglesia*, 28–29.

58. Bp. Jorge Mejía, "L'Église et l'économie: les enseignements de l'encyclique *Sollicitudo rei socialis*," in *Sociétés et développement, à propos de l'encyclique* Sollicitudo rei socialis (Paris: Desclée, 1989), 63–65.

59. John Hellman, "John Paul II and the Personalist Movement," *Cross Currents* 31, no.4 (Winter 1980–81): 409–19.

60. See SRS 27.

61. See SRS 26, 34.

62. Cf. *GS* 1.

63. See *SRS* 41.

64. See Rom 8:20.

65. See Rom 8:22.

66. Cf. *GS* 22.

67. See Luke 17:21.

68. See *SRS* 42–43. G. Gutiérrez, "Option for the Poor," in Ellacuría and Sobrino, *Mysterium Liberationis*, 235–50.

69. *Med* Poverty 4. Gutiérrez, *A Theology of Liberation*, 162–73.

70. *Med* Poverty, 5.

71. *Med* Poverty, 9–11.

72. Gustavo Gutiérrez, "Expanding the View: Introduction to the Revised Edition," in *A Theology of Liberation*, xxvii.

73. Gutiérrez, "Option for the poor," 241–44.

74. Considering the entire encyclical, Gutiérrez dismisses any substantial difference between the two phrases. The same is true for Rodriguez. However, others like Curran and Dorr note that "preferential love" and "preferential option" are not the same thing, and that this suggests a certain hesitancy of John Paul II about accepting the concept of a preferential option for the poor, because of the dimension of confrontation and conflict it implies. Gutiérrez, "Option for the poor," 240. Rodriguez, *La urgencia de transformaciones*, 152–62. Dorr, *Option for the Poor*, 298. Charles Curran, *Catholic Social Teaching 1891–Present: A Historical, Theological, and Ethical Analysis* (Washington, DC: Georgetown University Press, 2002), 183.

75. Victor Codina, "Sacraments," in Ellacuría and Sobrino, *Mysterium Liberationis*, 654–76.

76. Codina, "Sacraments," 660.

77. Codina, "Sacraments," 665.

78. *"Deus interior intimo meo et superior summo meo"* ("higher than my highest and more inward than my innermost self"). Augustine, *Confessions* III, 6, 11.

3. DEVELOPMENT IN CHARITY AND LOVE

1. See *LG* 1.

2. See *GS* 4, 11.

3. Edouard Herr, "L'encyclique *Caritas in veritate*. Une lecture," *Nouvelle Revue Théologique* 131 (2009): 728–48.

4. Benedict XVI, *Homily on January 1, 2009*, www.vatican.va.

5. Luis González-Carvajal, *La fuerza del amor inteligente. Un comentario a la encíclica* Caritas in veritate, *de Benedicto XVI* (Santander, Spain: Sal Terrae, 2009), 83–104.

6. Cf. Darío Múnera Vélez, *La encíclica* Caritas in veritate *del Papa Benedicto XVI. Claves de lectura y comprensión desde la Universidad* (Medellín, Colombia: Universidad Pontificia Bolivariana, 2010), 18.

7. González-Carvajal, *La fuerza del amor inteligente*, 87–88.

8. González-Carvajal, *La fuerza del amor inteligente*, 70. Translation mine.

9. Lieven Boeve, "Europe in Crisis: A Question of Belief or Unbelief? Perspectives from the Vatican," *Modern Theology* 23, no. 2 (2007): 205–27; Joseph A. Komonchak, "The Church in Crisis: Pope Benedict's Theological Vision," *Commonweal* 132, no. 11 (2005): 11–14.

10. Joseph Ratzinger, "Europe and the Crisis of Cultures," *Communio* 32 (Summer, 2005): 347.

11. Joseph Ratzinger, *Homily at Mass Pro Eligendo Romano Pontifice* (April 18, 2005).

12. Ratzinger, "Europe and the Crisis of Cultures," 355.

13. Stefano Zamagni, "Fraternity, Gift, and Reciprocity in *Caritas in Veritate*," in *The Crisis of Global Capitalism: Pope Benedict XVI's Social Encyclical and the Future of Political Economy*, ed. Adrian Pabst (Cambridge: James Clark & Co, 2012), 155–17. Amelia J. Uelmen, "*Caritas in Veritate* and Chiara Lubich: Human Development from the Vantage Point of Unity," *Theological Studies* 71 (2010): 29–45.

14. Donal Dorr, *Option for the Poor and for the Earth: Catholic Social Teaching*, 3rd ed. (Maryknoll, NY: Orbis Books, 2012), 374–77.

15. Herr, "L'encyclique *Caritas in veritate*," 733.

16. Drew Christiansen, "Metaphysics and Society: A Commentary on *Caritas in Veritate*," *Theological Studies* 71 (2010): 10.

17. See GS 40–45.

18. Luk Bouckaert, "Tensions between Proclamation and Dialogue," in *The Moral Dynamics of Economic Life*, ed. Daniel K. Finn (New York: Oxford University Press, 2012), 119–20.

19. Joseph Ratzinger with Vittorio Messori, *The Ratzinger Report:*

An Exclusive Interview on the State of the Church (San Francisco: Ignatius Press, 1985), 36.

20. Karl Rahner, "On the Theology of Worship," *TI*, vol. 19 (New York: Crossroad, 1983), 147.

21. Johan Verstraeten, "Dialogue in Light of the Signs of the Times," in *The Moral Dynamics*, 121.

22. Kenneth Himes, "Benedict's View of the Person," in *The Moral Dynamics*, 31–33.

23. Cf. *PP* 15. See also *CiV* 16, 17, 18, 19, 20.

24. Cf. *PP* 42. Henri de Lubac, *Le drame de l'humanisme athée* (Paris: Spes, 1945), 10.

25. See also *CiV* 11.

26. See also *CiV* 36.

27. See *CiV* 41, 46.

28. James Franklin, "*Caritas in Veritate*: Economic Activity as Personal Encounter and the Economy of Gratuitousness," *Solidarity: The Journal of Catholic Social Thought and Secular Ethics* 1, no.1 (2011), art. 3, http://researchonline.nd.edu.au/solidarity/vol1/iss1/3.

29. Cf. messages for the World Day of Peace in 1990 and 2010. John Paul II, *Peace with God the Creator, Peace with All of Creation* (January 1, 1990); Benedict XVI, *If You Want to Cultivate Peace, Protect Creation* (January 1, 2010).

30. See *CiV* 51.

31. See *CiV* 53.

32. Hans Urs von Balthasar, "*Communio*—a Program," *Communio: International Catholic Review* 33 (Spring 2006): 155. Originally published in 1972.

33. Von Balthasar, "*Communio*—a Program," 156.

34. Von Balthasar, "*Communio*—a Program," 160.

35. David L. Schindler, "The Anthropological Unity of *Caritas in Veritate*: Life, Family, and Development," in Adrian Pabst, *The Crisis of Global Capitalism*, 214.

36. Cf. Lisa S. Cahill, "*Caritas in Veritate*: Benedict's Global Reorientation," *Theological Studies* 71 (2010): 316.

37. Bernard Laurent, "*Caritas in Veritate* as a Social Encyclical: A Modest Challenge to Economic, Social, and Political Institutions," *Theological Studies* 71 (2010): 515–44.

38. Pontifical Council for Justice and Peace, *Towards Reforming*

the International Financial and Monetary Systems in the Context of Global Public Authority (October 24, 2011).

39. Cf. Zamagni, "Fraternity, Gift and Reciprocity."

40. Christiansen, "Metaphysics and Society," 13.

41. For example, the words *Jesus, Christ,* and *Lord* appear independently thirty-six times in *CiV* (approx. 30,000 words), fifty times in *SRS* (approx. 23,000 words), and twenty times in *PP* (approx. 12,000 words).

42. Lisa Cahill, *Global Justice, Christology, and Christian Ethics* (New York: Cambridge University Press, 2013), 122–203; "*Caritas in Veritate*: Benedict's Global Reorientation," 291–319.

43. See *CiV* 78.

44. Cahill, *Global Justice, Christology, and Christian Ethics,* 130.

45. Joseph Ratzinger/Benedict XVI, *Jesus of Nazareth: From Baptism in the Jordan to the Transfiguration* (New York: Doubleday, 2007); *Jesus of Nazareth,* part 2, *Holy Week: From the Entrance into Jerusalem to the Resurrection* (San Francisco: Ignatius Press, 2011); *Jesus of Nazareth: The Infancy Narratives* (New York: Image, 2012). See also Joseph Ratzinger, *Introduction to Christianity* (New York: Crossroad, 1985).

46. Ratzinger, *Jesus of Nazareth. From Baptism to Transfiguration,* xxii.

47. Cahill, *Global Justice, Christology, and Christian Ethics,* 148.

48. Cahill, *Global Justice, Christology, and Christian Ethics,* 148.

49. Cahill, *Global Justice, Christology, and Christian Ethics,* 148.

50. Cahill, *Global Justice, Christology, and Christian Ethics,* 150.

51. Cahill, *Global Justice, Christology, and Christian Ethics,* 150.

52. Cahill, *Global Justice, Christology, and Christian Ethics,* 131. As representative authors for Spirit Christology, Cahill mentions Friedrich Schleiermacher, Shailer Mathews, D. M. Baillie, Geoffrey Lampe, Piet Schoonenberg, Jürgen Moltmann, Michael Welker, David Coffey, Ralph Del Colle, Roger Haight, James Dunn, Elizabeth Johnson, and Elisabeth Schüssler Fiorenza.

53. Cahill, *Global Justice, Christology, and Christian Ethics,* 126.

54. Cahill, *Global Justice, Christology, and Christian Ethics,* 151.

55. Roger Haight, *The Future of Christology* (New York: Continuum, 2005), 175.

56. Lucy Peppiatt, "New Directions in Spirit Christology: A Foundation for a Charismatic Theology," *Theology* 117, no. 1 (2014): 3–10.

57. Cahill, "Benedict's Global Reorientation," 291.

58. Cahill, "Benedict's Global Reorientation," 292.

59. Cahill, "Benedict's Global Reorientation," 304.

60. Benedict XVI, *Opening Address: Fifth General Conference of the Bishops of Latin America and the Caribbean*, May 13, 2007, no. 3; *Fighting Poverty to Build Peace: Message for the World Day of Peace* (January 1, 2009), no.15.

4. DEVELOPMENT AS INTEGRAL ECOLOGY

1. Oxfam, "Wealth: Having It All and Wanting More," January 2015, https://www.oxfam.org/sites/www.oxfam.org/files/file_attachments/ib-wealth-having-all-wanting-more-190115-en.pdf.

2. See Global Footprint Network, www.footprintwork.org.

3. "Repenser les inégalités face au défi écologique," in *Revue Projet*, online version, March 2017, www.revue-projet.com/articles/2017-02repenser-les-inegalites-face-au-defi-ecologique.

4. John Paul II, *First Greeting*, October 22, 1978. Quoted by George Weigel, *Witness to Hope* (New York: Harper Collins, 1999), 255.

5. Francis, *First Greeting*, March 13, 2013, www.vatican.va.

6. See Austen Ivereigh, *The Great Reformer: Francis and the Making of a Radical Pope* (New York: Henry Holt, 2014).

7. Juan Carlos Scannone, "Pope Francis and the Theology of the People," *Theological Studies* 77, no. 1 (2016): 118–35.

8. Walter Kasper, *Pope Francis' Revolution of Tenderness and Love* (Mahwah, NJ: Paulist Press, 2015), 16.

9. CELAM (Latin American Episcopal Conference), *Disciples and Missionaries of Jesus Christ So That Our Peoples May Have Life in Him "I Am the Way and the Truth and the Life" (Jn 16:4). Concluding Document of the Fifth General Conference of the Bishops of Latin America and the Caribbean*. Aparecida (May 13–31, 2007), https://www.ltrr.arizona.edu/~katie/kt/misc/Apercida/Aparecida-document-for-printing.pdf.

10. Leonardo Boff, "The Magna Carta of Integral Ecology: Cry of the Earth, Cry of the Poor," June 18, 2015, https://leonardoboff.wordpress.com/2015/06/18/the-magna-carta-of-integral-ecology-cry-of-the-earth-cry-of-the-poor/.

11. Francis, *Audience to the Representatives of the Communication Medias*, March 16, 2013, www.vatican.va.

12. Christoph Theobald, "L'enseignement social de l'Église selon le pape François," *Nouvelle Revue Théologique* 138 (2016): 273–88.

13. See *Ap* 19.

14. José Luis Franco Barba y Juan Carlos López Sáenz, "Método y Espiritualidad en la encíclica *Laudato si'*," *Revista Iberoamericana de Teología* 11, no. 21 (2015): 48.

15. See GS 34.

16. See *LS* 25, 30, 45.

17. Susana Nuin Nuñez, "Laudato Si', Inesperada Sorpresa de Comunicación Dialógica," in *Laudato Si'. Lecturas Desde América Latina*, ed. Grupo Farrell (Buenos Aires: Ciccus, 2017), 75–88.

18. Arguably, the door opened here could lead to much further developments. For example, Celia Deane-Drummond points out that *LS* is still short of a proper theology of creation fully aware of evolution and of the nonharmonious-static-equilibrium of nature. Celia Deane-Drummond, *"Laudato si'* and the Natural Sciences: An Assessment of Possibilities and Limits," *Theological Studies* 77, no. 2 (2016): 392–415.

19. Vatican II used the language of the "seeds of truth" (see Vatican II, *Ad gentes* 11, http://www.vatican.va/archive/hist_councils/ii_vatican _council/documents/vat-ii_decree_19651207_ad-gentes_en.html).

20. Virginia R. Azcuy, Diego García, and Carlos Schickendantz, "Introducción," in *Lugares e interpelaciones de Dios. Discernir los signos de los tiempos*, ed. Azcuy, García, Schikendantz (Santiago de Chile: Ediciones Universidad Alberto Hurtado, 2017), 13–14. Translation mine.

21. Cf. Alberto Parra, *Textos, contextos y pretextos* (Bogotá: Universidad Javeriana, 2003), 265.

22. Charles P. Arand, "Tending Our Common Home," *Concordia Journal* (Fall 2015): 312.

23. Descartes, *Discourse on Method*, part 6.

24. Idelfonso Camacho Laraña, *"Laudato si'*: el clamor de la tierra y el clamor de los pobres. Una encíclica más que ecológica," *Revista de Fomento Social* 71 (2016): 73. (Translation mine.)

25. See also *LS* 69; 84–88.

26. "Time is greater than space" (*EG* 222–25; *LS* 178); "Unity prevails over conflict" (*EG* 226–30; *LS* 198); "Realities are more

important than ideas" (*EG* 231–33; *LS* 110, 201); "The whole is greater than the parts" (*EG* 234–37; *LS* 141). For a review of these four Bergoglian priorities, see Scanonne, "Pope Francis and the Theology of the People," 127–30.

27. For an overview of Franciscan theology of creation, see Timothy J. Johnson, "Francis and Creation," in *The Cambridge Companion to Francis of Assisi*, ed. Michael J. P. Robson (New York: Cambridge University Press, 2011), 143–58.

28. Johnson, "Francis and Creation," 146.

29. Johnson, "Francis and Creation," 143.

30. Laure Solignac, *La théologie symbolique de saint Bonaventure* (Paris: Parole et Silence, 2010). Johnson, "Francis and Creation," 150–53.

31. Denis Edwards, "The Theology of the Natural World in *Laudato Si'*," *Theological Studies* 77, no. 2 (2016): 388.

32. Johnson, "Francis and Creation," 156.

33. Edwards, "Theology of the Natural World," 378.

34. Celia Deane-Drummond, "*Laudato Si'* and the Natural Sciences: An Assessment of Possibilities and Limits," *Theological Studies* 77, no. 2 (2016): 392–415.

35. Solignac, *La théologie symbolique de Saint Bonaventure*, 93. Translation mine.

36. Leonardo Boff, "'Split a Piece of Wood…and I Am There': The Cosmic Christ," in *Cry of the Earth, Cry of the Poor* (Maryknoll, NY: Orbis Books, 1997), 174–86.

37. Boff, "The Cosmic Christ," 174.

38. Boff, "The Cosmic Christ," 174.

39. Boff, "The Cosmic Christ," 177.

40. Boff, "The Cosmic Christ," 180.

41. Boff, "The Cosmic Christ," 182.

42. Boff, "The Cosmic Christ," 182.

43. Celia Deane-Drummond, "Who on Earth Is Jesus Christ? Plumbing the Depths of Deep Incarnation," in *Christian Faith and the Earth: Current Paths and Emerging Horizons in Ecotheology*, ed. E. M. Conradie, S. Bergmann, C. Deane-Drummond, and D. Edwards (New York: Bloomsbury, 2015), 31.

44. Niels Gregersen, "Deep Incarnation: Why Evolutionary Continuity Matters in Christology," *Toronto Journal of Theology* 26, no. 2 (2010): 173.

45. Niels Gregersen cited by C. Deane-Drummond, "Who on Earth Is Jesus Christ?," 34.

46. Deane-Drummond, "Who on Earth Is Jesus Christ?," 35; Elisabeth A. Johnson, "Jesus and the Cosmos: Soundings in Deep Christology," in *Incarnation: On the Scope and Depth of Christology*, ed. N. H. Gregersen (Minneapolis: Fortress Press, 2015), 133–57.

47. Deane-Drummond, "Who on Earth Is Jesus Christ?," 49.

48. Deane-Drummond, "Who on Earth Is Jesus Christ?," 49–50.

49. Deane-Drummond, *"Laudato si'* and the Natural Sciences," 404.

5. THEOLOGICAL REFLECTIONS

1. Immanuel Kant, *Critique of Pure Reason*, trans. Norman Kemp Smith (London: MacMillan, 1950), 41.

2. Christoph Theobald, "The Principle of Pastorality at Vatican II," in *The Legacy of Vatican II*, ed. M. Faggioli and A. Vicini (New York: Paulist Press, 2015), 26–37.

3. Karl Rahner, "The Historicity of Theology," in *TI*, vol. 9 (New York: Herder and Herder, 1972), 64–82.

4. Karl Rahner, "The Historicity of Theology," 65.

5. Karl Rahner, "Practical Theology within the Totality of Theological Disciplines," in *TI*, 9:101–14. See as well Karl Rahner, "Practical Theology and Social Work in the Church," in *TI*, vol. 10 (New York, NY: Seabury Press, 1977), 349–69.

6. Rahner, "Practical Theology within the Totality," 102. Emphasis mine.

7. Joseph Ratzinger, *Theological Highlights of Vatican II* (Mahwah, NJ: Paulist Press, 2009), 218–20.

8. Karl Rahner, "The Church's Commission to Bring Salvation and the Humanization of the World," in *TI*, vol. 14 (New York: Seabury Press, 1976), 295–313.

9. Karl Rahner, "The Church's Commission," 296.

10. Karl Rahner, "The Church's Commission," 304–5. Recall also Rahner's insistence on the unity of the love of God and the love of neighbor. Rahner, "Reflections on the Unity of the Love of Neighbor

and the Love of God," in *TI*, vol. 6 (Baltimore, MD: Helicon Press, 1969), 231–49.

11. Rahner, "The Church's Commission," 313.

12. David Hollenbach, "*Caritas in Veritate*: The Meaning of Love and Urgent Challenges of Justice," *Journal of Catholic Social Thought* 8, no. 1 (2011): 171–82.

13. Rahner, "History of the World and Salvation History," 98–99.

14. Rahner, "Love of Neighbor and Love of God."

15. Rahner, "Practical Theology and Social Work," 358.

16. See *SRS* 37.

17. Ellen Van Stichel, "The Ethical Potential of Communal Movements for Catholic Social Thought: The Trinitarian Anthropology of the Focolare Movement," in *Visions of Hope: Emerging Theologians and the Future of the Church*, ed. Kevin Ahern (Maryknoll, NY: Orbis, 2013), 133–47; "The Economic Crisis as a Crisis in Anthropology: Would a Trinitarian Anthropology Offer an Alternative to an Economic Individualist Approach?" *ET-Studies* 3, no. 2 (2012): 295–315.

18. Van Stichel, "The Ethical Potential," 142.

19. Cambón, quoted by Van Stichel, "The Ethical Potential," 143.

20. Karl Rahner, *The Trinity* (Wellwood, UK: Burns and Oates, 1970), 10–11.

21. Karl Rahner, *The Trinity*, 21.

22. Karl Rahner, "The Two Basic Types of Christology," in *TI*, vol. 13 (New York: Seabury, 1975), 213–23.

23. Karl Rahner, "The Two Basic Types of Christology," 216.

24. Karl Rahner, "The Two Basic Types of Christology," 218.

25. Karl Rahner, "The Two Basic Types of Christology," 220.

26. Karl Rahner, "The Two Basic Types of Christology," 221.

27. Julio Lois, "Christology in the Theology of Liberation," in *Mysterium Liberationis: Fundamental Concepts of Liberation Theology*, ed. Ignacio Ellacuría and Jon Sobrino (Maryknoll, NY: Orbis Books, 1993), 188.

28. Rahner, "The Two Basic Types of Christology," 222.

29. Rahner, "The Two Basic Types of Christology," 222.

30. See *SRS* 47.

31. Benedict XVI, *Inaugural Address to the Fifth General*

Conference of the Bishops of Latin America and the Caribbean at Aparecida (May 13, 2007), no. 3. Francis, *Evangelii gaudium*, no. 198.

32. Jon Sobrino, *Christ the Liberator: A View from the Victims* (New York: Orbis, 2001); Leonardo Boff, *Jesus Christ Liberator: A Critical Christology for Our Times* (Maryknoll, NY: Orbis, 1978); Julio Lois, "Christology in the Theology of Liberation."

33. Cristián del Campo, *Dios opta por los pobres. Reflexión teológica a partir de Aparecida* (Santiago de Chile: Universidad Alberto Hurtado, 2010). CELAM, *Concluding Document of the Fifth General Conference of the Bishops of Latin America and the Caribbean*, May 13–31, 2007, https://www.celam.org/aparecida/Ingles.pdf.

34. Del Campo, *Dios opta*, 77. Translation mine as in all the following citations.

35. Del Campo, *Dios opta*, 77.

36. Del Campo, *Dios opta*, 80–90.

37. Del Campo, *Dios opta*, 31.

38. Juan Luis Segundo, "Disquisición sobre el Misterio Absoluto," *Revista Latinoamericana de Teología* 6 (1985): 225–26.

39. Del Campo, *Dios opta*, 98.

40. Del Campo, *Dios opta*, 100.

SELECT BIBLIOGRAPHY

Antoncich, Ricardo. *La preocupación social de la Iglesia. La encíclica Sollicitudo rei socialis y sus proyecciones en América Latina.* Buenos Aires, Argentina: Latinoamerica libros, 1988.

Baum, Gregory, and Robert Ellsberg. *The Logic of Solidarity: Commentaries on Pope John Paul II's Encyclical On Social Concern.* Maryknoll, NY: Orbis, 1989.

Boff, Leonardo. *Cry of the Earth, Cry of the Poor. Ecology and Justice.* Maryknoll, NY: Orbis, 1997.

Cahill, Lisa Sowle. "*Caritas in Veritate*: Benedict's Global Reorientation." *Theological Studies* 71, no. 2 (2010): 291–319.

———. *Global Justice, Christology, and Christian Ethics.* New York: Cambridge University Press, 2013.

Camacho Laraña, Idelfonso. "*Laudato si'*: El clamor de la tierra y el clamor de los pobres. Una encíclica más que ecológica." *Revista de Fomento Social* 71 (2016): 59–79.

Campo, Cristián del. *Dios opta por los pobres. Reflexión teológica a partir de Aparecida.* Santiago de Chile: Universidad Alberto Hurtado, 2010.

CERAS, ed. *Le discours social de l'Église catholique: de Léon XIII À Benoît XVI.* Paris: Bayard Centurion, 2009.

Dorr, Donal. *Option for the Poor and for the Earth: Catholic Social Teaching.* 3rd ed. Maryknoll, NY: Orbis, 2012.

Ellacuría, Ignacio, and Jon Sobrino, eds. *Mysterium Liberationis: Fundamental Concepts of Liberation Theology.* Maryknoll, NY: Orbis, 1993.

Endean, Philip. "Has Rahnerian Theology a Future?" In *The Cambridge Companion to Karl Rahner,* edited by Declan Marmion and Mary E. Hines, 281–96. New York: Cambridge University Press, 2005.

Gímenez Cassina, Alfredo. *Comentario a la* Sollicitudo rei socialis. Madrid: Acción Social Empresarial, 1990.

González-Carvajal, Luis. *La fuerza del amor inteligente. Un comentario a la encíclica 'Caritas in veritate' de Benedicto XVI.* Santander, Spain: Sal Terrae, 2009.

Grupo Farrell. Laudato Si'. *Lecturas desde América Latina. Desarrollo, exclusión social y ecología integral.* Buenos Aires: Ciccus, 2017.

Gutiérrez, Gustavo. *A Theology of Liberation: History, Politics, and Salvation.* 2nd ed. Maryknoll, NY: Orbis, 1988.

Hebblethwaite, Peter. *Paul VI: The First Modern Pope.* New York: Paulist Press, 1993.

Henriot, Peter J., and Joe Holland. *Social Analysis: Linking Faith and Justice.* Maryknoll, NY: Orbis, 1983.

Himes, Kenneth R., ed. *Modern Catholic Social Teaching: Commentaries and Interpretations.* Washington, DC: Georgetown University Press, 2005.

Hug, James E., Peter J. Henriot, and Edward P. De Berri. *Catholic Social Teaching: Our Best Kept Secret.* 4th rev. and exp. ed. New York: Orbis, 2003.

Ivereigh, Austen. *The Great Reformer: Francis and the Making of a Radical Pope.* New York: Henry Holt and Company, 2014.

Kasper, Walter. *Pope Francis' Revolution of Tenderness and Love: Theological and Pastoral Perspectives.* Mahwah, NJ: Paulist Press, 2015.

Komonchak, Joseph A. "Benedict XVI and the Interpretation of Vatican II." *Cristianesimo Nella Storia* 28, no. 2 (2007): 323–37.

Lopez Jordan, Rafael. *El manifiesto social de Pablo VI. Comentarios, presupuestos conciliares y repercusión posterior de la encíclica* Populorum progressio. Madrid: Studium, 1967.

Marmion, Declan, and Mary E. Hines. *The Cambridge Companion to Karl Rahner.* New York: Cambridge University Press, 2005.

Myers, Kenneth A. *Aspiring to Freedom: Commentaries on John Paul II's Encyclical "The Social Concerns of the Church."* Grand Rapids: Eerdmans, 1988.

O'Brien, David, J., and Thomas A. Shannon. *Catholic Social Thought: The Documentary Heritage.* Maryknoll, NY: Orbis, 2010.

O'Malley, John. *What Happened at Vatican II.* Cambridge, MA: Harvard University Press, 2008.

Pabst, Adrian. *The Crisis of Global Capitalism: Pope Benedict XVI's*

Social Encyclical and the Future of Political Economy. Cambridge: James Clarke and Co., 2012.

Rahner, Karl. "Basic Theological Interpretation of the Second Vatican Council." In *Theological Investigations*, vol. 20, 77–89. New York: Crossroad, 1981.

———. "The Concept of Mystery in Catholic Theology." In *Theological Investigations*, vol. 4, 36–73. Baltimore: Helicon Press, 1966.

———. *Foundations of Christian Faith: An Introduction to the Idea of Christianity*. New York: Crossroad, 1982.

———. "History of the World and Salvation-History." In *Theological Investigations*, vol. 5, 97–114. Baltimore: Helicon Press, 1966.

———. "Practical Theology and Social Work in the Church." In *Theological Investigations*, vol. 10, 349–69. New York: Seabury, 1977.

———. "Reflections on Methodology in Theology." In *Theological Investigations*, vol. 11, 68–114. New York: Seabury, 1974.

———. "Reflections on the Unity of the Love of Neighbor and the Love of God." In *Theological Investigations*, vol. 6, 231–49. Baltimore: Helicon Press, 1969.

———. "Theology and Anthropology." In *Theological Investigations*, vol. 9, 28–45. New York: Herder and Herder, 1972.

———. "The Two Basic Types of Christology." In *Theological Investigations*, vol. 13, 213–23. New York: Seabury, 1975.

Ratzinger, Joseph. *Introduction to Christianity*. New York: Crossroad, 1969.

Ratzinger, Joseph, and Vittorio Messori. *The Ratzinger Report: An Exclusive Interview on the State of the Church*. San Francisco: Ignatius Press, 1985.

Riga, Peter J. *The Church of the Poor: A Commentary on Paul VI's Encyclical On the Development of Peoples*. Techny, IL: Divine Word Publications, 1968.

Rodriguez, Gabriel Ignacio, and Mario Franco Espinal. *La urgencia de transformaciones personales y sociales para la paz. Análisis y comentarios sobre la encíclica* Sollicitudo rei socialis. Bogotá, Colombia: Cinep, 1989.

Rowland, Christopher. *The Cambridge Companion to Liberation Theology*. 2nd ed. Cambridge: Cambridge University Press, 2007.

Ruíz-Giménez, Joaquín. *Comentarios de Cuadernos para el dialogo a la* Populorum progressio. Madrid: Edicusa, 1967.

Sanchez Agesta, Luis. *La proyección de la "Populorum progressio" en la sociedad contemporánea.* Madrid: Centro de estudios sociales de la Santa Cruz del Valle de los Caidos, 1969.

Scannone, Juan Carlos. "Pope Francis and the Theology of the People." *Theological Studies* 77, no. 1 (2016): 118–35.

Stichel, Ellen Van. "The Ethical Potential of Communal Movements for Catholic Social Thought: The Trinitarian Anthropology of the Focolare Movement." In *Visions of Hope: Emerging Theologians and the Future of the Church,* edited by Kevin Ahern, 133–47. Maryknoll, NY: Orbis, 2013.

Theobald, Christoph. *La réception du concile Vatican II : Tome 1, Accéder à la Source.* Paris: Éditions du Cerf, 2009.

————. "The Principle of Pastorality at Vatican II." In *The Legacy of Vatican II,* edited by Massimo Faggioli and Andrea Vicini, 26–37. New York: Paulist Press, 2015.

Weigel, George. *Witness to Hope: The Biography of Pope John Paul II.* New York: Cliff Street Books, 1999.

INDEX

Discipleship, 39, 106, 133
Docetism, 21, 135, 166
Dorr, Donal, 73n74

Ecclesiam suam, 23–24, 123
Ecology: deep, 139; ecological
   footprint, 114; environmental,
   97; human, 97; integral,
   110–43
Économie et Humanisme
   (Economy and Humanism), 17
Economy of communion,
   85–86, 95
Edwards, Denis, 132
Eschatology, 5, 43, 75, 80, 109,
   131, 136, 140, 167
Etchegaray, Roger, 56
Evangelii gaudium, 119, 121,
   129, 134, 152, 165, 168

Focolare Movement, 85–86, 87,
   89, 95, 109, 148
Food and Agriculture
   Organization (FAO),
   32–33, 82
Fourth World, 48
Francis (Jorge Cal Bergoglio),
   2, 11, 110–43, 152, 156, 160,
   165, 167. See also *Evangelii
   gaudium*; *Laudato si'*
Francis of Assisi, 5, 11, 12, 111,
   112, 116, 119, 125, 130, 141,
   164
Fraternity (brotherhood), 14, 23,
   32–34, 36, 40, 64, 70, 95–96,
   127, 133, 141
Freedom: economic, 67; as
   feature of transcendent
   humanism, 28–29, 30–31,

153; and liberation, 65–67;
   religious freedom, 46, 93; as
   responsibility to do good, 94;
   and sin, 61

García Gómez, Matías, 19
Gaudium et spes, 7, 38, 123,
   127, 157
Gift (gratuitousnesss), 94–97
Globalization, 80, 82–83, 112
Global South, 106, 154
González-Carvajal, Luis, 61,
   82–83
Gorbachev, Mikhail, 48
Greenhouse gases, 82, 114
Gregersen, Niels, 139
Gutiérrez, Gustavo, 49, 65,
   73n74

Haight, Roger, 106
Henriot, Peter J, 51n17, 53
Heraclitus of Ephesus, 89
Hermeneutical circle (spiral), 2,
   147, 166
Historical Jesus, 11, 39–40, 105,
   133–35, 138, 140, 160–65
Historicity (and theology), 7,
   145–51
Holland, Joe, 53
Human dignity, 27, 46, 49, 98,
   127, 156, 167
Humanism: cannot exclude
   God, 93, 109; integral, 17;
   transcendent, 26–31, 58–60
Human rights, 29, 46, 48, 63,
   71, 94, 108, 128, 153, 156
Human vocation, 26–29, 36, 42,
   58–60, 67–68, 92–94, 153,
   155, 157